Marlborough Street
The Story of a London Court

Marlborough Street
The Story of a London Court

by

JOAN LOCK

ROBERT HALE · LONDON

Photoset by
Specialised Offset Services Ltd., Liverpool
Printed in Great Britain by
Lowe and Brydone Ltd., Thetford, Norfolk
Bound by Weatherby Woolnough, Northants

Contents

Illustrations

IT'S THE COURT THAT MAKES THE HEADLINES – MARLBOROUGH STREET MAGISTRATES' COURT, THE 'COURT OF CONTROVERSY', IN THE HEART OF LONDON'S WEST END.

Daily Mirror, 1964 ('The Magistrates of Headline Court')

MARLBOROUGH STREET, THOUGH REGARDED AS A PROMOTION, IS ALSO RECOGNIZED AS THE MOST TROUBLESOME COURT OVER WHICH A MAGISTRATE IS CALLED UPON TO PRESIDE, AND IT HAS, IN FACT, PROVED THE GRAVE OF MORE THAN ONE MAGISTERIAL REPUTATION.

The Times

THAT ECLECTIC COURT.

Stanley French, Clerk of the Court.

I HAVE SAT AT ONE TIME OR ANOTHER IN EVERY METROPOLITAN COURT, AND IN MY OPINION, MARLBOROUGH STREET IS BY FAR THE PLEASANTEST OF THE LOT.

J.B. SANDBACH KC, Magistrate

MARLBOROUGH STREET IS QUITE A FASHIONABLE AND *DISTINGUE* POLICE-OFFICE ... CRIME TAKES ON A MORE DANDIFIED ASPECT. IT ASSUMES GLAZED BOOTS AND ACHIEVES AN EXCEPTIONAL TIE TO ITS CRAVAT.

The Illustrated London News, 9th October 1847.

TO LEN ALMAND
who recognizes a good story when he sees one
and is generous with it.

Acknowledgements

Grateful thanks to the following for permission to quote: Weidenfeld (Publishers) Ltd (*The Cleveland Street Affair*); Mrs Ann Monsarrat (*Life is a Four Letter Word*, Cassell); Stanley French (*Crime Every Day*); William Kimber & Co Ltd (*The Jester and the Court*); and the *Evening Standard* (*My Court Case Book*). Full details of these books are given in the bibliography.

Picture Credits: 1, reproduced by Courtesy of the Trustees of the British Museum; 2, 4, 5-9, 13, 14, 16 and 17, R.B. Lock; 12, Len Almand; 15, David Hopkin *Hamilton Studios* photo; 18, by permission of the *Evening News*; 19, by permission of the *Daily Mirror*; 20 and 22, Commissioner, Metropolitan Police; 23-25 and 27-32, reproduced by permission of the British Library Board.

I would also like to thank Mr E.L. Yabsley (Senior Chief Clerk) for kindly allowing me access to the court's early records; Len Almand for the loan of his invaluable Press cuttings; Lord Justice Lawton; my husband Bob Lock, and various other lawyers and policemen for their helpful reminiscences. I would also like to thank my husband for editorial assistance, photographs and for compiling the index.

J.L.

1

The Next Case, Your Worship

Just around the corner from our Bloomsbury flat was the only undamaged telephone-box in the area. One Sunday evening I had managed, for once, to get Bob out on a stroll and, passing the said telephone-box, we noticed that the light was out – not only that, there seemed to be an awful lot of activity going on in there, much more than was required to press button B – a banging noise too. We exchanged suitably rueful glances. Goodbye walk.

"You slip around the back," said Bob decisively, "and I will approach from the front."

It was an oddly placed box, tucked in at one end of a solid block-house (rumoured to be a bomb-proof telephone-exchange built in the Second World War, but we never saw any sign of life there), which in turn fitted into a shallow crescent made by the four-storey buildings behind it. The solidity of the building and the box's situation made it difficult to see what was going on in there, but I obediently filtered around the back and sidled as close as possible so as to 'observe', an exercise which, even when I was a serving police-officer, had always made *me* feel peculiarly criminal.

To my relief, no sooner had I begun observation than the box emptied of two youths who walked off nonchalantly towards a car in the street opposite. On examination, the box appeared only slightly scratched and dented, and that could have happened at any time. That was a relief. No need to do anything. They must just have been trying to get their money back. We were becoming over-suspicious, a boring tendency which we must curb. Gratefully resuming our stroll, we met the aforesaid youths, returning – only now they were equipped with hammer, chisel and crowbar and were soon banging happily away at the coinbox.

Their recklessness astounded and puzzled us: were they workmen or something? We consulted two Post Office employees who were conveniently working in a nearby, but out of sight, hole in the road. They agreed with us that it seemed most unlikely, due to their youth and repair-technique, and accepted the guardianship of Bob's umbrella and his instruction that, should what was about to happen get out of hand, they would give or get help. Mind you, they were not the least bit happy about the latter and gave only half-hearted assurances which left us with the distinct impression that our second line of defence was tacky, to say the least.

Fortunately, Tony, a policeman neighbour of broad shoulders and quick mind, happened along on his way home after 'late turn' duty, and the arrest of the two youths was quickly effected before the astonished gaze of the Post Office employees.

"As a matter of fact," said one of them grudgingly when I collected hubby's gamp, "we thought *you* looked very suspicious, sneaking around like that!"

The youths turned out to be up from the country and had decided, on the spur of the moment, to try the coinbox-smashing that was so much in the news. That an out-of-order public telephone could cost a life just had not occurred to them. The arrest made an impression though. It frightened the life out of them, and, gratifyingly, their shocked parents decided to rub it in by refusing to bail them out that night. Consequently they spent a night in a police-station cell, which gave them time to ruminate.

What seemed to shake them most was that a policeman (Bob) should appear at the moment of misdemeanour – moreover, a policeman giving no indication that he was one, despite being of the uniformed branch, not a member of the CID. It was not fair, really. Like a great many people, they had the impression that no one noticed what happened in Central London, while, in fact, it is a group of villages. Also, and we chose not to enlighten them on this, they had chosen a very bad venue for their first sortie into crime, since around the corner resided another sixty or so members of the Metropolitan Police, some of even more suspicious turn of mind than we.

Next morning they became even more unnerved when a now-uniformed Bob checked them off the van and placed them in their court cells. Inexperienced though they were, they seemed vaguely aware that this was a little too much like personal service: the arresting officer, who had been fingerprinting them at 2 a.m., being there at 8 a.m. to welcome them to magistrates' court. Further, when they were called from the corridor into court, it was Bob who shouted their names, ushered them into dock, announced, "The next case, Your Worship ...", then dashed round into the witness-box to give evidence. A one-man police-force.

"We'll not do anything like that again," exclaimed one of the awed young men after sentence.* "You're blooming everywhere!"

Not really. He was just a policeman who worked at Marlborough Street Magistrates' Court.

Marlborough Street Magistrates' Court is situated in the heart of London's West End, next door to the London Palladium Theatre and opposite tourist-happy Carnaby Street. It serves the northern parts of Soho and Mayfair (being actually in the first and a few hundred yards away, across Regent Street, from the second) and, until recently, Hyde Park and Chelsea. Such a grandly situated dame can afford to be a bit perverse, and she is, for the street she is situated in is not Marlborough Street at all but *Great* Marlborough Street. Some people make the mistake of calling it Great Marlborough Street Magistrates' Court, which gives other people the chance to correct them. The English love to fool people with names.

But the court is an aged lady, so perhaps we can forgive her. The decision to set up the court was taken in 1792, following on the success of Bow Street Magistrates' Court, when six more 'Public Offices' were introduced. Westminster, Hatton Garden, Shoreditch, Whitechapel, Shadwell and Southwark came into being at the same time, and Thames was added in 1800. Marlborough Street and Thames were to join Bow Street as the most famous and written-about summary courts in the land, and Marlborough Street is the only one of the eight still occupying its original site.

It has seen a lot of action. Clare Sutton, the present court-keeper, says, "I love this place. It feels so full of history but always has a friendly feel, never frightening, even when you walk through alone at night."

Dickens reported the court's proceedings; Oscar Wilde took there the fatal step which sent him hurtling downwards; Napoleon III has stood in the witness-box; suffragettes have mercilessly harangued its magistrates, and The Rolling Stones have answered drug-charges therein. Marlborough Street Magistrates' Court certainly has some good tales to tell.

---

* *They received fourteen days in 'the Scrubs'. In desperation a Birmingham magistrate was giving out short, sharp sentences, and London was beginning to follow suit.*

2

Plank & Co

These days magistrates and the police employed in the running of the court normally have nothing to do with the detection of crime and the apprehension of the offender (apart from executing warrants), but it was not always so. Originally this was organized by Justices of the Peace, lazy and corrupt though many of them were. Thomas de Veil, a lecher of the first order and probably somewhat corrupt also, nonetheless applied himself to his task with great zeal when he began operating from a house in Bow Street in the mid-eighteenth century. As he received some payment from public funds, he could lay claim to being the first stipendiary magistrate.

He was followed by the vigorous and incorruptible Henry Fielding, who, after his death, was succeeded by his kindly half-brother, John Fielding. Between them they established Bow Street as a properly organized and government-funded public (police) office and the place to go for something resembling real justice.

Eventually, in 1795, long after the proposal for more Bow Streets had been mooted by John Fielding, the other seven were set up. Each had three magistrates, on a salary of £400 a year, and paid clerks. Present-day stipendiaries must have a law degree, but these originals were a very mixed bunch and included a poet, a clergyman and one barrister.

Bow Street and Thames, having their own 'police' or 'patrols' to assist the magistrate, proved far more efficient than the others, whose performance was at first disappointing. Gradually they too began to employ a few 'runners', Marlborough Street acquiring eight to cope with the misdeeds of a population of 270,000.

One of the runners was a man called Plank, and the following reports from *Cobbett's Evening Post* of 1820 give us a glimpse of the variety of his life:

MARLBOROUGH STREET – Yesterday the examination of Sarah

East, for having set fire to the house of Mr Walsh, the King's Messenger, of No 7 Charles Street, St James's Square, was resumed before J.E. Conant Esq., the sitting magistrate. Several gentlemen from the neighbourhood of St James's Square etc attended, in consequence of the great interest the case excited. All the former evidence was confirmed; in addition to which, Mr Waldrop, surgeon, in the King's service, deposed that he was applied to by the prisoner, who complained of having fits, in consequence of a plethora, a disorder which is sometimes accompanied with insanity; although he could not say the prisoner was insane, he should be warranted in saying she was at times deranged.

Plank, the officer, stated that the prisoner had told him privately, when ordered by Mr Conant to take her aside, that one day last week, a woman, who was a fortune-teller, came to Mrs Walsh's door, with some flowers in a basket; she forced herself in at the door and would not leave until her mistress turned her out; she beckoned the prisoner to follow her.

Mrs Walsh shortly after gave her sixpence to buy myrtle from the woman; she followed her to Waterloo Place, when she began abusing her mistress and said she might want a bit of bread herself, and persuaded her to set fire to the house, and threatened her, if she did not, that she would do it herself; she being a fortune-teller, and the fear that she would do something bad to her if she did not set the house on fire, urged her to do it. She said she did not do it from hatred or malice towards her employers. In her first confession of setting the house on fire, she said it arose from a quarrel with her mistress.

She was fully committed to Newgate for trial, and the parties were bound over to prosecute.

Of course Plank got out and about too on the court's business – not always to good effect as the second report shows:

EXTRAORDINARY DEATH OF A MANIAC – For some time past a family of distinction residing at the west end of the town has been thrown into considerable anxiety in consequence of the sudden disappearance of one of its members – a clerical gentleman, who of late has been observed to labour under alarming symptoms of derangement. He quitted his home in an abrupt manner, without any apparent cause, and from his absenting himself during several days, it was deemed proper to issue handbills. On Thursday last, information was received that a person supposed to be the above gentleman was wandering about the neighbourhood of Greenwich in a state of nudity and was living in the fields by night but could not be approached. One of the members of the family, accompanied by Plank, the officer at Marlborough Street office, repaired thither and traced the person through Greenwich, Eltham etc, until they arrived at Dartford, where the unfortunate being had retreated. On being pursued by Plank and the gentleman through the town of Dartford, he at length plunged into Dartford creek and escaped to the other side, and all hopes of overtaking him were given up by them. The following morning, on searching Dartford Wood, they found him lying on his back, cut and mangled in a dreadful manner; the soles of his feet were cut from running over the flint stones, and from forcing his way through the bushes he had cut his flesh dreadfully. His face was disfigured also, but he was found not to be the above clerical gentleman; a letter was found by his side, from the contents of which there is little doubt but he is Mr —, a surgeon of Inverness. The parties returned disappointed, and no tidings have since been received of the former fugitive. The above particulars Plank stated to Messrs Farrant and Dyer, Magistrates.

Not one of Plank's better efforts.

Apart from being hopelessly overworked, these assistants received very low wages and no recompense should they be injured apprehending a criminal – or a poor lunatic in Dartford Wood. Thus they became open to corruption, and things were back where they started. The new offices were supposed to be the magic solution to the rampant crime and violence, and there was much disappointment in their performance.

To protect themselves and their property, the public increasingly took the law into their own hands by means of citizens' patrols and mantraps. Eventually, in 1829, the Metropolitan Police were formed, and ten years later the magistrates in the newly named police-courts had their powers curtailed. They were responsible only for trying cases, not for the organization of the court or the apprehension of prisoners. It was a change which some of them did not appreciate.

Now specially seconded police run the court list, look after the prisoners and execute warrants for non-appearance or non-payment of fines. For this purpose they are divided into two groups: the gaoler's office and the warrant office. The gaoler's office day begins at 8 a.m. Soon after, charge-sheets, which have arrived from the catchment-area police-stations, are sifted into order. The minor, quickly-dealt-with matters will come on first, followed by the increasingly serious and then the remands from previous lists. Those in custody will usually go into number One Court, since Number Two Court does not have a security 'cage' outside the court-room.

Once sorted, the lists are typed, with copies, on a typically ancient typewriter, by a policeman who has never been taught to type. (Policemen are expected to be born with the ability to do certain things, and typing is one of them.) The list is then copied, by hand and in more detail, into the Magistrates' Register, and, since it is the official Court Record, it has to be right. This puts the highly trained, learned and well-paid judicial gentleman at the absolute mercy of the calligraphic abilities of the plain PCs, some of whom write like angels and others like demented spiders. However, some courts have gone over to typewritten loose-leaf registers, and it is possible that, by the time you read this, Marlborough Street will have done the same.

Prisoners arrive at the cells in the rear of the court via two main procedures. Those who have previously been remanded in custody are collected by the big prison-vans which leave Lambeth Depot at the crack of dawn and set off in all directions, taking on offending persons from Wormwood Scrubs, Brixton and Pentonville Prisons and so on. The vans then proceed to exchange-points: police-stations with backyards large enough to accommodate several of the monster vans and walls high enough to deter all but the most athletic of prisoners from escape-attempts. Once there, a van which has been to, say, the Scrubs, will hand over several prisoners to a South London van, which will, in turn, give them some prisoners from Brixton and Wandsworth. This is simplifying it but gives the general idea. It certainly looks most impressive in practice, and one wonders how they get it right since it all looks so chaotic.

On the way to the courts, the vans also pick up the 'overnights' from the police-stations – those arrested the day before. Thus, although the prisoners come from several directions, only one or two prison-vans arrive at Marlborough Street's huge back doors. Prisoners who are already serving another sentence are brought in separately by prison-officers.

Prison-vans are a fairly awful way to travel – in little individual cells on each side of a long central corridor. It was worse when they were horse-drawn, since bumping along and not being able to see out made people feel very sick. Though the vans are far from perfect now, it is difficult to think of another way to transport so many people securely. The vans are reasonably escape-proof, so one does not find instances such as that featured in the *Hue and Cry and Police Gazette* on 4th July 1818:

POLICE NEWS.
John Bond escaped on the 2nd instant, from a coach in which he was being conveyed from Tothill Fields, Bridewell, for re-examination before the fitting magistrate at the Public Office, Great Marlborough Street, on a

charge of Fraud. He is twenty-three years of age; about 5 feet 10 inches in height, stout made, pale complexion, somewhat marked with the smallpox, with very light hair; much the appearance of a stage-coach man*; and has general acquaintance with that class of men, particularly those drivers to and from Windsor. Is also known in town as a Duffer.**

The attitudes of the prisoners towards their police gaolers vary considerably. Some are surly or aggressive, many, especially the old lags, matter-of-fact or friendly. Some are too hung-over to assume any stance, and others are mentally disturbed. Their 'estates' vary considerably too, traditionally more at this court than most. East End courts, for example, tend to have East Enders, but Marlborough Street gets the full human mixture – as *The Graphic* of 16th July 1887 pointed out:

> In Great Marlborough Street all kinds of persons of all degrees of society rub shoulders together; here extremes meet with a vengeance. Peers and pickpockets, Members of Parliament and members of the swell-mob, the army, navy and the bar, literature and the fine arts, representatives of all the clubs in Pall Mall appear here in turn as prosecutors and prisoners, according to the Fates and their lucky and unlucky stars.

Among those usually the most difficult to deal with are the mentally unstable who may have a disturbing tendency to rip off all their clothes or, worse, to shout and bang (sometimes their own heads against the wall) endlessly. The noise, while moderately irritating to the police who have their office just down the corridor, can be purgatory for their fellow-prisoners. "Here, for God's sake, can't you shut him up?" is the frequent plea. One such prisoner screamed so hard and so unendingly that it penetrated Court One, some distance from the cells, and caused the waggish magistrate, Mr St John Harmsworth, to murmur, "Gaoler, is that someone assisting police with their enquiries?"

Among the more pleasant prisoners to grace the cells at Marlborough Street Court were the Welsh-language demonstrators who, not so long ago, lay down in the road outside the BBC. The high, bare cells which so echo the yells served as excellent acoustics for the beautiful choral singing with which they whiled away part of their

---

* Stage-coach drivers had a reputation for being rough and independent.
** Someone who 'duffed things up' to make them look new and/or valuable.

waiting-time. The police, having been thus sung through their tedious early-morning clerical tasks, gave them a well-deserved round of applause, and no one asked for them to be silenced.

The cells, being old, are pretty dismal and Dickensian: tiled to above head height, with stark wooden benches, a half-partitioned loo with suicide-proof, push-button flush, and dim lighting. In 1885 Louise Twining, a Poor-Law Guardian, described the police-court cells as cold, horribly insanitary and overcrowded. Today they are warm, clean and rarely overfull (in fact they are often the cosiest places in the building) – not warm enough for some, however: one 'nutter', who did the clothes-removing trick, carefully piled them in the middle of the floor and set fire to them. Shouts from prisoners in other cells brought police running to find the place filled with smoke and the clothes in charred flakes. He had secreted a match about his person which had not been found when he was searched.

The risk of fire is rather a problem, but one cannot refuse a light for a cigarette for a prisoner who has hours to wait. One such prisoner stuffed the dog-end down behind some radiators where fluff, cigarette-packets and similar debris pushed down there by other prisoners over the years caught fire. Soon the cell was full of smoke. As it happened, these particular prisoners had demanded constant attention so the PCs were being fairly leisurely about answering their bell until they heard shouts of "Fire! Fire!" and found gasping faces at the cell peephole. But even if the police did not give them lights, remand prisoners may have their effects returned by the prison authorities, and these sometimes include matches or lighters.

However, there are worse cells than those at Marlborough Street, as evidenced in a most unusual way by a detective constable in 1975. He was giving evidence about a young man who had skipped bail and whom he had had to collect from Edinburgh. The policeman took the opportunity to protest about the conditions in which the prisoner had been held for six weeks, in punishment for offences committed there. "It was," he told Mr McElligott, "spartan to say the least. It was a dark, dank place, and the walls were running with water. It was almost medieval conditions, almost unbelievable. I found him almost to be a broken man." "CID MAN STARTS STORM OVER JAIL OF SHAME", announced the *News of the World* later, quoting an Edinburgh councillor who agreed with him: ' "The cells are in a dreadful state. Everyone is ashamed of them. They should not be used, but it would cost thousands of pounds to renovate them, and today everyone screams about spending public money."

Mind you, waiting about in any court cells must be very boring, and some occupy this time in Marlborough Street by practising the age-old craft of graffiti-writing, executed under especial handicap since the tiles extend to well above head-height. To reach the suitable paintwork surface necessitates clambering on to the wooden bench or loo seat and stretching. It helps to be tall.

Obviously, the prisoners have an obsessive need to record why they are there and what happened to them: "I got six months for burglary," "Joe Bloggs, suspended sentence," etc. There are lots of these. Then there is the odd warning or accusation: "I was stitched up by D.I. Jones," "All the Sweeney are bent," or "Smith and Smith are bleedin' useless briefs!" – a kind of *Which* for villains. Woven into this tapestry is the occasional advertisement, useful if you happen to be looking for a gentleman with an extra long appendage (measurements supplied) – in the men's cells this is. And, as befits the polyglot nature of the clientèle, there are one or two epithets in foreign tongues. You can tell they are epithets by the rows of exclamation-marks after them and the odd recognizable rude word in the text. "Down with the Shah!" takes its rightful place here, even though he has been down for some time now. (This exhortation is also inscribed on the walls of Warren Street Underground Station. I see it on the way to work. Do numberless Iranian revolutionaries travel on the Northern Line, I wonder, in the vague manner of one whose brain does not start to function properly until well after the coffee-break. However, the cell-wall writer was certainly sure of an appropriate audience since a disproportionate number of his countrymen got to, and still get to, occupy these places.) My favourite graffito is, "I was here, but you were not. Now you are here, and I am not." It has a Pinterish ring to it.

As the day wears on, there is much changing over in the cells. Some leave on bail, or forever; others replace them to await the prison-van. This can be a knife-edge procedure when a defendant is waiting for a friend or relative to come up with his fine or stand bail for him so as to prevent his incarceration. Will the van arrive before the rescuing relative? He can still be released from prison, of course, but the fine-payer will have to go there to get him out.

This tight-rope walking can be the fault of the prisoner. Some, particularly foreign shoplifters, will appear at court with insufficient money, though they are obviously well-heeled and have been warned to expect a hefty fine if found guilty. They have the strange delusion that, should they bring less money, they will be fined less.

Keeping track of all the comings and goings in the cells is quite a job, so it is remarkable that so few errors are made. However, once, when doing a customary home-time check, the gaoler was disconcerted to find a man still in occupancy when everyone was supposed to have gone. Fortunately there is no chance of Marlborough Street's paralleling a recent 'accident' in an Austrian cell, where a young man lay forgotten for eighteen days and lost fifty pounds in weight; when found, he had to be rushed to intensive care. And he had been put in the cell only while his friend, the driver of an offending car, was being questioned!

The other extreme, finding themselves one short, is a heart-stopper for police. Such an incident occurred at Marlborough Street not so long ago when a bunch of bank-robbers – 'Category A' prisoners – while being escorted from the court along the cell corridor by accompanying police-officers (*many* accompanying police-officers, since they were 'up' for such a big job and thought so liable to try to escape, but not court staff). As often happens in a case of too many cooks, each thought the other had tabs on a particular one, who, in fact, had slipped out of line, into a doorway, while his fellow-robbers passed on. Then, being dressed sufficiently smartly to pass for a solicitor or one of the sharp-suited CID men who abound at such busy periods, and carrying papers under his arm, he was let out of the police-office along with others. It was a very cool operation, though 'cool' is not the word for the feeling he left in his wake. It was a futile exercise in the end, for several months later he was recaptured after having had a pretty uncomfortable time on the run. When he reappeared at Marlborough Street for his committal to Crown Court, the court staff police looked after him very carefully. He did leave a lasting impression on all those concerned – and some new prisoner-guarding rules at Marlborough Street.

Fortunately, not all prisoners want to try to escape, and some even become somewhat worried if a chance presents itself. One morning not long ago the noise of a throat being cleared made the gaoler look up from his task of compiling the Magistrates' Register to see a vaguely familiar face gazing anxiously at him.

"Excuse me, guv'," said its owner, "but shouldn't my cell door be locked?"

3

The Squabbles

Before the start of the morning list proper in a magistrates' court, the 'applications' are heard – applications from local authorities and police for summonses and arrest- or search-warrants. Most are fairly straightforward and are often applied for in batches, fifty non-payment of television-licences or electricity-bills, or twenty-five London Transport ticket-frauds, for example.

More interesting are the private applications, for all the raw edges of life are there: squabbles between next-door neighbours, tenants and landlords, cabbies and fares, bus-conductors and passengers resulting in pleas for summonses as regards noise, dirt, bilking fares, obscene language or common assault. Again, little is new – witness the following report which appeared in *The Illustrated London News* in 1842:

MARLBOROUGH STREET – Mr William Black of Lansdowne Cottage, Islington, summoned Wm Rhodes, the driver of one of Hardwick's Hammersmith omnibuses, before Mr Maltby for abusive language. The complainant, an elderly gentleman, stated that he got into the defendant's vehicle at the Mansion House, intending to go as far as Hyde Park Corner; but the omnibus was upwards of an hour and a half getting as far as Down Street, Piccadilly, and when he remonstrated he was assailed by the defendant with the filthiest abuse. A police sergeant came forward and corroborated Mr Black's statement regarding the slow pace at which the defendant was driving along Piccadilly. The defendant denied the charge of bad language. With respect to driving slow, it was always the custom for omnibuses not to be in a hurry on Sundays. The usual time was *one hour* from the Mansion House to Piccadilly (this is a piece of useful information for those who ride in omnibuses on that day by way of expedition), and drivers were not particular to a few minutes more.

To rebut the charge of bad language, the defendant called a witness who was outside the omnibus at that time. This witness merely said he did not hear any abuse given. Mr Maltby said he was entirely satisfied of the entire truth of Mr Black's statement. It was impossible to conceive a more flagrant outrage than that which the defendant had committed on a respectable gentleman, by applying to him, in the public streets, language so disgraceful and disgusting. He (Mr Maltby) felt it to be his duty to protect the public as far as possible against such conduct, and he should, therefore, inflict the highest penalty the law permitted, without listening for a moment to any application for mitigation. The fine of £3 and expenses was inflicted and paid.

These days the altercation would probably arise because the passenger felt he had been waiting too long for a number 11.

Some applications do have more a ring of the times in which they were made. A Mrs Cubley was "grossly insulted" and "driven away without redress" by the magistrates at Bow Street and Marlborough Street when, in May 1914, she applied for a summons against a man who assaulted her while she was making a suffrage speech in Hyde Park. These private summonses were necessary, it was claimed in a subsequent report in *The Vote*, because police would not give suffragettes the protection afforded ordinary citizens in these circumstances but stood by and smiled. The law did, however, manage to snap into action a few months later when Mrs Cubley was brought before magistrates for non-payment of tax – one of the suffragettes' methods of protest against non-representation.

From time to time a more unusual application comes up at Marlborough Street. One such occurred on 4th February 1903 when a Mr W.A. Coote of the National Vigilance Association applied for a warrant for the arrest of a Frenchwoman, Mme Spitzner, and her manager, Leon Dekaesmaker, for holding an indecent exhibition. Mme Spitzner was more than a little upset at this, since before bringing her exhibition to London and after its arrival, she had several times asked the police to inspect it to see whether she was contravening British law. They had replied that this was not their function; they could act only should a breach of the law be established – which meant, of course, if anyone objected. Of course, someone did. It was a foreign exhibition for a start, as the *Daily Express* announced: "A PUBLIC SCANDAL, SHAMELESS EXHIBITION OPENED BY ALIENS IN LONDON." They would refrain, they said, from giving the exact situation in Oxford Street lest the organizers should benefit from this. After giving a short description of the exhibits and mentioning that some "could not be described", they went on: "The place is run by aliens, apparently of French origin. '*Caisse*' is over the booking-office; '*Entrée*' and '*Sortie*' are inscribed on the doors. The staff peruse the *Petit Journal*." You cannot get much lower than that! Finally the newspaper quoted a gentleman resident of the neighbourhood who felt " 'The sooner these aliens and their undesirable show are cleared out of our midst, the better for the health of the public.' "

Meanwhile, Messrs Shocked and Disgusted were in touch with the Yard, who were busy debating what action to take when Mr Coote pre-empted them. Consequently, a raid took place on the premises of (I feel it is now safe to reveal) 95-97 Oxford Street.

Mr Coote was backed up by about fifteen plain-clothes police-officers and took away some eighty-four exhibits.

It was, in fact, an "anatomical exhibition" consisting of waxen, life-size figures suffering from diseases and/or being operated upon. Mme Spitzner's late husband, a doctor, had shown it on the Continent over the previous thirty years. Among models seized were some of women giving birth, having a Caesarean section and being delivered by means of "an instrument called a crochett", and there was one of a woman with twins inside her uterus, which had been "cut open". Later Mme Spitzner claimed that Mr Coote had also asked her staff to show him "obscene scenes which never existed except in his imagination".

At Magistrates' Court, Mme Spitzner pleaded that she had repeatedly asked permission from the police, finally sending her manager to "the Chief of Police", whose secretary had assured her it was all right as long as she was showing only what was in the catalogue, though he had suggested they consult a solicitor. The solicitor's only suggestion was that she cover up some of the faces since it was against English law to show faces of persons being operated upon! That sounds curious, but she obeyed, covering the four in question, who happened to be the pregnant ladies.

It was to no avail. The case went on to the Central Criminal Court, where Mr Coote agreed to withdraw his prosecution if all the catalogues were destroyed and Mme Spitzner took herself and her exhibition out of the country. This she did, insisting, however, that she had been coerced into it, since her counsel had threatened to withdraw if she would not do what he suggested, even though she wanted to fight. So back to France she went, a wiser and much poorer woman, who must have wondered greatly at the ways of the English, whose streets were thick with poverty and vice but who could not allow childbirth and disease to be seen in public. But, to be fair, it was more likely money than enlightenment which drove the lady; and Mr Coote was in fact also a leading fighter against the infamous White Slave Traffic. Incidentally, the exhibition was for male eyes alone, although Mme Spitzner claimed that she "had under consideration to appoint a day for ladies".

Probably the most famous private summons issued at Marlborough Street was that granted a few years earlier to one Oscar Fingall O'Flahertie Wills Wilde against the Marquess of Queensberry. Who knows when Wilde's recklessness would have caught up with him had he not reacted as he did to the card inscribed, "To Oscar Wilde, posing as a somdomite" (wrongly spelled in the original), left by Queensberry with the hall-porter at his club. It is probable that his indiscretions would eventually have led to his downfall since attempts had been made to blackmail him. Moreover, people with whom he was acquainted through his sexual activities had been brought before the magistrate at Marlborough Street not long before. And it is unlikely that Queensberry, whose fury had been roused by his son 'Bosie's' involvement with Wilde, would have given up since he had already been persecuting Wilde for two years.

On the advice of friends, Oscar Wilde did not tear up the card but applied for a warrant for Queensberry's arrest on a charge of criminal libel. Heaven knows how he thought he could lie his way out of the libel's being proved. There was much evidence available for anyone who looked hard enough, although his solicitor, whom he had assured there was no truth in the allegation, was not aware of this. Maybe he was confident that his quick mind would save him, for he was no stranger to courts of law. He had attended Bow Street for the hearing of charges against Burns and Graham in connection with the sensational Trafalgar Square Riots in 1887 and had been in the public gallery when his fellow-countryman Parnell was on trial for treason. Moreover his family had been involved in a libel suit (as the defendants) when he was a child — a suit which had brought no benefit to either side. So he knew of the backfiring qualities of litigation.

The warrant was duly executed, and Queensberry made his appearance, in custody, the following day. When the case came up again a week later, Marlborough Street Magistrates' Court was under siege; now everyone wanted to watch him, and there was not even standing-room. 'Bosie' and his brother only just managed to get in but were soon instructed to leave by the testy seventy-four-year-old Mr

Newton. This was probably because he was so pertinent to the case against his father that there was a strong likelihood he would be called to give evidence – something he always swore he wanted to do but, in fact, never did. Even here, Oscar could not resist showing off in the witness-box. This, and his inattention, earned him a rebuke from Mr Newton. Showing off was to contribute to his downfall when the case was at trial: during his brilliant cross-questioning repartee with Sir Edward Carson, he went too far with his reply to: "Did you ever kiss him?" – "Oh, dear, no. He was a peculiarly plain boy."

At the initial Marlborough Street hearing Mr Newton would not allow the introduction of letters (containing more libels) from Queensberry to 'Bosie', on the grounds that they were inadmissible. They also contained mention of the fact that the Solicitor General's son had been seen in bed with Wilde, and later the judges also managed to keep them out of the proceedings. One slight oddity about the magistrates' court hearing was that, after the evidence in chief, Mr Newton asked both lawyers to accompany him to his rooms, where they remained for ten minutes. The contemporary *Times* report mentions this, but I have seen no other references to the incident nor reports of what was said there.

During the famous and damning cross-examination of Wilde at the libel trial, a previous Marlborough Street case was dragged in, and it did not do him any good. The case concerned admitted friends or acquaintances of his. Alfred Taylor, Charles Parker and Arthur Marling, who had been among eighteen men arrested during a raid on a house in Fitzroy Street. Marling was one of two who had been wearing female attire and had subsequently appeared in the dock at Marlborough Street in "a fantastic female garb of black and gold". He claimed that he was a female impersonator and had been employed as such at a 'benefit concert' at the house. The case had been dismissed, but the knowledge of it was used again at the *final* trials of Wilde and Taylor, as in this examination of Parker (who had turned Queen's evidence), by prosecuting counsel Frederick Gill:

Mr GILL:
In August 1894 something happened to you and Taylor? – Yes, we were arrested.
Mr JUSTICE WILLS:
Arrested? On what charge? [Witness appeared to hesitate, and his lordship continued:] I only want to know, you know. You leave the

impression that there is something mysterious. What were you arrested
for? – For being in a house in Fitzroy Street.
Mr GILL:
Really for being there for a felonious purpose. There were men dressed as
women.
Mr JUSTICE WILLS:
Then I suppose they were charged with consorting together to commit
acts of indecency. Much better have the whole thing out.
Mr GRAIN [Defence] – In that case, then, better at the same time have it
out that both Taylor and Parker were discharged by the magistrate.

Marlborough Street was also to see a rather sordid sequel to the
Wilde case. On the day that Taylor was found guilty, a jubilant Lord
Queensberry was proceeding up St James's Street towards his hotel
when he bumped into his other son, Lord Douglas of Hawick, who
had stood bail for Oscar Wilde. Lord Douglas asked his father to
refrain from sending his wife obscene letters. In reply the pugilistic
Lord Queensberry blew a raspberry, and soon the two men were
fighting in the street. A constable separated them, but they resumed
the punch-up soon after.

When they appeared at Marlborough Street the following day (the
day on which Oscar Wilde was due to begin his *final* trial), they were
both bound over in sureties of £500 to keep the peace for six months.
Three days later, on Saturday 25th May 1895, the even more jubilant
Queensberry saw Wilde receive two years' hard labour, as an earlier
News of the World headline had predicted: "QUEENSBERRY
RULES."

4

The Night-Charges

"In the matter of night-charges, Great Marlborough Street probably bears the palm as to number and variety." (*The Graphic*, 16th July 1887)

After the applications have been dealt with, the list proper begins. First come the 'overnights', once known as 'night-charges', in ascending order of gravity. The 'overnights' are those arrested the day or night before and now making their first appearance before the magistrate. When they have been dealt with, the remanded cases from previous days are taken.

First come the very trivial, quick and easy-to-deal-with beggars, vagrants, drunks, prostitutes and street traders. Since the Vagrancy Act of 1824, beggars have always figured prominently on Marlborough Street's list due to the wealth of the residents, and even today there is a regular trickle.

At the beginning of the nineteenth century there were thousands of beggars.* Even Dorothy Wordsworth, tucked away in the Lake District, mentions the continuous flow on the roads, and these were soon to increase when the end of the Napoleonic Wars in 1815 threw thousands of sailors out of work. When they banded together, they could be pretty intimidating, as this report from *The Illustrated London News*, 4th November 1842, shows:

THE PLEASURES OF MEMORY
Mary Ann Jameson, Mary Ann Smith, Ann Giles, Caroline Johnson and Mary Holcombe, five elderly women, were brought in before Mr Hardwick, charged with having begged from, and otherwise importuned for money, Mr Samuel Rogers, of St James's Place, an elderly gentleman well known in the poetical world. Horsford, one of the Mendicity Society's** constables, said he watched the proceedings of the defendants

* Due mainly to the 'Speenhamland Act' and the Corn Laws. For a good run-down, see G.M. Trevelyan's *Illustrated English Social History* (Pelican).
** The Mendicity Society was an organization for saving beggars.

for nearly an hour. He saw them surround the old gentleman and solicit him for money. Mr Rogers tried to avoid them, but they followed him to a clubhouse in Waterloo Place, waiting until he again made his appearance. When Mr Rogers came out, they renewed their importunity, and it was quite evident their object was to extort money, either through the fear or compassion of the old gentleman. He got the assistance of another constable and succeeded in taking all five into custody.

A police constable corroborated Horsford's statement and added that one of the defendants was so violent that the old gentleman, to get rid of her, was obliged to inflict "a poke on her stomach with his umbrella".

Mr Hardwick asked Jameson what she meant by the conduct imputed to her?

Jameson said she had been intimately acquainted with Mr Rogers for forty years. Mr Rogers, in consideration had settled upon her an annuity of 10 shillings a week for life. It was therefore, very unlikely she should have acted in the way described by the constable.

Mary Anne Smith gave the magistrate to understand that, when a mere child, Mr Rogers became intimate with her. Mr Rogers had frequently given her money, and if the magistrate caused him to attend, he would not deny it.

The other three women made various excuses. None of them, however, claimed any acquaintance with Mr Rogers. Mr Hardwick said the practices of these women had grown to such a height that he was determined to put a stop to them. He should, on this occasion, send all five to the House of Correction for one month, with this caution, that if brought before him again he should make a term of imprisonment three months with hard labour.

According to Henry Mayhew, in his surveys of *London Labour and the London Poor* (fourth volume), published in 1862, begging had become an industry. Also, by his reports, it had become something of an art as well. He divided his 'Beggars and Cheats' into a mind-boggling array of 'ashamed' beggars, 'swell' beggars, 'clean family' beggars, naval and military beggars, foreign beggars, 'disaster' beggars, 'petty trading' beggars and 'distressed operative' beggars.

The 'ashamed' beggar went in for pathos with well-brushed shabbiness, a handful of lucifer matches or sticks of sealing-wax for sale and a nine-year-old half-starved boy in tow. On his neck was an 'ashamed notice' asking people to buy and regretting that he had been brought to this pass. His eyes would roll imploringly, but no sound would escape his lips, and in wintertime he introduced a little shiver and stifled cough into his performance which, he intimated by a despairing drop of his eyelids, was slowly killing him. One such, said

Mayhew, had a regular beat in the West End and was popular with the ladies, who would slip coppers into his hand quickly as if afraid they would hurt his feelings.

The 'swell' beggar was a decayed gentleman who ran around sweeping crossings and dabbing out puddles in the path of ladies and gentlemen. The 'clean family' beggars wore clothes falling into rags but had faces that shone with cleanliness; they would operate in an artistically arranged family group. Naval or military beggars included the 'turnpike' sailor, who had never been to sea but adopted salty slang, a sailor's roll and dress. However he cannot really have fooled many people since his face "bore the stamp of diabolically low cunning", and it was "impossible to look at him without an association with a police-court". Mayhew describes how one was unmasked to him by a real sailor who had seen the man spitting to windward.

Foreign beggars divided themselves into the French beggar, destitute Poles, Hindu beggars and Negro beggars, many of whom used their bewilderment in a foreign country to prey on "John Bull's partiality for foreigners"! Hindu beggars were evidently very easy to spot, "those spare, snake-eyed Asiatics who walk the streets, coolly dressed in Manchester cottons or chintz of a pattern commonly used for bed-furniture, to which the resemblance is carried out by the dark, polished colour of the thin limbs which it envelops". They often affected, he claimed, to be converts to the Christian religion and distributed tracts. The Negro beggar would represent himself as a down-trodden ex-slave, and several years before, when the slave trade had been suppressed, they had been so successful that many white beggars, "fortunate enough to possess a flattish or turned-up nose, dyed themselves black". What a droll image that presents. Mayhew does admit, however, that the Negro beggars would always work if they could get it, but getting it was the problem. Occasionally they could become silver-buttoned servants, but otherwise life was pretty hard. In 1887 Marlborough Street had its own Negro beggar, 'Robert the Devil,' who was often brought in on other charges as beggars frequently are. He was, *The Graphic* explained, "a well-known Regent Street nigger". The report went on:

A notorious character is 'Robert the Devil' at Great Marlborough Street, giving no end of trouble to the police and constantly being run in for disturbing the peace and endangering the safety of Her Majesty's liege subjects. Known to all the little boys from the back streets, too, who 'chivey' him when in his cups, and form a whooping *cortège* after him when he is running like a madman after the omnibuses and cabs, or orating to the general public outside the gin-shop from which he has just been 'chucked'. A constant attendant at Socialist meetings is 'Robert the Devil' also, where his general deportment is not to be admired, and where he constantly disturbs the harmony of the proceedings.

Poor Robert.

Mayhew's 'disaster' beggars seem to have been the most colourful of all, since their ranks included shipwrecked mariners, blown-up miners, burnt-out tradesmen, lucifer-droppers, bodily affected beggars, those "having swollen legs", cripples, blind beggars, beggars subject to fits, beggars "being in a decline", shallow coves, famished beggars and offal-eaters, not to mention those who did "the choking dodge" or had been "seventy years a beggar". Some, he claimed, changed their disaster according to the latest news. "After a serious coal-mine accident, 'blown-up miners' swarm in such numbers all over the town that one might suppose the whole of the coal-hands of the north had been blown south by one explosion." Lucifer-droppers were children who carried trays of matches or peppermints and would place themselves so that gentlemen bumped into them and spilt their wares into the mud. For this, white peppermints were really more effective scattered in mud, he suggested. The broken-hearted child would soon wring some money out of the gentlemen. "Having swollen legs" had almost been suppressed by the police now, said Mayhew (they achieved this by application of poisonous ointment or ligatures), but beggars subject to fits (with the aid of soap) still abounded, and many still fell into the Serpentine deliberately so as to be revived with brandy by the Humane Society.

"Shallow coves" were half-clad and shivering, and "famished" beggars were duly made up to look starving, sometimes with notices to that effect around their necks. It was these types who, to capture attention, would 'choke' on a mouldy old piece of bread or pick up scraps (offal) thrown out for the birds. Starved-out manufacturers, frozen-out gardeners (ground too hard) and distressed operatives completed Mayhew's lists, apart from the many varieties of begging-letter writers. The distressed operatives apparently kept an eye open for the list of patents and watched for the effects of new inventions on the operatives in Lancashire and Yorkshire!

Even in 1910 Marlborough Street's lists still showed a great number of beggars, many with children or babies in arms, but the numbers dropped right down during the First World War. The present-day trickle of regulars is much less colourful, and rarely are they professional beggars but usually alcoholics or drug-addicts who beg merely to support the habit. They are liable to turn up among the 'overnights' in various guises: as a beggar, drunk and disorderly, drunk and incapable or (though more rarely these days) as a vagrant sleeping rough and refusing to go to a place of shelter.

The regulars are often on first-name terms with the police-court staff, who, along with the probation-officers, are often the only regular caring human contact they have. Those who frequent Marlborough Street are various: refugees who have never quite made it back into the normal world, fallen gentlefolk, 'boffins' who have worked and worried their way into alcoholism, and kitchen porters and road-sweepers. 'The Duchess', who has a beautiful dark-brown voice, always makes up her face in the van *en route*, so as to be presentable on arrival. "How are you darlings?" she will enquire of the gaolers. However, though she is utterly charming once sober, it is a rather different story when she is in her cups, when she becomes one of the raging, fighting drunks. She is aware of this. "Was I a beast, darling?" she will enquire of the rueful young officer who had the pleasure of arresting her. In marked contrast to the Duchess was May Allen, who was always as nasty as possible to everyone all the time and who had the less than charming habit of defecating and urinating where she stood, whether it be in the cell or in the queue outside the court. J.B. Sandbach, magistrate at Marlborough Street from 1934 to 1946, recalls three old-lady regulars who went on regular meths binges together. Two of them were obviously of the duchess variety, and one treated the court with suitable, well-bred disdain. The third, who would always present herself at the station when she thought it was time she was arrested, felt she had a right to one particular cell and that anyone else occupying it should just be woken up and moved. Regulars have rights. Some, who have no fixed abode, will sometimes go out of their way to get arrested to escape the particularly cold spells or for a bit of Christmas cheer. 'Mary' used to get very cross if Hyde Park police refused to oblige when she had made up her mind to spend the night inside. To help them change their minds, she would break the station window, which predictably became known as 'Mary's window'. On one occasion, when this attempt was foiled, she lay down in the path of the area car.

By no means all the regulars appreciate a prison sentence. 'Michael', an inebriate little Irishman, for instance, always chants, "I only had one bottle of wine, Your Worship" when asked by the magistrate if he has anything to say. Once he was arrested after being found crawling round and round a bottle of a certain well-known tonic wine waving a Union Jack. "I admire his patriotism but not his choice of beverage," said Mr Harmsworth. However, Michael's exuberance or temper when in his cups sometimes lands him inside – as when he applied his 'one bottle of wine' to the head of an innocent passer-by, or when he grabbed an American lady tourist and swung her into the oncoming traffic, giving her a holiday to remember – in hospital. The longer sentences thus acquired produce a remarkable difference in Michael's appearance, and he returns to the West End a much improved man, though not, sadly, for long.

Sometimes, when we are having a drink in a West End pub, we bump into one of Marlborough Street's regulars, and they always insist on buying us a drink. To refuse is just not on – not if you care about other people's dignity. The implication will always be that Bob will chat to them in friendly fashion in court but does not think they are good enough to drink with. Recently one very charming (when sober) Scottish gentleman demanded we join him in a Christmas drink. He was still sober (well, sort of) when he proudly went off to get them in, and the journey back was achieved, by dint of great concentration, without spilling a drop. Alas, just as he reached our table, he tripped over a brief-case, carelessly left on the floor, and crashed to the carpet, throwing our drinks all over the people at the next table as he went. His bewilderment and disappointment were unbearable to watch, and it seemed so unjust to be tripped up when sober (well, practically).

Back in court, the police staff can sometimes assist the magistrate with a little information about the regulars, particularly if he is a visiting magistrate or is on a bench of JPs.

'Pawel', though not really a regular, had been to Marlborough Street before, Bob told the bench. "JAILER HELPS GESTAPO VICTIM," said a headline in the next issue of the *South London Press*, followed by this graphic account:

Assistant jailer Robert Lock made a timely intervention in a case at Marlborough Street, and his words served to shed a new and knightly light on a prisoner who until then had seemed to be a shabbily-dressed little man with grey hair and a foreign accent.

Pawel Malkiewicz, a fifty-eight-year-old Pole, unemployed and homeless, had denied but was found guilty of assaulting Darcy Yarde, of Kellet Road, Brixton, and damaging his spectacles.

Yarde said that when he asked Malkiewicz to move himself and his bundle from an arcade in front of a shop in Brompton Road, Chelsea, one night, Malkiewicz hit him on the forehead with a shoe, causing cuts and breaking his spectacles.

Malkiewicz denied striking the blow. He had taken off his shoes to clean them, he said, and had one in his hand when Yarde tried to retain his bundle and prevented him from getting it.

The magistrate found the charges proved and was about to deal with Malkiewicz when PC Lock intervened.

"Some two or three years ago he was arrested for wandering abroad," he said, "and the police went deeply into his background. He is a war hero who did sterling service with the Polish Army. He was very highly decorated, and he suffered tremendous injuries at the hands of the enemy and the Gestapo." The magistrate fined Malkiewicz £1 on each charge.

Of course, not all drunks charged at the court are regulars. Often they are one-offs. Some are people who live or work locally, but more are out-of-towners who have been on a binge, be it post-cup-match or business dinner. The reasons for getting drunk are very varied, and so are the morning-after attitudes. Some are hung over, some bewildered ("Did I really do that?"), others ashamed or worried – worried about how they are going to explain missing the train back to Glasgow, or not being at work that day, or how they can keep it out of the papers. Rarely are they the same aggressive creatures arrested the night before, though naturally some do strenuously deny the charge. One man, arrested just post-war, disputed that he was drunk and disorderly. He had merely been striking matches in St Anne's Churchyard in Soho, in search of Hazlitt's tomb, he said, when a constable told him to go away and alluded to him as "a spiv". Now there is an expression which brings back memories.

'Nanny', however, pleaded guilty and looked most demure in dock, so one could scarcely believe what *she* had been up to the previous day. While travelling on a bus she had suddenly electrified her fellow-passengers by announcing that she was about to give birth. The bus was cleared immediately, and the ambulance and police were called. The police arrived first and noticed that not only did Nanny's breath smell of drink but her speech was slurred. She refused to get into the ambulance when it arrived and eventually was put into a police-van instead – by three officers. In hospital she was found not even to be pregnant.

For her court appearance she wore a neat nurses' uniform and white cap. She apologized to the magistrate and explained that, before boarding the bus, she had been to a party. A fine of £2 was imposed, and, of course, there was *no way* it was going to stay out of the newspapers. "NANNY CLEARED THE BUS", sang the headline.

The younger drunks sometimes get a special ticking-off, for their own good. Mr Eric Guest (when he was a guest magistrate at Marlborough Street!) had some strong words for three teenagers brought before him: "If you could be in court with me for a few years and see the stinking wrecks who think it is grand to get drunk at your age and then go on with it, it would frighten you off drink a great deal more than anything I am able to do. If you come here again, I will take every unpleasant step the law allows to see that you don't become yet one more of this rotting humanity."

Blunt, but one can see his point. There is no sadder sight than a real old soak as he straightens his lapels and pulls his clothes about in a vain attempt to tidy himself before entering court. Then, with painful concentration, he aims for the dock trying to make it in a straight line and without falling over.

5

The Magistrates

"What is he saying?" asked the magistrate.

"He says: 'If you do not release me, there will be something happen to you that will not be good,'" replied the interpreter.

It was not very good grammar, but it was no idle threat. Only the previous day, a quiet, sunny Sunday afternoon, the accused had, with others, murdered an El Al hostess and seriously injured nine more people with the aid of hand-grenades and a machine-pistol.

David Hopkin, the magistrate, peered over his spectacles at the Arab's glowering face and enquired mildly; "Is that a formal application for bail or is it a threat?"

"It is a threat," the interpreter assured him.

"Thank you. You will be remanded to 31st August. The remand will be in custody."

One way and another, Marlborough Street Magistrates' Court has always been regarded as a hot-seat for magistrates, though more often as a threat to their good names than to their lives. *The Times* once referred to the court as "the grave of more than one magisterial reputation". There are dual reasons for this vulnerability: the wealth and social prominence of many of the prospective customers, which make likely attempts to pressurize the magistrates into certain decisions, then maximum publicity once they have made them. The West End venue also ensures more than usual Press attention.

The authorities, not unaware of these problems, ensure that the magistrates are usually well experienced at other courts before being appointed to Marlborough or Bow Street and that these particular appointments are made directly by the Home Office and with the approval of the Lord Chancellor.

The dangers of magistrates being too intimately acquainted with possible defendants was evident very early on, as this report from the *Observer* of 7th May 1799 indicates:

PUBLIC OFFICE, MARLBOROUGH STREET – Wednesday Mr Mathias O'Byrne was convicted in the penalty of £50 for laying and betting at a certain unlawful game called Faro. The offence, like those determined on Saturday, took place in the house of the Right Hon. the Countess of Buckinghamshire in St James's Square. The same witnesses viz Geo Evett and Joseph Pafford (the two discarded servants) were brought forward to establish the fact. They positively swore to have frequently seen the defendant play Faro at Lady Buckinghamshire's house, particularly on the night of 30th January last, the date specified in the information ... Some time after, Mr O'Byrne appeared at Marlborough Street before Mr Conant, *in proprie persona*, to answer charges against him.

Mr O'Byrne insisted he had not played on the night in question but

that he had played Faro within the six months was a fact, and he should, no doubt, amuse himself in the sáme manner again; how far he had acted contrary to the laws of the realm he was not able to say but, as the present and later Lord Chancellor of England had stood at the back of his chair whilst he was at play, he conceived that had he violated the laws of his country to any great extent, one or other of the noble Lords would unquestionably have admonished him for his offence; nay, he was not clear but that the Chancellor of His Majesty's Exchequer also had been an eye-witness of his conduct on similar occasions. Mr O'Byrne added that it was well for justice herself that informers had not been so vigilant a short time since or one of the magistrate's brethren, acting, he believed with him in that office, might have been in similar jeopardy, for amusing himself had been in his (O'Byrne's) company, at the game of hazard, which he had frequently done! He closed his Philippic by saying that he should now pay his penalty of £50, which he immediately did.

Peel had already begun some of his penal reforms when, in 1824, Frederick Roe became a magistrate at Marlborough Street. Roe was still there when Peel's New Police came into being in 1829, and he was to prove their most implacable enemy, quite prepared to fight in any dirty and underhanded way to bring about their downfall. He must have been delighted when the Whigs came into power in 1830 and Lord Melbourne was appointed Home Secretary, for the Whigs had bitterly opposed the idea of police. Though they now realized they would be better off with them than without them, they (and especially the new Home Secretary who had direct control of them) were determined to be cynically unsupportive towards them, encouraging all blame and no credit for everything they did. As David Ascoli points out in his police history, *The Queen's Peace*, the two new commissioners, Rowan and Mayne, fought a lone battle.

Roe was a crony of Lord Melbourne and kept the lazy, indecisive Home Secretary fed with ammunition to use against their common enemy. In 1833 he received his reward when he was appointed Chief Magistrate at Bow Street. It was, comments David Ascoli, "a deliberately provocative appointment". While holding the post, he continued to use the then illegal Bow Street Runners and did some of his worst mischief, almost succeeding in his aim of bringing the New Police down. He pushed an allegation of rape, which was regarded as having no foundation and had been thrown out by a jury, against two officers and goaded the new Home Secretary (also in his pocket and a brother-in-law of Melbourne) into giving an order that they be dismissed. The two commissioners, who were convinced of the men's innocence, knew that, if they did not comply, they would have to resign and leave their infant, struggling-for-life organization in the hands of the jackals; they complied.

Fortunately, magistrates have to retire sometime, and the next Whig Home Secretary, Lord John Russell, was not quite so unsupportive. It was during his office that the position and responsibilities of the New Police were consolidated and defined and also spread to the provinces.

Marlborough Street was also to acquire one of the best of the nineteenth-century magistrates, John Hardwick. As reformist feeling grew, the number of newspapers grew also and the London stipendiaries came under stiff attack from Cobbett, Black, Dickens and Co (see the chapter entitled 'Press and Public'). Dickens is credited with the removal of Alan Laing of Hatton Garden Court by exposing his dreadful ways; he used him as a model for Mr Fang in *Pickwick Papers*. However, even Dickens admired one or two magistrates, one of whom was 'Hardwick of Marlborough Street'.

John Hardwick was the son of a famous architect. A Fellow of Balliol College, Oxford, he was called to the Bar in 1816, becoming a stipendiary magistrate at Lambeth in 1821. In 1841 he was transferred to Marlborough Street, where he stayed until 1856. "His decisions were remarkably clear," states the *Dictionary of National Biography*. "He was popular on the bench and noted for his courtesy and linguistic ability." *The Illustrated London News* of 9th October 1847 thought the fact that he was "a capital linguist" was a most advantageous quality in a "police judge" presiding over a locality so "swarming with foreigners" and where applications for assistance from distressed Poles and "other expatriate unfortunates" were so frequent an occurrence. His works "on police-style subjects" were said to have influenced the organization of the Metropolitan Police, they assured their readers. "A rather elderly mild-looking personage," they went on, "he conducts the business in an easy and conversational, yet by no means undignified, style and is not above receiving a hint from any of the minor officials who surround him."

His popularity did not protect Mr Hardwick from occasional attack for his decisions, though more often they were used as a stick to beat others. The campaigning reformist voices in the newspapers had long complained about inequality of punishment, particularly with regard to petty offences. On 3rd October 1846 the *Daily News* pointed out that:

Any rich man may enjoy the luxury of an assault by paying for it. The fine imposed is the price of the article. The 'gentleman' buys his knock-down blow, or wrenched knocker, or smashed lamp, at Bow Street, as he does his coat at Stultz's or his boots at Hoby's. The tariff varies at different police offices. A Mr COMBE, for example, lets such things go very cheap indeed; a HARDWICK is disposed to put the very highest price on these dangerous luxuries.

But, they argued, whoever the magistrate was, there was always a choice between fine and imprisonment for a rich man, while the poor had no such option. Most just could not pay the fines and had to leave their wives and children unprovided for, not to mention doing a turn on the treadmill when they were incarcerated. Mr Hardwick had recently " ... to his honour, carried out the equalization principle, by awarding to a gentleman (who drove up to the office in his cab, and no doubt expected to be asked to a seat on the bench) a severe term of imprisonment for assaulting a policeman under most aggravated circumstances". Hardwick was able to do this, the paper explained, because the offence was the only one for which he was not obliged to offer an alternative of a fine.

Unhappily, the *Daily News* went on, his example had now been followed by a less judicious magistrate, Mr Ballantine, who had given a solicitor's clerk, who had, when intoxicated, merely pushed a policeman in the chest, seven days in a house of correction. The clerk told the magistrate that this sentence would ruin him, since his employer particularly needed him at this time, and also he was subject to fits which internment would bring on. He had, in fact, fallen down in a fit when sentenced. Policemen were not *that* sensitive the newspaper protested: "A thump or two, we apprehend, comes quite in the way of business to a policeman; and the unsteady 'wipe' of a drunken man is the least formidable of such visitations." Furthermore, the young man was of a class where a fine *would* be punishment, they insisted, and added, "We wish, when Mr BALLANTINE was bent on following Mr HARDWICK's example, that he had chosen his opportunity as wisely." Of course policemen were only just beginning to get a little protection from the law themselves.

Magistrates were also chastised, usually by the establishment Press, for being too lenient generally. E.H. Maltby was Hardwick's colleague at Marlborough Street for five years. Soon after he arrived, in June 1842, *The Illustrated London News* thought fit to guide him in the way he should go. They included one of his cases in the round-up of more interesting news from the courts – an Italian complaining of harassment, threats and finally assault from one of his fellow-countrymen of whose gang he said he was in fear for his life, as were many of his compatriots. Mr Maltby fined the offender 10 shillings. The magazine reported this, then added in brackets: "(With all respects to the worthy magistrate, we think the punishment in this case hardly commensurate with the offence – Ed. *ILN*.)" The glare of publicity was to continue to shine on the Marlborough Street magistrates, and often this was tied up with the pressure to do a bit of judicial covering up. 'The Case of Miss Cass', in 1887, which involved Robert Milnes Newton, and 'The Cleveland Street Affair', which put James Lennox Hannay on the spot in 1889, were typical. But the man who drew the most Press and public attention in the court's history was also its longest-serving and probably most controversial magistrate, Frederick Mead.

Mr Mead came to Marlborough Street in 1908 and served there until his retirement in 1933, when he was eighty-six years old – small wonder that, by the end of his term, his judgments were becoming a little wilful and eccentric. However, Stanley French, a clerk of the court who worked with him during some of those later years, found him "mentally agile and as acutely perceptive as any of his younger colleagues" and, though formidable, always compassionate. A very small man who always wore mittens when on the bench as he got older, he had very decided views, one of which was that women were to be protected from the nastier side of life whether they liked it or not and that their place was certainly not in political and public life. The suffragettes found his attitude towards them aggressive, and while a previous Frederick (Roe) had undertaken to sabotage the New Police, Mead took on the women police who began to emerge in the Great War. He was horrified that women should presume to do such things: they did not agitate to stoke the boilers of ships going through the Red Sea but only wanted to do some of the nicer things, he claimed, and this particular aim was warped and perverted. When they began to get mixed up in "filthy cases" from Hyde Park, he blocked their evidence and attacked their motives in court.

While he harassed women who stepped out of line, he did follow through and protect them even when it meant trouble for him, as in the case of Sir Almeric Fitzroy in September 1922. Sir Almeric, for many years a trusted Court official and Clerk to the Privy Council, was charged with "wilfully interfering with and annoying women in Hyde Park". Due to his royal connections, the case attracted a great deal of headline publicity, and Marlborough Street was besieged by interested onlookers.

Mr Mead found him guilty, a decision which caused considerable outcry. "May not a man walk in the Park?" the (entirely male-run) newspapers asked. Sir Almeric had, in fact, admitted to speaking to one of the women, but only because, he claimed, he had mistaken her for a friend. He had realized his mistake as soon as he had spoken, but did not want to seem rude so had carried on talking – similarly when he sat down beside her on a seat, asked her what she was doing there and suggested she take a walk to warm herself; it were merely manners. Since he had spoken to her once, he could not ignore her. He denied looking into the faces of other women and following them and was unaware that the police "knew of his presence in the park". He was waiting there to meet his wife, and the lady herself came forward and verified this. She also confirmed that the woman he had spoken to twice was, indeed, very much like a friend of theirs. By the time of the appeal, defence counsel had been able to dig up some dirt about the woman to whom he had spoken. She was not, as claimed, married but was living with a man.

When the conviction was quashed and costs given against police, Mr Mead came under fire – a fire which, claimed J.B. Sandbach who followed him, became rather persistent and unfair. "At one time" he says in his book, *This Old Wig*, "a certain section of the Press, for some reason which I have never understood, made a point of giving prominence to all the cases in which Mead's decision had been reversed upon appeal. It by no means followed that Mead had been wrong."

It seemed that whatever the Marlborough Street magistrates did in these 1920s 'gentlemen in the park' cases was wrong. In 1927 Mead's colleague, Henry Cancellor, found another influential gentleman 'not guilty', but the accused was not even satisfied with that, even though it is now pretty obvious that he was guilty and that Mr Cancellor had not only refused to allow the lady involved to be cross-examined in case it upset her but had awarded costs against the police.

The gentleman in question was Sir Leo Chiozzo Money, an ex-MP and writer on financial affairs who had been arrested for behaving indecently in Hyde Park with Miss Irene Savidge, a twenty-two-year-old valve-tester from New Southgate. Sir Leo immediately used his influence to cause questions to be asked in the House of Commons about the case, then skilfully switched the spotlight of accusation against the police, who had been a little cavalier in their handling of Miss Savidge (as they always were with women witnesses) when questioning her about the affair on behalf of two arresting officers who had been suspended.

More uproar in the House followed. Subsequent tribunals on the behaviour of the police in handling Miss Savidge resulted in massive publicity, massive public expenditure, massive attacks on the conduct of the Metropolitan Police and another 'case' about nothing, to be enshrined and dignified with the title 'The Savidge Affair'. Sir Leo was kept right out of all the bother and was not even properly questioned since he had now become a Knight on a White Charger. Eventually the investigating police were largely exonerated, and the case did result in more care being taken with women witnesses and more use being made of women police. The next time Sir Leo was arrested (for indecent assault), he was allowed to take his medicine without involving the Government or the calling of tribunals.

The 1930s brought the very popular J.B. Sandbach KC to the court. He liked sitting there since it enabled him to lunch at his club, the Oxford and Cambridge, whence he hastened, carnation buttonhole *in situ*, every lunch-time. A large, florid and jovial man who admitted to being not a very good lawyer, he was nonetheless extremely articulate and shrewd. "You couldn't throw dust in his eyes," comments Lord Justice Lawton, who often appeared before him as counsel. Sandbach, while sensible, was also impish, he recalls, and "one felt he was always enjoying some personal joke, getting a lot of amusement out of life." Another contemporary thinks he was probably the 'nicest' magistrate ever and the one most capable of expressing himself.

He first expressed himself in print when he was an impecunious young barrister. He had noticed that the newly enforced Motor Car Act of 1903 was receiving some rather conflicting interpretations in magistrates' courts and sought to remedy this, as well as to draw attention to himself and earn a little money, by producing a textbook on the subject. His only qualifications were, he admitted later, that he had once driven a car – on one occasion, that is, and then right into his own gatepost. This did not deter him, however, from writing *The Law and the Motor Car*, which, to his astonishment, got quite good reviews. He was pleased when a friend, later to be a County Court Judge, said: "Sandbags, I bought a copy of your book the other day." They were sitting in his club, and, since each sale meant a much-needed royalty in his pocket, he "leaned forward to touch the bell" but checked his hospitable impulse when the friend added, "It is, without any exception, the foulest book I have ever consulted." But, 'Sandbags' admits in his book, "I'm quite sure he was right."

Mr Sandbach became a favourite of the barrow-boys who attended the court on charges of footway-obstruction, and when he retired, in 1947, they presented him with a silver snuff-box inscribed, "To Mr J.B. SANDBACH KC, a grand old English gentleman, from the street traders of the West End." At his funeral, four years later, three West End barrow-boys carried a replica of the magistrate's chair executed in white, mauve and blue carnations and hydrangeas and surmounted by a gilt crown.

Following Sandbach came a contrasting character and one of the court's most respected magistrates, Paul Bennett VC MC. Handsome and well dressed in formal striped trousers and black jacket, and with a crown of wavy silver hair, he looked the part. In practice he was tough but not hard, fair but not gullible – one of his occasional pertinent questions could demolish in a flash a whole edifice of lies carefully built up and presented to him as truth. His Victoria Cross had been won on the Somme on what he referred to as "a very long day", when he had led his men over the top against insuperable odds, then, though wounded, consolidated their position and encouraged them to hold on.

Some thought him a rather cold man, and he certainly never played to the gallery or displayed much emotion on the bench. One thing he did get rather cross about though were the Hyde Park 'bustle-bumpers'. "I wish," he once said, "that women would turn around and slap the faces of men who behave in this way." No sooner the word than the deed, for, shortly afterwards, he was congratulating a woman who had turned around and broken one such man's nose! "I wish more women would turn around on men like this," he said, "or use their umbrellas." (The umbrella had long been one of Marlborough Street's favourite offensive weapons, though mostly used by 'gentlemen'.)

Like most of the court's magistrates, Bennett came from a background of some privilege, but his colleague broke that mould with a vengeance. Daniel Hopkin was anything but privileged. Maurice Wiggin, in *My Court Casebook*, describes Hopkin's early days most eloquently:

He has hewn his own life out of the most grimly unpromising material ... His father, a farm-labourer in the parish of Llantwit Major in Glamorgan, died when Daniel was seven. His mother's income thereafter was never more than 10s 6d a week. Young Dannie did every job that came to hand: hewed wood and drew water for the local parson; fetched and carried; did a turn for the farmers; slaved at his lessons. He won the King's Scholarship and at prodigious, grinding sacrifice did two years at teachers' training college at Carmarthen. He taught himself Latin, took a teaching job at Cambridge and entered himself at Saint Catherine's College. He then achieved the prodigious physical and psychological feat of transplanting his mother, brother and sister from Llantwit to Cambridge. He clocked in for early-morning chapel, taught all day, missed every lecture except a few at odd tea-time hours, taught at evening classes, borrowed a friend's notes and read halfway to morning. He took an extra weekend job, kept his family out of his earnings and paid his fees; and took the degrees of MA and LlB.

On the bench he was volatile, witty, decisive and popular. Lord Justice Lawton remembers him as "a warm-hearted, delightful fellow to appear before, providing your client had not done any real harm to another human being". When welcomed, as all new magistrates were, by the senior regular solicitor, then Claude Hornby, Mr Hopkin replied that he wished to uphold the traditions of fairness and justice set by Frederick Mead and other famous magistrates and added, "I know I can only do that with the help of the very loyal staff, of all the legal practitioners who come here and not least the Press." He was to prove a boon to the latter and was soon hitting the headlines with pronouncements that he was going to get to the bottom of the "absolute mystery" of why highly respectable women went shoplifting.

The Press delightedly kept track of his progress with headlines such as "NINE MORE CLUES FOR MR HOPKIN" and "MR HOPKIN CALLS SECRET CONFERENCE". The latter referred to a meeting he had held with the Drapers' Chamber of Trade on the question of shoplifting, while the former topped an item which reported his questions to a defendant who had stolen nine items. "Would you like to tell me why you did this? I am most anxious to know," he asked the woman.

Sadly, the 'mystery' was to defeat him, and, typically, he admitted he was beaten. When yet another shoplifter claimed she did not know why she stole, he commented; "No, and I don't think I shall ever know as long as I sit here." "SHOPLIFTERS BEAT ME, Mr Hopkin Makes a Confession," the Press announced. But he was to make more headlines during his short stay at the court.

Daniel Hopkin had earlier been Labour MP for Carmarthen West for $8\frac{1}{2}$ years and, while so employed, had begun his habit of getting out and about among all kinds of people, from farm-labourers on Welsh hilltops to milling crowds at Hyde Park Corner, as well as mixing with the mighty and living well, both of which he enjoyed. His wide experience, which he felt all magistrates should have, made him sympathetic to the less privileged, and, being Welsh, he probably also enjoyed the drama of the grand gesture.

Once he instructed the court to buy some paints for a down-and-out artist, while advising him to stick to "a good English school" rather than imitate van Gogh; on another occasion he gave the Christmas present of 'a chance' to a man who had expected a prison sentence. He did it on the grounds, he explained, that he had done similarly a year and a half before and had just received a letter thanking him and saying it had worked. The second man, benefiting from the chance utilized by the first, promptly fainted in the dock. "HIS CHRISTMAS PRESENT WAS FREEDOM", said a headline. The man had wit enough to respond to the role thus thrust upon him by later saying, "It was the perfect Christmas present – goodwill to all men."

Mr Hopkin would doubtless have stayed in the headlines, but, after only four years at Marlborough Street, he collapsed while in court and later died – on the day before Mr Sandbach's funeral.

They were followed by two more 'characters', another Welshman, the extraordinary Rowland Thomas, and the quaint Clyde Wilson. "Oh you must put about how Rowly used to jump up and down and run around his chair in a rage – and *some of the things he used to say*!" people insisted when they knew I was writing this book. Then the reminiscing would begin, eyes widening in continuing disbelief at his outrageousness. Frankly, I felt it all must be a little exaggerated – until I read his Press-cuttings! Unbelievable! How *did* he get away with it?

Mr Rowland Thomas served at Marlborough Street for only two years (just before my police service in the area) but left an indelible mark, nonetheless. First of all it was evident that Mr Thomas ("a Welsh terrier", as one onlooker describes him), was not over-keen on foreigners of any kind or dark-skinned persons with British passports, added to which his ideas were rather behind the times – as was his Boys' Own Paper language, full of 'rotters' and 'cads'. But no one could call him a coward. He always said what he thought. "Well, really that was because he was never sober," comments one lawyer who knew him.

He publicly regretted not being able to give corporal punishment to a man who, while living on the immoral earnings of a woman, had also assaulted a policeman; Mr Thomas was very pro-police. "FLOGGING NEEDED!" yelled the headline.

A black man who was found guilty of having three grains of Indian hemp about his person was treated to a harangue about the appalling effect that that "wicked drug" had on white girls who mixed with these coloured men. Rowland vowed that he would like to deport all those found 'in possession'. Sometimes even the police or prosecution felt the need to protect the accused against Rowly's wilder flights, and in this case the detective sergeant assured Mr Thomas that, although the accused was a 'stowaway', he had worked well since he had arrived.

"That," agreed Rowly, "is very much in his favour. As a rule these stowaways from Africa have only one port of call here – the public assistance!"

It was not just black people who earned his contempt. Once a Pole who had, as the contemporary parlance put it, 'associated' with another man's wife who was now up on a charge of soliciting, was given the full treatment.

"Fellows like you should be horse-whipped," he was told. "If there were not rotten fellows like you about, these girls would stick to their husbands. It is time some of you learned the law. A large number of you do nothing good in this country. Keep away from this woman and clear out!" Rowland concluded by adding, to the woman, that he would save her from this "wastrel and scallywag".

Being white and British through and through was no guarantee of escape, but the language employed was liable to be more 'boy-scout'. "You young bloods try to be clever," he told a couple of young men who had been accosting women in the park, "but you are nothing but a couple of cads."

Sometimes even the beloved police felt the edge of his tongue.

"Who," he asked one day, "is responsible for this magnificent prosecution?" A man had been brought before him for stealing, by finding, five bars of chocolate from a carton outside a kiosk at Hyde Park Corner. "If this man had eaten the rest of the chocolate," he declared with undeniable logic, "there would be no prosecution!" Then he gave the man an absolute discharge, telling him, "You should have eaten the other four bars."

To see him perform was, I understand, the most unbelievable experience. Instead of listening impassively, as most magistrates do, to the tale of evil doings of the person in the dock, he would react with tutting, exclamations and facial expressions of disgust and anger and even (people insist) jump up and down in his chair in a fury.

Clyde Tabor Wilson was also a one-off personality, though not so outrageous in style. Basically a kind man and well-thought of by the court staff, he also, it is rumoured, proved resistant, on one particular occasion at least, to pressure from above. He reminded me of nothing so much as a querulous gnome sitting up there on his toadstool piping his set comments on his twin dislikes, London Transport fare-dodgers ("Don't do it again – it's dishonest!") and homosexuals. (Heaven help you if you were a homosexual fare-dodger!) Seriously, he was not unkind to the latter, though a trifle disgusted by the thought of them, and he particularly disliked the idea of the soliciting some did in certain favourite lavatories and the fact that police had to supervise these to stop its getting out of hand. "The usual lavatory-patrol, officer?" he would cut-in, scarcely able to hide his distaste.

He did not think too much of psychiatrists either. When a civil-service staff-officer, told him that a man, who was accused of stealing from a colleague, had refused to see a psychiatrist, Clyde piped, "In that he showed his good sense, didn't he?"

Stanley French remembers him as a compulsive woolly-toy giver:

> He was the patron of a home for girls where the principal activity seemed to be the production of woolly toys and dolls. Wilson kept a stock of these with him and was constantly on the look-out for children for whom they would make suitable gifts. Probation-officers called into his room after he had heard a case in which a child had figured used to groan because they knew they would come out with their arms full of button-eyed lambs and cuddly dolls which would probably have no attraction at all for the little recipient.

Leo Gradwell took us back to something more akin to the Paul Bennett style of magistrate. A kindly, cultured and much-loved man, he had served in both world wars, in the first as a midshipman in a destroyer on the Western Approaches and in the second in command of various escort-vessels on the dreaded Russian runs. In 1942, while escorting the notorious PQ 17 convoy bound for Murmansk and Archangel, he won the DSC. As his obituary in *The Times* relates:

> After the convoy had been ordered to scatter, Gradwell in *Ayrshire* collected the vessels *Silver Sword, Ironclad* and *Troubadour* and took them 20 miles into the ice in the north Barents Sea. They stayed there for two days, camouflaged themselves by painting their upper works white and then continued their journey southward to reach Matochkin Strait in Novaya Zemlya safely. ... His conduct in this desperate enterprise earned him an almost legendary reputation for valour and unconventional resourcefulness.

In 1951, soon after becoming a magistrate at Thames, he contracted polio but refused to give in to his disabilities and carried on with calipers and sticks. In 1961 he was appointed to Marlborough Street and was, Stanley French declares, "full worthy of that eclectic court" in that he could be relied upon to keep his head in all circumstances. The sea was still a great love: any seaman who appeared before him captured his especial attention, and little bits of naval knowledge escaped now and then in his judgements. For example, during a strip-club prosecution he announced that Soho ought not to be worse than any other place in Europe, including Port Said.

Most magistrates mutter the odd quiet aside to themselves or meant only for the clerk or court staff to hear, for it can be lonely up there, and it helps to relieve the strain sometimes. Once, when a recalcitrant mongrel was brought before Leo Gradwell for being a nuisance and biting someone, he asked that the dog be brought into court and, after struggling around to see the now tail-wagging defendant, he was heard to murmur, "If you bite me now, it will be the worst thing you ever did." Fortunately the hound took the hint and licked his hand, and the case was dismissed.

Shortly after Leo Gradwell arrived, he was joined by Edward Robey, son of the comedian George. The current strong measures being used in an attempt to curtail shoplifting, the many famous persons being brought in on drugs charges, and the publicity attending the many ban-the-bomb demo arrests brought new focus to Marlborough Street around this time and led to Gradwell, Robey and Sir John Aubrey Fletcher's being dubbed "The Magistrates of Headline Court".

Robey is another clubbable man, though it is the Garrick with its historic connections with the stage, law and literature which he enjoys, smitten as he is with a rather natural love of greasepaint. Gilbert and Sullivan's operettas are his chief passion and one which afforded him a short-lived elevation to the heights when he played the Lord High Chancellor. With his father in mind, defendants could occasionally be heard to murmur "Give us a song" or "I liked your dad's act better", but his chief memories of the court, apart from the Monday morning demo-defendants, were of having to remand the ex-chef of his beloved Garrick for the murder of his wife and of seeing a blue film backwards. The film, the subject of obscenity charges, consequently started with a couple "behaving as one would have expected" and ended with the man going backwards out of the room, raising his hat to the lady in question, who was by then demurely seated in an armchair. The projectionist had offered to rewind it, but Robey had told him not to worry, as he would get the idea that way just as well.

His own autobiography gives the impression of his being a rather sheltered man, admitting, as it does, that he was more or less kept by his father until he was over thirty, due to his lack of success as a barrister. (Both Mr Sandbach and Mr St John Harmsworth have also claimed, perhaps partly in jest, that the reason they became magistrates was that they were struggling as counsel!)

Eventually he did a long stint as prosecutor for the Director of Public Prosecutions – not, one would think, good training for a magistrate, but my husband, who listened to him for long periods, found him very shrewd and thought he made reasoned decisions and was not too hard. (Despite what one would imagine, police are not necessarily fond of the over-tough magistrate.) Nevertheless, I must add that a friend who attended the court with his fellow political demonstrators who had been arrested, thought him "unnecessarily severe". These cases were, however, his pet hate, as he makes evident in his book. He certainly did not appreciate a court which went on too long, and court staff, who get to know the magistrates' little idiosyncrasies, would always know the danger-signs when long sighs began to emit from the bench.

Neil McElligott, who arrived there in 1972, was thought by some to be severe, because he insisted on the dignity of his court being maintained, but Bob always felt he was one of the best magistrates he had heard – tough when toughness was necessary and kind when kindness was called for. "He had tremendous guts, even when a counsel," remembers Judge Lawton fondly. Police and solicitors were, however, expected to do their jobs properly, and if they did not, he would tell them so. One policeman was told to speak up: "I remember the time," McElligott told him, "when a policeman went into the witness-box, threw back his head, expanded his chest – and you could hear him in the adjoining street. Now you all whisper. For heaven's sake speak up!"

His name caused some confusion, and he was always referred to by one regular offender, very incongruously, as 'Mr McGigglygot'. Like many of the magistrates at that time, he found it necessary to try to resist the onrushing power of the social and psychiatric report which (if taken too much notice of, as by some benches of JPs) can result in 'trial by social worker'.

"It says here," said Mr McElligott wonderingly, as he read one such epistle, "that he had a comfortable bedroom in pastel colours and a colour TV set. What on earth has that got to do with a man touching the backside of a woman?"

Nowadays Court Two is largely left in the hands of a bench of JPs, and Court One's business attended to by David Hopkin, son of Daniel, and St John Bernard Vyvyan Harmsworth, nephew of

Viscounts Northcliffe and Rothermere. Mr Hopkin is I hear, "very shrewd", though he sometimes makes decisions which some find a little puzzling, and Mr Harmsworth is a highly articulate joker who makes very quotable quotes.

6

A Man at the Top of his Profession

The middle-aged man looked pleadingly at Mr Harmsworth, who had just fined him £20 for obstructing police by warning gamers of their imminent approach.

"I'd like you to make it a little bit less if you could," he said.

"Certainly not," replied Mr Harmsworth. "You are a man at the very top of your profession. It would only expose you to the scorn and ridicule of your friends and colleagues if I fined you less than the maximum."

The gamers, or three-card tricksters, invite passers-by to 'find the lady' or their own pound note from under one of three cards – an impossible task, of course. They form part of the regular clientèle at Marlborough Street and engender in those who deal with them at court a very ambivalent attitude. It is hard to approve of what they do, as really it is all a big cheat (though one wonders at the naïveté of people who fall for it), but it is harder to dislike the men themselves. They are friendly and cheeky and can be very funny with police and magistrates, with whom they often form an odd kind of relationship. Mr Harmsworth's riposte was certainly a clever way of bridging this ambivalence without giving way to it.

The street traders, who are usually among the footway-obstructions (or have been trading without a licence), often have a similar relationship with magistrates and police. They are charged merely in an attempt to keep them under some kind of control, to prevent complete congestion of the pavements and too much friction between them and the local shop- and store-owners, who, not unnaturally, get somewhat upset when they see their profits being creamed off by people who pay neither overheads, rent nor rates. However, police did not care for one JP who mistook her role for that of a social worker and fined street traders more than shoplifters. After all, street traders are working, not committing crimes.

Their wares vary with the fashion and season, but some are perennials, such as the fruit-and-veg merchants, the 'Paris perfume' purveyors and the sellers of fluffy jumping-toys. Currently in fashion are leather belts and 'growy' umbrellas, but in Sandbach's time exorbitantly priced black-market elastic was the big attraction.

Not all street traders appear as defendants. Their permanent position on the street means that they sometimes get dragged in as witnesses in other cases or become complainants themselves. The latter was the case with one hot-dog man.

Two very ordinary, mild-looking girls stood in the dock charged with criminal damage to a hot-dog barrow and contents. Apparently there had been a difference of opinion between them and the stall-holder as to the price he had initially stated for his hot dogs. When they handed over their money, he said it was not enough. They insisted that that was what he had asked for. He disagreed. All right, they said, have your hot dogs back. He declined. The girls saw red, and soon so did he, for one of them grabbed hold of the ketchup.

"You should have *seen* it when I got there!" exclaimed the still-bemused arresting officer. "He and his stall were covered in tomato ketchup and mustard; there were rolls and sausages all over the road, and one of the girls was slowly squeezing ketchup into his hair! It was amazing!"

Others who come in for footway-obstruction include street photographers, (often with their monkeys) street entertainers and the 'apricot priests', as the police have dubbed those saffron-robed, mohican-headed Hare Krishna monks who wander along Oxford Street ringing their bells and banging their drums. Since 'peace' is their 'thing', as they keep telling everyone, they are normally quite easy to deal with, though they can become a little too persistent in their importuning of passers-by, to whom they offer records or tracts – for a 'donation' (Just try to keep a record they thrust into your hands without making payment!) Their constant chanting of "Hare Krishna, Hare Krishna, Hare Krishna", as they fiddle with their beads, does, however, sometimes make the police feel a little less than peaceful, so they allowed themselves a small smile recently when one of the monks was brought in on a charge of causing actual bodily harm to another. Peace, evidently, has its price.

'Santa Claus' denied causing footway-obstruction, as did his companions, nine more Santas and three eskimos. It was Christmas 1969, and they had come all the way from Greenland to picket

Selfridges in a protest against the employment of under-paid, non-union santas being used to exploit the dreams of children. Led by 'Super Santa' Ed Berman, an American writer, they had formed, they said, a Santas' Union. Mr Robey obviously did not care whether he got his stocking filled or not, for he found them guilty and fined them £10 each, enquiring drily whether he could expect a militant Snow White and Seven Dwarfs next year. The real aims of the demonstration seemed a little woolly and smacked of a publicity stunt, though for what, was not apparent.

The late-1960s 'battle of the boutiques' in Carnaby Street also brought a spate of rather unusual obstruction charges, when the shop-owners endeavoured to attract attention to their particular businesses by the cynical display of the female form. Caged girls, half a dozen naked girls sitting in the window of a newly opened boutique and even a girl pressing her bare bosom into concrete, *à la* Grauman's, were featured. Huge crowds gathered, but the resultant charges were not exactly fretted over, bringing as they did, wide publicity.

All these less serious 'overnights' are speeded through the court by the gaoler. In fact, he is an assistant gaoler, the real gaoler being the sergeant behind the scenes, but to everyone in court, he remains 'the gaoler'. A police constable or, sometimes, a sergeant, usually of long service, he stands by his lectern adjacent to the dock and consults his list for the next case. Then he walks to the door, calls in the defendant and ushers him into the dock. Alternatively he walks to the door, calls the case and no one answers, so he curses the policeman concerned who has not produced his prisoner, and goes back to find the next name on the list.

If the case is found proved, he gives details of any offences against the accused at that court. If remanded, he finds a date for the next hearing in the court's diary. It is a seemingly simple procedure which, at the beginning at least, is carried out at a fast lick – in theory. What can throw a spanner in the works at Marlborough Street is a gaoler who has not been born knowing (or having since casually acquired the ability to pronounce) all the world's languages, so that foreign defendants will instantly recognize their names and answer to them. BBC newsreaders should come here for practice.

Another stumbling-block are the hoverers. These are a small knot of people who hover just behind a gaoler with a view to catching his attention, then persuading him that there are good reasons why their particular case should be heard earlier than scheduled: "The PC is on night-duty and wants to go to bed now, please"; "The counsel is wanted in the other court (or at the Old Bailey) in twenty minutes time," and so on. The sensible and experienced hoverers realize that their plea stands a much better chance if they do not forward it in the middle of the first rush of quickie cases. If they tug at the gaoler's arm while he is whipping people in and out of dock, or stand in his path and block his wham-bang progress they impair their chances – not to mention risk their lives.

While the longer cases are proceeding, the gaoler, again in theory, just stands there. However, having advantage of uninvolved listening, a good gaoler often takes on more tasks, such as seeing that the law is properly carried out in 'his' court. Stanley French describes one such gaoler at work:

> I would be busily engaged in the next case when I would have the feeling that someone was looking at me from behind. Then I would notice that the usher was gazing pointedly beyond me. I would look round. There was the gaoler, a slight smile on his lips and a large black book in his hands. "Excuse me," I would say to the magistrate, "I think Sergeant Saunders wants to point out a blunder." Then the gaoler would come up to my empanelled enclosure and whisper, "Sorry to interrupt you, sir, but that last case – I don't think the magistrate can do that." ... My mistakes were pointed out and put right so quietly and unostentatiously that there was little likelihood of the occupants of the public gallery knowing what was happening.

Magistrates can be aware of the gaoler too. One admitted to Stanley French that he always glanced over to one particular gaoler after he had made his decision, as he could tell by his expression whether it was the right one. And a JP friend of mine says he could not keep his eyes off another gaoler when they were being told a particularly outrageous lie. His face was so totally without expression at those times that it spoke volumes; however, when credulity was being stretched beyond all bounds, his face would still remain deadpan but his glance drift ever so slowly up into the upper-right-hand corner of the room and remain fixed there.

Being uninvolved in the outside police work, the gaoler can, as I have shown, be quite as helpful to the defendant as he might to a police-officer, in that, if he knows something about the case which he feels the court should know, he may occasionally intervene and address the bench. At one time gaolers intervened a great deal and

mostly not to the advantage of the defendant, as in the case of the
intimidated Italian on page 42 when the gaoler put his oar in and
advised the magistrate that the defendant was a "desperate
character"! Nowadays it would frequently be something in the
accused's favour and may even amount to a plea of mitigation.
"FORMER NANNY GETS LENIENCY" (nannies, as you may
have noticed, make good copy), "Gaoler Better Than Counsel", said
the *Kensington Post* of one of my husband's interventions. Like Plank,
he had repeated to the bench what she had told him during the lunch-
adjournment – that her employer had previously given her permission
to take her car (she was now charged with doing so without
permission), and she had no idea that she was not insured. She would
have said this herself but had been struck dumb by nervousness. The
bench told her that, thanks to the police, who had spoken up for her
better than counsel, they would deal with her leniently. And, in case
you are thinking that she should have had legal aid – have you heard
some of the lawyers you can get that way?

7

"I do not understand"

A pretty, dark-haired policewoman was standing alongside a Greek shoplifter who was speaking rapidly into the phone, in her native language, "getting a friend to stand bail". When the woman had finished, she put down the phone and glanced at the policewoman, scarcely able to conceal her smile of triumph, tinged with disdain. The policewoman smiled back and murmured, in Greek, "I think I should tell you that I understood every word you said and intend giving it in evidence at court tomorrow." Collapse of stout alien. She had been instructing her friend to go to certain stores, buy certain goods and make sure she retained the receipts and carrier-bags. Not surprisingly, these goods were identical with the ones she was accused of stealing. She was cooking up a defence.

The mainly monolingual British sometimes give foreigners a false sense of security, but these days there are many second-generation immigrants in the police, and the Greek shoplifter had been unlucky enough to land an officer of Cypriot parentage to whom it was not 'all Greek'.

Foreigners have always attended Marlborough Street in far greater numbers than any other magistrates' court, Soho long being the haunt of *émigrés* and refugees. The White Slave Traffic, rampant in the nineteenth century, also brought many foreign prostitutes to London's West End, so many that they were always taken first on the court's list of night-charges, "to save time and expense" – the expense, one presumes, of the interpreter, who was 'a well-known face' at Marlborough Street. Contrary to our prejudices, these foreign prostitutes were nowhere near as excitable or easily reduced to tears as the British girls. As *The Graphic*, of 16th July 1887, reported:

The foreign element is more composed, more conservative, more bland and businesslike. When a policeman's evidence is very strong against an offender of this class, the lady will shrug her shoulders, spread out her gloved hands and appeal to the magistrate direct.

"*Oh! m'sieur, ce n'est pas vrai!*" escapes in silvery accent and with 'tears in the voice'.

This lack of excitability was still true of the Continental prostitutes in my service in the 1950s. 'Businesslike' was the word. Indeed, I, from the sticks, sometimes found their poise and élan somewhat intimidating. They were so 'got-together' in appearance as well, with beautifully tailored, very expensive suits over elegant figures. Their lives, too, were organized: regular VD checks, fines and rents paid on time. They kept out of trouble. Most were French or Belgian, and this coolness continues today in the French shoplifter who does all the expected disdainful shoulder-shrugging and makes sure one registers her scarcely-concealed contempt for the proceedings – an attitude which makes the French one of the three most unpopular races dealt with by the police, store detectives and interpreters. The other two are Arabs and Iranians, who think it is all the fault of those doing the arresting and often have abominably whining children in tow. If those children are boys, they are totally unbearable, being so spoilt.

Argentinians do not mind whose character they blacken in their attempts to escape justice, and the Italians are, well, Italian. Most dignified, and also least likely to land up in the dock, are the Northern Europeans, North Americans and Orientals. Although they are generally well off, this cannot be the only reason, since the Arabs and South Americans who steal are often not just financially secure but very rich.

The people through whom the aliens (I wish there was another word besides this, and 'foreigners' – both sound so bigoted) often speak, the interpreters, work on a free-lance basis. Courts and police-stations have lists of their names and languages, to which they refer whenever one is needed. Since it can be seasonal work, the good interpreter gets his holiday over before the summer or Christmas rush. If they want a lot of work, they must make sure they are easy to find (some carry 'bleepers') and be willing to attend at sometimes not very social hours. Crime is not nine to five.

Many speak several languages, especially those brought up in the Middle East in particularly multi-lingual centres such as Cairo or Beirut where English, Arabic and Greek are commonplace, with French or Italian sometimes thrown in for good measure. The best interpreters are those sufficiently interested to be of use to both prosecutor and accused in making sure they understand each other and that the accused knows what is going on. A few go over the top and become partisan. They try to fight the defendant's case or act as extra prosecutors. The worst are those who think that natives of their own country cannot have done wrong, and this can even result in their putting words into a defendant's mouth instead of taking them out. Those with such tendencies will be politely warned to desist and stick to their jobs, which requires quite enough skill and grey matter if done properly. If they do not accept the warning, they can be struck off the official list.

Josephine Bacon, an interpreter writing in *Police Review*, 27th July 1979, claims that police have told her that they positively welcome working via an interpreter, since, as impartial observers, the latter are valuable witnesses in court against the two-common accusations of police 'verballing' of an offender or using brutality.

There is no doubt they get some odd things to translate.

"What is she saying?" asked the clerk of the court recently, when one Arab woman shoplifter suddenly held out her arm and, gabbling excitedly, pointed to it.

"She is saying," explained the interpreter, "that you should cut off her hand."

"Tell her we don't usually do that," said the clerk.

Afterwards, the clerk, Mrs Gubbay, realized that that was perhaps not quite the right statement of our policy. "It made it look as if we *did* do it, occasionally."

Rarely does an alien get as far as the dock without an interpreter if needed, but it does happen now and then, usually with those who insist they speak English "perfectly well, thank you," and are most insulted if you suggest otherwise. The magistrate might decide that they do not, in fact, speak it well enough to understand the rather formal law language, and they are 'put back' until an interpreter is found. Once Mr Harmsworth found one himself without moving from the bench.

"Do you speak Turkish by any chance?" he enquired politely of a street trader up on a charge of footway obstruction. Mr Ahmet Hassan did and agreed to act as go-between for a Turkish Cypriot drunk.

"I am much obliged to you, Mr Hassan," Mr Harmsworth assured him afterwards. "In all the circumstances you are conditionally discharged, and you are also entitled to an interpreter's fee."

Some gaolers find all this foreign pronunciation business, which is forced upon them, a bit of a trial. Others, with an ear for languages and a penchant for showmanship, rather enjoy it all. The exuberant deliveries of singsong Chinese and lisping Spanish became quite a feature of a Number Two Court gaoler and caused many a magistrate to widen his eyes or hide his face behind his hands in suppressed giggles. "We always wait to hear how *you* will pronounce it," one of his JP fans told him. Of course he did have the advantage of knowing, since the British are generally so ignorant about these things, that if he did get it wrong, no one (with the exception of the interpreters and defendant) would ever know.

He could also manage, "Hello", "Goodbye" and "Stand over there, please", in several languages, but, should his masterly delivery of these tongues spark off long, gabbling replies in said tongue, he would conveniently find himself much too busy to respond. But it says much for his style that he has been the recipient of delighted exclamations: "You speak Serbo-Croat!" and "You speak Hebrew!" Well no, not quite.

Not all the court's shoplifters are foreign, but most of them are female and steal mostly clothes, make-up and jewellery. There are one or two seemingly national obsessions with certain garments: Iranian women, for example, tend to steal countless pairs of briefs, which predilection won them the typical police dubbing of 'the Persian knicker-nickers'. Every one a gem!

When men do have a go, it is often for books or records. Sometimes they are students stealing textbooks; sometimes they are straightforward thieves intending to re-sell; sometimes they are people who feel one should not have to pay for books since "they are our heritage really, aren't they?"; sometimes they have an obsession about the subject the books deal with, and sometimes they just cannot resist books.

One man, who had an obsession with magic, the occult and so on, was recently charged with stealing a library-book entitled *The Book of the Sacret Magic of Abra-Melin the Mage*, written in 1932 by S.L. MacGregor-Mathers and out of print since 1934.* The magistrate pointed out, as they often do in such cases, the selfishness of such an

---

* Although it has recently been republished by A. Thomas & Co, whose advertisement states: "This hitherto rare work, claimed to be the most genuine and magical manual ever published, has released strange, uncanny and sometimes terrifying phenomena – even in modern times!"

act, in that the thief was depriving other members of the pleasure of borrowing the book. In this case, however, the officer permitted himself a small smile, as he had been informed by the library that the book had been on the shelves since 1933 and taken out only twice since then.

When those who just cannot resist books are apprehended, great piles of books are often found, filling whole rooms where the thieves live. One such, who had managed to steal fifteen hundred books without being caught, finally came unstuck when he tried to make off with nine at once. Another, a Chinese gentleman, had a too tidy mind, which proved his undoing: when he was caught for one theft, his diary revealed full details of all his previous offences. He had neatly entered the name of each volume, venue of appropriation, normal selling-price and how much he had actually received on re-selling. He had no choice but to plead guilty to such well-documented crimes. Not so clever!

Most of the shoplifters are culled from Oxford Street, a mecca for shoppers since before the court opened. This is how one lady, Sophie von la Roche, saw it in 1786:

We strolled up and down lovely Oxford Street this evening, for some goods look more attractive by artificial light. Just imagine a street taking half an hour to cover from end to end, with double rows of brightly shining lamps, in the middle of which stands an equally long row of beautifully lacquered coaches, and on either side of these there is room for two coaches to pass one another; and the pavement, inlaid with flagstones, can stand six people deep and allows one to gaze at the splendidly lit shop-fronts in comfort. Behind great glass windows absolutely everything one can think of is neatly, attractively displayed.

Even then some ladies did not stop at looking – they 'lifted' too. Later, during an epidemic in 1830, a broadsheet ballad on shoplifting had the pleading title *Ladies, Don't Go Thieving* and began:

Oh don't we live in curious times.
You scarce could be believing,
When Frenchmen fight and Emperors die,
And ladies go a-thieving.

And they meant 'ladies', or at least those who appeared to be, not just women, who were something else again in those days.

The Illustrated London News of 9th October 1847 mentions the style of the "flaunting West End 'Lady Thief' ", who rustled in satin at Marlborough Street's fashionable bar while Clerkenwell and the East End courts saw merely mouldy-bread stealers. However, this was scarcely surprising, they thought, since:

> Marlborough Street presides over fashionable squares and gay West End streets; regions of coroneted carriages and cold stately town residences, or else glittering thoroughfares; gaudy shops, brilliant with every graceful luxury, every winning trifle, every fashionable bagatelle; a quarter of dashing men-milliners, and elaborate confectioners, and incomparable modistes, and trouser-makers from Berlin, and boot-makers from Paris, and music-sellers, and bouquet-sellers, and print-sellers, and lace-sellers ... flashing their brilliant fancy wares and rich stuffs.

The area, especially after the advent of Regent Street, was felt to be the best shopping-centre in the world. The lady thieves stole mostly small items, such as gloves and jewels, but rolls of silks or 'stuff' were not beyond them. Mayhew describes how they tucked them under their arms, which were well-covered with large cloaks or stoles. Often they lined their dresses from the pocket downward which provided "a large repository all around the dress". The ampleness of the crinoline, fashionable in the mid-nineteenth century, made their consequently bulky outlines seem not unusual.

However, Marlborough Street was not without its own need-rather-than-greed offences. Food and boots loomed large in the lists of goods stolen even up until the First World War. The Court Register for 1910 features many a dead fowl and leg of mutton, and even "one loaf of bread". In those days, of course, butchers and poulterers hung their goods outside their shops, so it was relatively easy to whip away the chickens and joints. *The Graphic* of 1887 describes a typical boot-stealer and also demonstrates that pity is not the prerogative of our age, as we sometimes like to think:

> A bare-footed, half-starved, shivering wretch is hustled into dock to answer a charge of stealing a pair of boots, and here is a worthy constable with the boots *en evidence*. There is no getting out of this case – the prisoner can only plead as Harold Skimpole* pleaded for spring lamb: the

---

* Harold Skimpole, a character in Dickens's *Bleak House*, who was innocently ignorant about finance and sponged off his friends. Said to be based on Leigh Hunt.

Marlborough Street Police-Station and Court, 1854. (From the
Crace Collection, British Museum).

Marlborough Street Magistrates' Court, 1979.

A view from the court doorway, showing the North End of Carnaby Street. To the right: Liberty's; left: the offices of Claude Hornby & Cox, the court's most regular solicitors for many years.

View from the dock in Number One Court.

View when approaching the dock. Note the door at the rear – curved to follow the concave panelling.

The road to the cells.

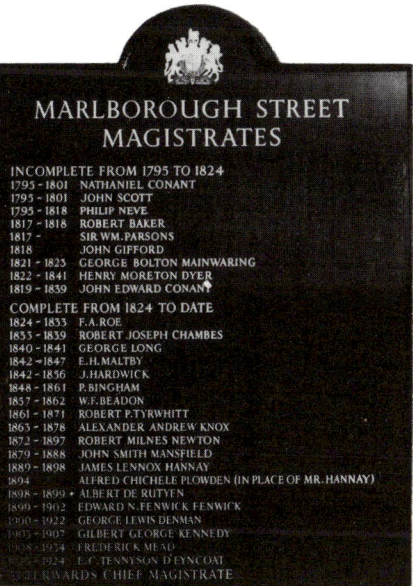

The (stipendiary) Magistrates' Room.

The Magistrates' Boards, listing those who have sat permanently at the court. (Mr Cancellor's name is incorrectly spelt).

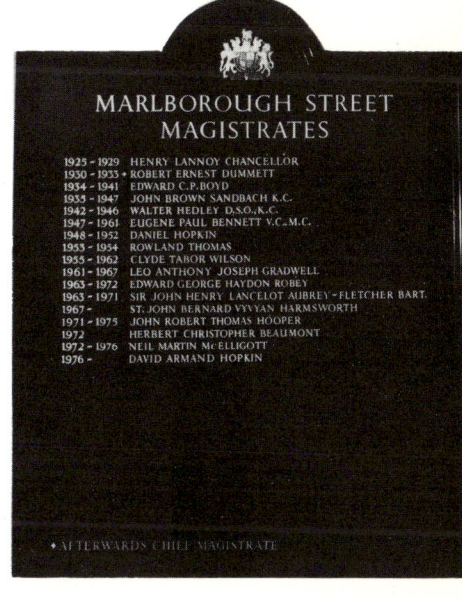

MARLBOROUGH STREET MAGISTRATES

INCOMPLETE FROM 1795 TO 1824

1795 - 1801	NATHANIEL CONANT
1795 - 1801	JOHN SCOTT
1795 - 1818	PHILIP NEVE
1817 - 1818	ROBERT BAKER
1817 -	SIR WM. PARSONS
1818	JOHN GIFFORD
1821 - 1825	GEORGE BOLTON MAINWARING
1822 - 1841	HENRY MORETON DYER
1819 - 1839	JOHN EDWARD CONANT

COMPLETE FROM 1824 TO DATE

1824 - 1833	F. A. ROE
1833 - 1839	ROBERT JOSEPH CHAMBES
1840 - 1841	GEORGE LONG
1842 - 1847	E. H. MALTBY
1842 - 1856	J. HARDWICK
1848 - 1861	P. BINGHAM
1857 - 1862	W. F. BEADON
1861 - 1871	ROBERT P. TYRWHITT
1863 - 1878	ALEXANDER ANDREW KNOX
1872 - 1897	ROBERT MILNES NEWTON
1879 - 1888	JOHN SMITH MANSFIELD
1889 - 1898	JAMES LENNOX HANNAY
1894 -	ALFRED CHICHELE PLOWDEN (IN PLACE OF MR. HANNAY)
1898 - 1899 •	ALBERT DE RUTYEN
1899 - 1902	EDWARD N. FENWICK FENWICK
1900 - 1922	GEORGE LEWIS DENMAN
1903 - 1907	GILBERT GEORGE KENNEDY
1908 - 1934	FREDERICK MEAD
1923 - 1924	L. C. TENNYSON D'EYNCOAT

• AFTERWARDS CHIEF MAGISTRATE

MARLBOROUGH STREET MAGISTRATES

1925 - 1929	HENRY LANNOY CHANCELLOR
1930 - 1933 •	ROBERT ERNEST DUMMETT
1934 - 1941	EDWARD C. P. BOYD
1935 - 1947	JOHN BROWN SANDBACH K.C.
1942 - 1946	WALTER HEDLEY D.S.O., K.C.
1947 - 1961	EUGENE PAUL BENNETT V.C., M.C.
1948 - 1952	DANIEL HOPKIN
1953 - 1954	ROWLAND THOMAS
1955 - 1962	CLYDE TABOR WILSON
1961 - 1967	LEO ANTHONY JOSEPH GRADWELL
1963 - 1972	EDWARD GEORGE HAYDON ROBEY
1963 - 1971	SIR JOHN HENRY LANCELOT AUBREY - FLETCHER BART.
1967 -	ST. JOHN BERNARD VYVYAN HARMSWORTH
1971 - 1975	JOHN ROBERT THOMAS HOOPER
1972	HERBERT CHRISTOPHER BEAUMONT
1972 - 1976	NEIL MARTIN McELLIGOTT
1976 -	DAVID ARMAND HOPKIN

• AFTERWARDS CHIEF MAGISTRATE

Well-known faces at Marlborough Street Magistrates' Court, past and present. Above, *from left to right:* Magistrate Frederick Mead; Arthur Newton, the court's best-known solicitor of late Victorian times (from *Vanity Fair*, 1893); Len Almand, the court reporter from 1926-76. Below: Magistrates (*left to right*) Leo Gradwell, John Aubrey-Fletcher and Edward Robey (in the background, Charlie Morgan, Chief Probation-Officer at the Court for many years); solicitors A. E. Cox (of Claude Hornby & Cox) and Victor Lissack— both now judges.

The two present magistrates: David Hopkin (left) and St. John Harmsworth.

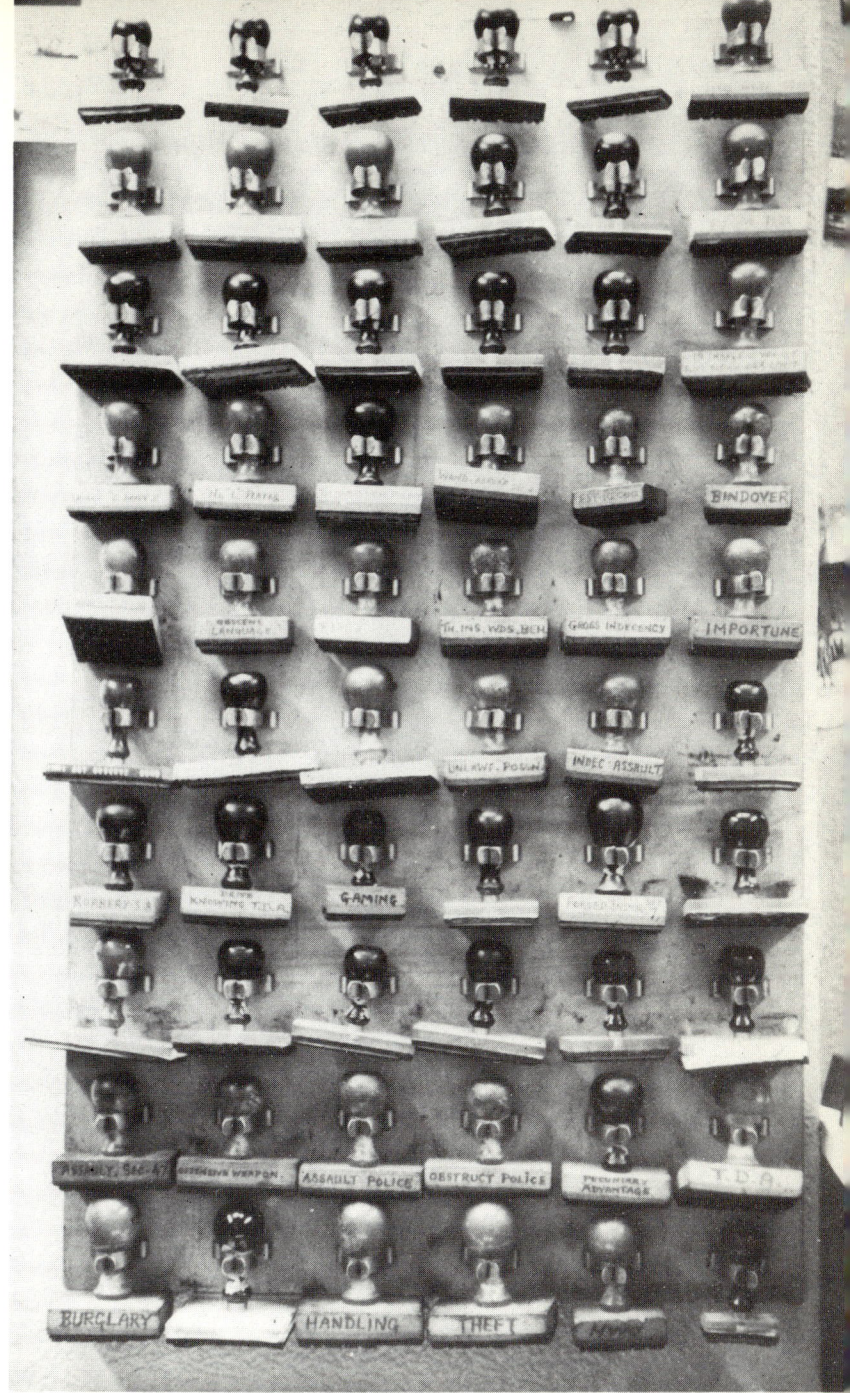

The stamp-board in Number Two Court gaoler's office. Each stamp carries details of a regular offence.

Caption: THIS FREEDOM –
"Please, ladies and gents, be
reasonable. Whatever the
arguments, everybody's
agreed that you shouldn't
get on the old bus at least
until it's *stopped*!"

This cartoon comments on
the furore following a Marlborough Street decision on a
case brought by the author's
husband. (London *Evening
News*, 2nd September 1954).

An extract from the *Daily
Mirror*, 1964.

The magistrates of
Headline Court

IT'S the court that makes the headlines
—Marlborough-street Magistrates' Court,
the "Court of Controversy," in the heart
of London's West End.

The grey, gaunt building next to the London
Palladium's stage door is in the centre of a big
rumpus.

Since the beginning of the
year, more than 200 motorists
have been arrested on warrants
issued by the court's three stipendiary (paid) magistrates for
minor motoring offences. This is
many more than were issued at
any other London court.

Only yesterday, two motorists—
the Marchioness of Londonderry
and Ann, Lady Crofton—appeared
at Marlborough-street after being
arrested on warrants for minor
motoring offences.

Only the day before, one of the
three Marlborough-street magistrates spoke about Britain's
"clogged-up courts." "There aren't enough
courts, and there aren't enough magistrates,"
Mr. John Aubrey-Fletcher said.

Marlborough-street sees all kinds of people in
trouble—Mayfair playboys, suburban housewives
caught shoplifting in Oxford-street, vice-mongers
from Soho. And, of course, motorists. The Keeler-
Profumo-Ward affair burst into the news there
last year, with the appearance of
John Edgecombe on a shooting
charge.

These are the three £4,000-a-
year-plus magistrates who sit
at the court:

MR. LEO GRADWELL, 63,
the senior magistrate. Stern,
but with a sense of humour.

MR. AUBREY-FLETCHER, 51,
an ex-Guards officer. "Regulars"
regard him as a fair man.

MR. EDWARD ROBEY, 63, son
of the famous comedian, Sir
George Robey. Known for his
kindness.

Three valued, busy men. Three
Headline Magistrates.

Mr. Edward
Robey.

Mr. Aubrey-
Fletcher.

shoemaker had boots − plenty of boots in stock, and the former was without them − stockings as well, for the matter of that − and wanted boots badly − the old question of demand and supply. Did it give all these sturdy officials, the witness to his arrest, much trouble to effect his capture, we wonder? It does not look like it in the daylight of Great Marlborough Street Police Court.

The 'ladies' went thieving again with a vengeance in and just after the Second World War − mostly real, rather than pretend well-to-do ladies, probably because wealth was no longer enough to obtain scarce goods. Coupons were also necessary. There was often anything from two to six shoplifting charges every day, Sandbach reports. At the time of writing, it can be anything from twenty to forty.

1956 brought the most famous shoplifting case of all. At first, to the experienced store detective Margaret Belson, it was just another case. She saw a handsome young woman push a red woollen hat up her sleeve, and sandwich four feathered hats between some brown-paper bags and then walk off without paying for any of them. When arrested outside, the woman was found not to speak English. Growing ease of travel was making the foreign shoplifter common by then, but no one could at first discover what language she did speak. Eventually, to their surprise, they realized that it was Russian. She was Nina Ponomareva, a Soviet discus-thrower, soon to be enveloped in a deluge of publicity which would enshrine her for ever in the history of shoplifting: 'The case of Nina and the Five Hats'.

It is difficult today to describe, let alone believe, the sensation her arrest caused − a sensation due entirely to the climate of the times. A chink in the Iron Curtain had just been glimpsed. The Russians had only recently begun creeping back into international athletics and games but always kept their teams in camps well away from those of other nationals. Now they had consented to send a team to participate in competition with the British at White City as a warm-up to the Olympics in Australia three months later. Much excitement ensued. Actually to *see* a Russian was very unusual; to see one in our charge-room at West End Central, where I was then serving, was staggering.

The Russians were, of course, still going through a time of severe austerity, and the temptation was very understandable. Nonetheless, Nina strenuously denied the charge of stealing five hats, worth £1 12s 11d, from C&A Modes. She was bailed to appear at court, left the police station with her Embassy advisers – and promptly disappeared. An International Incident, of huge proportions and awe-inspiring implications, was born.

The Russians were livid. It was 'dirty provocation' aimed at preventing Ponomareva's taking part in the games just so Britain could beat them – and no, they did not know where she was. Tass admitted that the Russians had tried to get the British Foreign Office to withdraw charges, but they had replied that they had no power to do so. A warrant was issued for her non-appearance at Marlborough Street and the whole Russian team withdrew from the games and, shortly afterwards, returned to the Soviet Union.

Five days after the arrest, West End Central's Detective Superintendent and thirty Special Branch men 'swooped' on an aircraft about to leave Heathrow for Copenhagen, on which a seat had been booked for Nina Ponomareva. She was not found. Was it a blind to stop them inspecting a TU 104 taxi-ing only 300 yards away, the detectives, and soon the Press, asked. Every move and every character involved received the maximum publicity, from the store detective, who had her next cases well reported, to Clyde Wilson, who had issued the warrant and who was photographed leaving the court 'smiling' after her non-appearance. As it happens, it was strongly rumoured that he resisted considerable pressure from above to allow the charges and warrant to be dropped. The store would probably have co-operated (shops initiate such charges, police merely acting as their agents) since their chief was quoted as saying, from his home in Hilversum, "I don't think we should upset the world for a mere 30 shillings." The principle, however, was not 'mere'.

Weeks passed and still no sign of Nina. Where was she? Had she caught that TU 104? On 12th October 1956 she ascended the steps of West End Central Police Station and gave herself up, saying she had "misunderstood the situation" and apologizing for her non-appearance at Marlborough Street.

She had, of course, been expected by them, but it had been kept very dark. There was no advance notice of her appearance, and her name did not appear on the regular court list, so technically the Press did not know. Nevertheless, by the time she arrived at the court, escorted by Detective Sergeant Shirley Jennings (later to become head of the Metropolitan Women Police and the first woman Commander in the country), Court One was packed to the gunwales, and the street outside had been brought to a standstill by crowds of sightseers.

Frederick Lawton, who prosecuted, says it was all the result of the astute eye of a court reporter who realized that something was afoot when Mr Lawton, Mervyn Griffiths-Jones (defending), Gerald Gardner (watching for C&A) all ascending stars in the world of counsel, and the Director of Public Prosecutions began to drift casually into the court. He still finds astonishing the speed with which that grapevine worked, nonetheless.

Thus, before the day was out, the world knew of every gesture used, word spoken and item of clothing worn by the defendant; each movement in the drama was given its due, and even the assistant gaoler, Donald Hunting, got his mention for announcing "Charge No. 25" and ushering her into the dock. Nina was found guilty, given an absolute discharge and required to pay 3 guineas costs on this simple, most commonplace Marlborough Street charge. Incident closed — well, almost. Mr Lawton remembers that Clyde Wilson, horrified by the paltry sum the athletes had been allowed to bring in with them and sorry for the woman, asked someone to go out and buy a gift for Nina to take back to her child: a woolly toy.

In the 1960s it became the fashionable thing to shoplift from the boutiques or to exchange the dress one was wearing for a new one and walk out in it. Annabel and Amanda from Knightsbridge joined in with the best of them, conveniently embracing the current dictum that ownership was theft, despite the fact that that probably made mummy and daddy the criminals of all time. The term 'shoplifting', with its curiously uncriminal ring, did not help. It also sounds modern, but it is not; Mayhew used it. Recently the big stores have endeavoured to put shoplifting in its proper criminal perspective by putting "Thieves will be prosecuted" stickers on their doors, rather than "Shoplifters ..." and it is a curious fact that nothing upsets shoplifters more, especially Middle Eastern shoplifters, than the reminder that they are thieves. They will, in fact, angrily deny it. Even an Annabel, unaware of my husband's occupation and boasting to us about her dress-swopping and stealing activities ("Well, everyone does it, darling") in the sixties, was furious when Bob said to me, "Watch your purse, darling. She's a thief." And of course they are, and it is we who pay extra for our goods to compensate for their activities.

Nowadays, the stealing has reached such proportions that permanent police shoplifting squads, with their own vans, continuously patrol Oxford Street, sometimes filling up from store to store until they have a van-load of offenders, many of them well-to-do or even very wealthy. Foreign delegates, police chiefs, magistrates, surgeons, judges, nuclear physicists and pilots all stand in the dock on the charge, for shoplifters seem not to be from any one section of the community these days, and the number of men, too, is growing. Sometimes one gets one of our European brothers who is living in a squat, drawing social security (never having worked here) and shoplifting to fill in the time when we are working – a situation which induced one of the magistrates to come out with the statement that we are "the mugs of Europe".

Occasionally, however, the genuine kleptomaniac, or someone who appears to be, turns up, and these are treated with sympathy. Then there are the dear old ladies, scraping by on a pittance, who are suddenly overcome by longing for some little luxury. Comforting weeping and ashamed grannies and telling them that it does not matter, is then the role of store detective, police and even magistrates. Some old ladies are not charged, but those who will not desist have to have a little brake put on them. "I just don't know how to punish you at your age," confessed Paul Bennett to a seventy-five-year-old with twenty-six convictions for shoplifting. "I need a good horse-whipping, sir," she suggested helpfully.

Not being charged was a gesture which a certain Martha Ann would not, however, have appreciated. She had had a difficult enough time getting arrested, thank you, and was still rather cross about it when she reached the court. "My boy," she said to the forty-five-year-old gaoler, "I really don't know what the store detectives are coming to these days."

Apparently, she had stolen an umbrella and walked straight out of the store with it. Nothing happened. After hanging around outside in the cold for a bit, she went back in, replaced the umbrella and stole another one, this time looking around surreptitiously first then slowly picking it up, holding it high and carrying it off. Again, nothing. She was getting a bit cross by then and huffily marched off to another store, where she pinched a stuffed toy and left – alone. It was incredible. What did she have to do? She marched back, picked up the biggest toy in the place, a huge stuffed panda, wrapped her arms around it and sallied forth again. Realizing that she had not acquired a tail, not even aroused interest, she kept going until she got to the nearest police-station, where she dumped the toy on the counter, announced that she had just stolen it and said would they *please* arrest her.

The lads obliged but suggested that such a dear old lady should have a good defence counsel who could explain that 'something had come over her'. Martha Ann made it very plain she wanted no such mealy-mouthed excuses. But, they said, she would probably get off with only a small fine or probation. Probation! Probation! Did they seriously think she had gone to all that trouble just to get probation? Martha Ann wanted a month inside *at least*. Surely she deserved it? "After all," she told the gaoler, "I *have* got form." What was more, she knew she was doing wrong and, if they let her off, would go straight back and do it again. You see, Martha Ann loved Holloway Prison. It was so much livelier than the old people's home she lived in. The latter was, well, simply full of boring *old people*, which depressed her. In any case, Holloway's linen-cupboards got into such a state if she was not there to organize them.

Her desire was discreetly conveyed to the magistrate, who looked skywards when she appeared, then lowered his head to look at her sternly, pronounce that this was a most serious offence and that she must go to prison for six weeks. In fact, what else could he do? Six weeks! A delighted Martha thanked him effusively and skipped out of the dock. Six weeks! What a lovely man. The country had not completely gone to the dogs.

8

The Toms

"Literally every woman who yields to her passions and loses her virtue is a prostitute, but many draw a distinction between those who live by promiscuous intercourse, and those who confine themselves to one man."

That male-chauvinist statement to end all male-chauvinist statements was made by Henry Mayhew in the mid-nineteenth century. Nonetheless, he devoted much of his energy to documenting the variety and experiences of the prostitutes of the time, and his writings include these observations on 'The Traffic in Foreign Women': "One of the most disgraceful, horrible and revolting practices (not even eclipsed by the slave-trade) carried on by Europeans is the importation of girls into England from foreign countries to swell the ranks of prostitution. It is only very recently that the attention of Mr Tyrrwhit, at the Marlborough Street Police Court, was drawn to the subject by Mr Dalbert, agent to the 'Society for the Protection of Women and Children'." The law regarding brothels was, he went on, so peculiar, that the women were virtual prisoners, and nothing could be done about it. And, indeed, nothing was done for a very long time, mainly because, its opponents claimed, it was so well-protected by members of the Government and establishment, many of whom were the brothels' best customers.

Nevertheless, in 1875 some progress was made as far as children were concerned, when the age of consent was raised from twelve to thirteen. Ten years later it was raised again, this time to sixteen, where it now stands, a decision which helped to curtail the then common child prostitution.

The Case of Miss Cass was a small step forward for women, in that after its conclusion they could not so easily be labelled prostitutes. Like most Marlborough Street *causes célèbres*, it began with an ordinary, everyday occurrence: one July evening in 1887 PC

Endacott arrested the twenty-three-year-old Miss Elizabeth Cass for soliciting in Regent Street. She was charged with being a common prostitute, annoying male passengers for the purpose of prostitution, despite the fact that she had no previous convictions and had never come in contact with police before, though PC Endacott claimed he had seen her "about" for several weeks.

Miss Cass, who had not been in London long, lived with her employer, Madame Bowman, a businesswoman of long standing. Madame Bowman was furious about the whole affair and turned up at court next day, where she found the proceedings most unsatisfactory, having tried to give evidence that it was all a mistake but being "brushed aside". The magistrate, Mr Newton, she wrote to the Commissioner, had been offensive, overbearing and in every way insulting. He had seen fit to caution Miss Cass, thereby casting "a lasting stigma of shame upon a poor, innocent girl". She also wrote to the Lord Chancellor in the same vein and accused the police of being "criminals". Soon *The Times* was announcing that the Lord Chancellor had commenced an enquiry into the conduct of Mr Newton during the hearing of the charge against Miss Cass.

On cautioning the girl, Mr Newton had said, "if you are a respectable girl, as you say you are, do not walk Regent Street or stop gentlemen at ten o'clock of a night. If you do, you will be fined or sent to prison. Go away and do not come here again." But it was not Mr Newton who was to be on unofficial trial at the subsequent enquiry but PC Endacott, for if women had few rights, so did the class to which the PC belonged, and it usually provided the necessary sacrificial lamb.

The tribunal was chaired by the Commissioner, and the Recorder of Lincoln acted as 'legal assessor' and his assistant. Two counsel appeared for Miss Cass and Madame Bowman, and a ruffled Mr St John Wontner for the constable. (Nowadays the Yard has its own legal department, but for many years the firm of Wontner & Sons represented the Metropolitan Police.) What was ruffling Mr Wontner was the fact that he had been advised of the case only the previous day and felt he did not know nearly enough yet properly to cross-examine the string of witnesses called for Miss Cass. He reserved his right to do so later and wondered aloud just what, exactly, they were all gathered there to do. He was alarmed, he said, by the preponderance of witnesses for the ladies, all of whom were giving evidence without taking the oath. Was the constable on any particular charge, he enquired, or was this "a roving commission to satisfy an angry public?"

The gist of the case against the PC and the charging officer at the station was, indeed, vague, but it loosely seemed to be that the constable was lying or mistaken about what Miss Cass was doing in Regent Street and that he had no right to describe her as a common prostitute, especially since she was so innocent-looking and respectably dressed. And why had not he and the other police taken Madame Bowman's word that the lady was not a prostitute and passed it on to the magistrate? Eventually Wontner called a halt to the proceedings so that he could prepare a defence.

When they returned, the police produced a weird and wonderful array of witnesses of the arrest and goodness and innocence of PC Endacott. If hearsay and speculation were on the agenda, the defence could give as good as it got, and did. The report submitted was also pretty woolly and inconclusive, but, before it came out, the PC was on trial for perjury.

The whole case rested, ultimately, on whose word could be taken as truth, so at the trial Miss Cass (by then Mrs Langley) was again presented as a fresh and cloistered girl only recently come to the big bad city from the provinces. However, the defence had been to the provinces themselves, making a few enquiries. They now cross-examined her about a married boy-friend there who had given her a diamond ring and who had spent some time alone with her in a hotel room, and about one or two other men-friends – none of which made her a prostitute but did make her seem less the innocent maid.

The defence once again played prosecution's game in that they presented PC Endacott as a thoroughly honest and truthful character too, though they did not suggest that he was sexually innocent. It was possible, they contended, that he had been mistaken about Miss Cass, but that did not warrant a charge of perjury. Eventually, the judge having whittled down the area in which he considered the constable could even be accused of perjury to his having said he had seen the lady on previous occasions, prosecution threw in the sponge. The judge ordered an acquittal and had some pretty sharp words to say about the wisdom of "holding a private enquiry, or an enquiry by a public authority, into the conduct of a man who is afterwards to be accused of crime, such an enquiry not being authorized by any statute". He was right, of course, so the case not only marked a little fighting back by women against the extremely one-sided morality laws and the cavalier way in which women could be handled, but made the point that policemen deserve some justice too.

There is no way of telling now, any more than then, who was telling the truth, but it certainly could not have happened in the 1950s, when I served in the West End. By then, prostitution charges were treated with great care, being acknowledged as one of the most fraught areas in which the police moved. Officers could not even make an arrest for soliciting until they had had a year's service, and the men always had to have a colleague accompanying them to avoid allegations of sexual impropriety. Most prostitutes were, in fact, arrested by the 'Tom Patrol' which was manned by experienced policemen brought out for a month on that sole duty. Not only that, no woman was arrested for soliciting until she had received two official cautions which had been duly noted in the pocket-book of the cautioning officer, then entered into the Cautions Book at the station. The situation was still very one-sided however, and it always struck me as rather droll that, when I went off late-turn duty after chasing, searching and fingerprinting prostitutes arrested for soliciting to the annoyance of male passengers, I would be so persistently annoyed by men soliciting me as I tried to cross the Bayswater Road. There was no specific charge for that, and there still is not. Mind you, when I produced my warrant-card, they would age ten years in two seconds. It was almost worth it for that.

Suffragettes and others carried on agitation against White Slaving but found that, even when a bill to curtail it had actually become law, protection of those involved was still possible. The first prosecution under the new act was against 'Queenie Gerald' in 1913 for procuring. The cover-up began, the suffragettes claimed, at the committal proceedings at Marlborough Street when Mr Mead "protected her alias and instructed the Press he was holding 'a secret enquiry' ". So claimed *The Vote*, the organ of the Women's Freedom League, which commented that, when Mead presided over Suffragist cases, he did not display any undue leniency; to the contrary, he turned himself into an additional prosecutor. The case was rushed through the higher court, they claimed, the Press being given little information and everything being made easier by the fact that 'Miss Gerald' pleaded 'Guilty', for which she was rewarded with a light sentence. It was all over before anyone outside knew anything about it.

But it was not to rest there. Suffragettes investigated, came up with many prominent names and passed the information on to the *Daily Sketch*, which began to ask just what was going on. "Letters have been found, signed by men of high position," they announced, "revealing an organization for procuring young girls and little children." But, they went on, the men were being protected. Eventually their agitation resulted in Questions in the House, but to no avail. "I was unaware," claimed the Home Secretary, "of any of the names until the trial was over." And he denied that any MPs were involved.

Before the 1959 Street Offences Act, the lists at Marlborough Street and Bow Street were dominated by queues of prostitutes of all types, from the classy to the brassy. There is no doubt that they added some eye-popping 'colour' as they were shuttled in and out of dock, with only the occasional pause when one pleaded a cross and defiant 'not guilty!'.

The arresting officers would stand just behind the witness-box as the parade passed by, keeping themselves ready to leap into it should the magistrate wish to know anything about their particular arrest or should his 'tom' plead 'not guilty'. Since it was all so routine, the magistrates mostly did not ask for any details and so were largely unaware whether the officer was there or not. Once, due to falling asleep while waiting to go to court from night-duty, I arrived after my prostitute had left the dock, but I had not been missed. Mind you, the Court Inspector refused to sign my time-off card, so it was a wasted journey all round.

At the time, many of the West End streets were wall-to-wall with prostitutes. The whole thing had got out of hand, the Press kept saying, and 'something had to be done'. We police were approached endlessly by members of the public asking why we could not clear the girls away, and we had to reply that we simply had not the power to do more than shuffle them around a bit – why did they not write to their MPs, who actually made the laws? Many of the complainants, especially of the male variety, were so enraged by this social evil that they spent hours studying it. Some became familiar figures – 'tom-watchers' we used to call them, as they stood on their own particular, busy corner in the land of vice, often with their hands in their pockets, furtively masturbating. One foreign connoisseur even asked me where he could find some better-looking prostitutes and acted as if I were personally responsible for the poor calibre of those he had come across so far.

I found similar vicarious interest in people I met socially. As soon as someone revealed that I was a police-officer in the West End, even before the incredibly old and coy women-police jokes and deliberate slurs on my character in relation to all the bribes I was taking, would come, "You must have your work cut out with 'the girls'?" or "Do the 'pros' give you a lot of trouble?", in suitably confidential tones.

The fifties, perhaps due to all the vice publicity, also brought a spate of married women to the West End for an afternoon's soliciting rather than shopping. Some pleaded loneliness, others boredom, and a few admitted they just liked the extra money. One "needed a little relaxation from looking after three children" and, since she was new to London and found the people reserved, had headed for Hyde Park, where the women were friendly to her and easy to get on with. Nonetheless, she did admit to the probation-officer that she had initially gone there because she had read so much about the vice therein, and even after a first conviction for insulting behaviour (which lost her husband the job they had come to London for), she returned and did a spot of soliciting and finally got a conviction for prostitution.

One young housewife, arrested for behaving indecently with a man in Hyde Park, received little sympathy from Paul Bennett when she told him she was bored to death and had gone out on a wild impulse as she was sick of staying in. He thought she had very strange ideas about enjoying herself, and to say she was bored was "perfectly ridiculous".

The fifties also brought shades of the White Slave Traffic, when the vicious Messina vice-ring was exposed by the *News of the World*. "So crowded was the court," the *Star* told its readers when Attilio Messina, the brains of the group, appeared at Marlborough Street charged with procuring and living on the immoral earnings of one woman for ten years, "that some of the public who wanted to get in had to be excluded." We may not have been permissive then, but we did like a good vice story.

Those unfortunates who did not get in missed Attilio's reported classic statement on arrest ("It is fantastic. I cannot understand it. Tell me, what does procuring mean?") and also the evidence about a woman's being kept his prisoner and acting as a prostitute under threat of being 'cut up'. Attilio, otherwise known as Raymond Maynard, claimed he was British, but the Home Office did not agree and declared him to be Italian, though Italy had refused to have him when, after an earlier conviction for living on immoral earnings, there had been an attempt to deport him thence. On this second occasion he got four years' imprisonment, and eventually the Italians conceded and took him back.

Eugene and Carmelo Messina had been sent to prison in Belgium on procuration and passport offences, but Carmelo, who had had only a short sentence, soon sneaked back and reappeared as 'Charles Maitland'. He too insisted he was British to the core, as he stood in Marlborough Street dock on a charge of illegal entry into the country. The prosecution solicitor alleged he was an Italian, born in Alexandria, but Detective Inspector John du Rose said Carmelo had papers on him saying he was a Maltese, born in Alexandria. (Many London ponces at the time were either Maltese or Cypriot.) Carmelo too ended up, involuntarily, in Italy, and he died in prison there shortly afterwards, having been a sick man when he appeared at Marlborough Street.

These days, only a thin trickle of toms pass through the court, and few of these have anything like the looks, style and variety of their fifties counterparts, possibly because competition was hot then and glamour was 'in'. Most are now the enthusiastic amateur type and are occasionally found loitering in Park Lane. Their fate at court depends largely on which magistrate they draw. Mr Harmsworth will treat them lightly and give them a small fine, while Mr Hopkin may enquire into their circumstances and possibly remand them for social reports before deciding on his action. Since the benches of JPs change all the time, their actions will be various too.

Of course, prostitution is a very risky business, and for this reason many professionals employ a maid just so there is someone around when clients call. Others are either less prudent or well-organized or not sufficiently successful to afford one, so Marlborough Street has seen quite a few prostitute murderers − not as many as it should have, of course, such murderers being so notoriously difficult to catch.

The murder of thirty-one-year-old Veronica Murray in December 1958 was just such a difficult case. When she was found dead in her room by her landlord on 19th December, it was not even certain when she had died: all that could be deduced was that it had been somewhere between the 12th and the 19th. It was a ferocious crime. She had multiple fractures on her skull, six wounds on her forehead, twelve completely circular one-inch marks on her skin and two coat-hangers thrust into her body. The wall was splashed with her blood, and nearby were two bloodstained dumb-bells weighing about 6 pounds each. The murderer had obligingly left fingerprints on the coat-hangers and on a teacup, but unfortunately the Yard had none in stock which matched up. They could not find the culprit, and the case faded from the news.

Nine months later, on 10th October 1959, a divorced woman named Jean (not a prostitute) was returning from a visit to a friend when she met a baby-faced, eighteen-year-old guardsman who told her he had been drinking rather heavily. He insisted on accompanying her home and then wanted to come in. Jean did not want him to as it was late and her three children were asleep inside, but he was just a young boy, and he promised he would only have a cup of coffee and then go. So she let him in. He did, in fact, sit in the kitchen and drink a cup of coffee, but when he had finished, he stood up and removed his shirt and jumper. Jean told him to put them on again, a request he did not appreciate.

Next morning a neighbour found Jean on the kitchen floor. Around her neck were two tightly tied nylon stockings, and her face and neck were swollen and covered in small haemorrhages. On her body were several circular marks made by an object with a serrated edge. Nevertheless, she was alive – unconscious, but alive – and was rushed to hospital.

When she came round, she could not remember anything after she had told the young man, 'Mick', to put on his jumper and leave.

A short while afterwards a young soldier named Mick was being investigated on suspicion of house-breaking in the area in which Jean lived. His fingerprints matched those in Jean and Veronica's rooms, and this time the victim could identify him.

Soon the police were telling the young guardsman that they thought he was involved in three attacks on women. He was glad it was all over, he replied. Everyone was against him. This business had worried him for a long time, and he had wanted to go to the doctor about it. It was the drinking that did it. He was all right when he did not drink. He would tell the detective all he could remember, which was that he had met Veronica in Trafalgar Square and had gone home with her. After intercourse, he had fallen asleep but later she had woken him up, and they had had a row, during which she threw a vase at him. She had then struck him on the back of the neck with something and scratched him on the nose and eyes, so he had knocked her down and struck her with the dumb-bells.

He first appeared at Marlborough Street on the housebreaking charge, but "graver charges" were mentioned, and he was remanded in custody. The principal medical officer at Brixton Prison found him to be a typical psychopath, aggressive without sufficient cause, lacking in remorse for his crimes, without any sense of shame when discussing perverted sexual behaviour, a suicide attempter (he had tried to hang himself in the guard-room two years earlier) and a sadistic violator of women's bodies. Not only that: his encephalograph reading was abnormal; he was vain and untruthful and unable to make friends, and he thought nothing of drinking two bottles of spirits a day. Although he had 'coughed' to the attacks and murder, he could not help the police about the circular marks, and the doctor felt that his amnesia, here at least, was genuine. The pathologist, Dr Donald Teare, could not explain them either.

On that first hearing, defence counsel had mentioned that, in view of the evidence of a sexual and sensational nature which might be given, he might well have to apply for the case to be held *in camera*. The magistrate replied that he had not much enthusiasm for justice behind closed doors, but counsel could raise the matter at the next hearing. When he did, Clyde Wilson refused, commenting; "I take the view that the right of trial by jury and freedom of the Press are twin cornerstones of English justice. The last, secret trial I can think of was that of Nagy* – a famous trial or infamous trial, whichever way you look at it. When you have a trial behind closed doors, you are halfway to the secret trial. I am going to hold this inquiry in public."

The charge was now one of the murder of Veronica Murray. By common consent, the housebreaking charge was dropped, and it was a hushed court which heard a nervous and tense Jean re-tell the circumstances of her meeting with the accused, who now sat quite still in dock, listening intently to every word. By the time she was finished, her slight figure in blue dress and cardigan was shaking with sobs. The hospital doctor gave evidence of her injuries, the police of the fingerprints and confession, and Dr Donald Teare of the similar markings on the body of Veronica Murray. The guardsman, who, according to one newspaper, was "a slight boyish figure with a spotted face", was committed for trial.

His defence was aimed at a manslaughter verdict due to diminished responsibility; to this end the Brixton doctor gave evidence of his psychopathic tendencies, and his Commanding Officer weighed in

* Imre Nagy, Hungarian Premier during the uprising of 1956, who was tried and executed in that year.

with a bad character reference. Though the opinions were for his own good, they could not have aided his self-esteem: his CO had always known he was "a bit odd", more, he was "known to have contact with people in foreign countries, which was most unusual for a soldier of that type"(!); he had delusions of grandeur, which were probably occasioned by the fact that he was "small, weak and insignificant", the senior officer went on, and there was a desire to impress people and to make out he was someone more important than he really was.

However, the CO and other army witnesses were not to come away unscathed, as the judge had some sharp words to say about the gross drinking-binges the lad had indulged in, seemingly with the knowledge of his colleagues but with no attempt on their part to restrain him. A verdict of manslaughter was brought in and a life sentence, without time recommendation, passed. The authorities must be able to detain him, said the judge, until they were satisfied he could mingle safely with his fellow-creatures again.

9

Not Such a Good Idea

He was a small, undistinguished Yorkshireman of amiable disposition but with one outstanding social drawback: he would keep showing his 'thing' to ladies. With a couple of dozen convictions for indecent exposure – or, in the parlance, flashing – behind him, he appeared on the list one day for exposing indecent photographs to view. Curious at this sudden change in a lifetime's habit, the gaoler asked him, in the usual subtle policeman's manner, "Here, what's all this then, George?"

His reply was unbelievable in the way only the truth can be. "I was trying to break myself of the habit," George explained earnestly, "so I thought I'd try weaning myself away, gradually." It would be a step in the right direction, he had reasoned, if, rather than exposing the real McCoy, he substituted a picture of same instead. So, thus motivated, he sought out a photographic booth of the type from which (should it be working) one obtains hideous passport pictures. Putting his money in the slot, he stood on the chair provided and positioned himself so that 'it' would be caught to best effect when the light flashed and the shutter clicked.

Having acquired his dubious snaps, he commenced on his regime of self-therapy. Whenever the urge to throw his coat open came upon him, he instead rushed up to the lady in question, thrust the picture into her hands and enquired her opinion of it. Evidently, most were not impressed for he was soon arrested and was now beginning to realize the basic flaw in his plan.

"It seemed such a good idea at the time," he confessed rather sadly, "but now I come to think about it, it looks worse, really. More premeditated, like." True. However, what keeps coming into my mind's eyes is a vision of George getting his snaps, and another customer, thinking there was no one in the booth because he could see no legs, throwing back the curtain. Had anyone done so, what would have been instantly borne upon them, as it was with me when I first started dealing with 'the public', is that there are some very funny people about.

When you are writing a book like this, people say to you, 'I expect you'll make most of it up?' Good grief, who needs to? And what kind of imagination do they think I have?

Not only men end up at Marlborough Street for showing parts of themselves that they ought not. Quite recently a young woman was arrested at Marble Arch underground station for wearing a very see-through mesh jumper which "fairly exposed" her breasts. A constable decided she was causing a sensation such as was likely to cause a breach of the peace. The magistrates agreed and bound her over 'to be of good behaviour' for one year.

Serious outdoor sexual assaults or murders rarely occur in the area, being offences naturally more endemic to open spaces, where a woman can be caught alone. Hyde Park is, of course, a very large open space, but it is well-frequented and policed, even having its own police-station.

The court does see plenty of the minor type though, such as the 'bustle-bumpers' – men who rub themselves up close to women in crowds or 'touch them up'. The offenders are often foreign tourists from cultures where women are kept out of sight more, cover themselves up more and are frequently held in low esteem. The sudden intimacy of department stores and underground trains inflames these men, and since they do not think too much about women's rights anyway, they happily gratify these inclinations, sometimes running amok and doing multiple 'touch-ups', occasionally including the store detectives in their rounds.

The manner in which they are reported scarcely helps. "Romeo Fined For Stealing Some Kisses" was the headline afforded a story concerning an Egyptian who, after asking a woman the way on an underground station, had kissed her hand, pulled her towards him and "planted more kisses on her cheek, neck and shoulder". "Sexy Arab Pinched Over a Bit of Cheek," announced another which told of a Saudi Arabian who pinched a shop-assistant's bottom twice (or "indulged an ancient Eastern custom") then grabbed her and held her close. It was all a bit of a giggle really, but just let one of those ladies try to indulge any ancient British customs of dress or freedom in his country and see how amused their newspapers are!

Mayfair being for so long the abode of the rich, its servants have been involved in many of Marlborough Street's cases, mostly to do with theft but occasionally sexual too. One report from *The Illustrated London News* of 25th June 1842 provides some interesting social comment plus an ironic twist in the form of a witness for the defence. Was he genuine or was he forced?

MARLBOROUGH STREET – Mr Thomas Edward Johnson, a gentleman of fortune, occupying a suite of chambers at 131 Piccadilly, appeared yesterday before Mr Maltby, to answer a summons obtained against him by Amelia Browning, a very good-looking young woman, for assaulting and otherwise ill-using her. The complainant, who appeared to be very indignant against the defendant, stated that she is a housemaid to Mr Cowling, of 131 Piccadilly, where the defendant occupied the whole of the second floor; and it was her duty to clean the rooms, make the beds etc., for all the gentlemen residing in the house. On Monday morning, while [she was] engaged in dusting the defendant's dining-room, he, about half-past eight, came in from his bedroom, with nothing on but his dressing-gown and slippers, and after giving her a slap on the back, proceeded to take most improper liberties and hustled her about the room for about twenty minutes, pulling her about and attempting to throw her on the sofa. Being very strong, she resisted his attack. The defendant, who had two or three times, while the girl was making her statement, broken into laughter, for which he was checked by the magistrate, said there was not the slightest truth in any part of her statement; it was all a lie, from beginning to end. The fact was that, when he, at nine o'clock, entered his dining-room in his dressing-gown, without his cravat (to be sure), but otherwise completely dressed, he found the girl there, at work. As the room ought to have been cleaned before that hour, he told her so and further desired her to leave the room. She put her arms akimbo and resolutely refused; he then laid hold of her arm to put her out, but she resisted, and, [she] being very strong, he was obliged to give up the attempt and to ring for her master to turn her out. The defendant's valet, having been sworn, said that in the consequence of hearing some high words, he was proceeding towards it, when the bell was rung, and his master desired him to fetch Mr Cowling to turn the girl out. She was abusing him very much. Mr Maltby said that as there was conflicting evidence on both sides, he did not think it a case fit to be summarily decided by a magistrate, but it was a very proper one to go before a jury; he should, therefore, call upon the defendant to enter into his own recognizance, in £100, to answer any charge that might be preferred against him at the Westminster sessions.

Paul Bennett, would, I think, have appreciated the lady's spirit.

The sexual fetishist has been an intermittent visitor to the court, particularly those who cut off women's hair while they are standing behind them at bus-stops or in stores. A man in his sixties got six months for removing some of an eleven-year-old's hair. It was his fifteenth conviction for the offence (it comes under stealing), and on one occasion he had 'stolen' plaits from four girls. Another man ran rampant on the underground slitting up the backs of women's skirts as they ascended the escalator ahead of him. The women would be unaware of what had happened until someone pointed it out to them or the station staff spotted it. Eventually he was seen at it and caught.

There is no end to the ingenuity employed in the quest to glimpse the tops of women's legs. One man carried an umbrella with a mirror attached to its tip and another donned a black hood with eyehole slits so that he would not be seen when peering up from under a pavement light near Tottenham Court Road.

Less understandable and much more serious are what I think of as 'the flingers' – for example, the man who grabbed a sixteen-year-old girl and tried to throw her onto the line at Tottenham Court Road Underground Station. (I hope I am not putting you off tube-travel. These things do not happen all the time.) This man had already caused bodily harm to a twelve-year-old schoolgirl at another station on that same day. Oddly similar was the case of the man who grabbed a girl passer-by on a landing in a museum and, with great ferocity, threw her down the next flight of marble stairs. There are some not-so-funny people about.

10

In the Box

The policeman giving evidence has long been a comic figure for his formalized, seemingly unimaginative, "I was proceeding up the High Street in a northerly direction", type of exposition. But there is, of course, a purpose to this parrot-like official phrasing other than to make him seem a dolt and a dullard.

The day-date-time-place formula has in fact been drummed into him at training-school, as the one way he can be certain not to miss facts which it is essential for the magistrates, juries and judges to know, and also as a basis for the clarity necessary in giving evidence. If, for example, you already know that the offence occurred at midnight, you do not need to be told why it seemed rather suspicious that a furniture-van was loading in a residential area; likewise if the accused was wearing a heavy mink coat when you already know she was arrested in August.

Sticking to a formula does not always result in dullness. Sometimes it aids the odd and whimsical, as when one young PC straightfacedly told the magistrate that, at 1.20 a.m. that day, he had been called to 'The Garden of Eden'. It was, of course, one of the many nightclubs in the Soho area, but such utterances are a gift few magistrates can resist, even when they are the usually rather sober-sides Paul Bennett. He murmured, "And were there only two people inside?" As the court laughed, the PC assured him that there were many more than that.

Police prosecutors and witnesses come in all forms: the young and nervous rooky; the natty and knowing detective with his slick delivery, and the laconic, deadpan traffic-cop, all shiny gaiters and technical gobbledegook, secure in the knowledge that many of the people he is addressing will not have a clue what he is talking about. His slightly world-weary air is the result of his having been handed every whopping lie human creativity can produce as an excuse for speeding or having faulty splinge-sockets.

Though inclined to be classics-trained, some stipendiary magistrates do put these experts more on their mettle with the odd searching question about overhead camshafts or down-draught carburetters. Such a one was Clyde Wilson, who had raced cars at Brooklands in his earlier days, and Leo Gradwell could bandy side-valves with the best of them. He surprised one policeman, giving evidence in a traffic case, by telling him that his first motorcycle was in the Science Museum at South Kensington, adding appealingly, "It gave great pleasure to my children when I took them to see Father's original machine."

The British motorist, being a fearsome and unpredictable animal, occasionally given to head-on charging when frustrated, ensures that traffic-cops sometimes double as prosecutors and victims. One police motorcyclist was deliberately knocked off his bike in Hyde Park by a motorist swerving into him while doing 50-60 miles an hour (the Park limit was twenty). The fact that the escaping motorist was only two years into a thirty-year driving-ban may have had something to do with this seeming over-reaction to being waved-down for speeding.

Foot-policemen can prove equally provoking. I remember two such cases while I was at West End Central – one where a woman drove first at one PC, waving his arms about on a double traffic-point at Oxford Circus and, having missed him, tried for the second one who, fortunately, was forewarned by his colleague's indignant yell and also managed to leap for safety. Not so lucky was a PC, who had been driven at by a woman who missed but who, when he attempted to execute a warrant for this offence, was knocked down by her as she made her escape. He was not seriously injured, fortunately, and she subsequently made her due appearance at Marlborough Street.

Some of the heat was taken out of the situation for policemen by the arrival of traffic-wardens who, the public found, made even better targets, since they seemed designed solely to annoy them and could not even be said to be, in mitigation, public protectors. During the first year or so of their employment (the pilot scheme for the whole of London was run from the office next door to Marlborough Street, and my husband was one of those employed), they were spat at, punched and, of course, driven at, by many upright pillars of the community. These offenders were used to dealing with policemen who were merely exercising their discretion as to whether an offence should be reported and could often be flannelled out of the idea. In any case the whole parking business was in such a hopeless mess that one ticket here or there was not going to make any difference. With the coming of the parking-meters, there was either an offence or there was not, and no amount of chat could alter that. As one PC remarked, "Parking-meters brought democracy to Mayfair at last."

But I digress, for we were talking about policemen in the witness-box. Sandbach found that they could never resist bringing in anything which might enliven the atmosphere of the court and particularly remembered one who obviously could not wait to tell him that, when arrested, the accused had indignantly denied being "under the affluence of incahol".

Policemen and store detectives expect to have their evidence attacked, to be called liars in fact. One can scarcely blame them for becoming rather cynical about it, for it is often done with great indignation by the counsel of defendants who are weaving mind-boggling webs of fantasy themselves. The defendant is, however, allowed to lie with impunity even if it means dragging down the reputation of others in the process. He stands very little chance of being charged with perjury, and, while I do not think it should become a habit to charge such people, I do feel that a few more prosecutions of the more outrageous cases might restore the balance a little.

The pity is that the continuous attack on prosecution evidence (police and store detective) does, in magistrates' court at least, tend to have the reverse effect of that intended. Like crying wolf, it is heard so frequently and is so often obviously untrue that genuine complaints stand less chance of being taken seriously. This is not true of cases which come before juries, as they lack the experience of hearing the constant cry of, "I was framed." Hardened criminals know they stand a better chance before juries, for this reason, even if they have no defence. Magistrates are well aware that an early and continuous attack on police honesty, or that of other prosecution, is often indicative of the paucity of the defence case. "If you've got no defence, attack the police," is the popular maxim.

The sad result of this constant attack is threefold. Some police-officers get so sick of being called liars, come what may, that they eventually do lie; genuine cries go unheard, and also really 'bent' policemen get practice in the unnecessarily important skill of stonewalling accusations and appearing totally honest. "What's he like in the box?" is a question frequently asked about a new colleague one is to work with closely.

Police Constable Battes was obviously very good in the box.

Edward Robey remembers that he stood up well under cross-examination and quietly maintained that he *did* find a piece of brick in a demonstrator's pocket. He seemed a truthful witness. Consequently Mr Robey found the prisoner guilty, despite the fact that he had dismissed the case against another man who had been similarly charged by Battes's senior officer, Detective Sergeant Challenor. Expert evidence had shown that the defendant could not have been carrying the brick in his pocket and that this brick fitted pieces found in two other defendants' pockets, including that of Battes's prisoner. As Robey admits, in his book *The Jester and the Court*, the PC's 'honesty' added credibility to the story. Doubtless the fact that the magistrate had heard umpteen other, usually patently untrue, "it was planted on me" stories influenced his judgement too.

Poor Mr Robey had his nose rubbed in this understandable error, for when Challenor, Battes and two other constables were eventually charged with conspiring to pervert the course of justice, they appeared before him at Marlborough Street, where he found there was ample evidence to commit them for trial. Challenor was found unfit to plead through insanity; Battes received three years' imprisonment and the two others four years each, ultimately reduced to three. Mr Robey acquired a realization of "how completely I had been deceived".

At one time, magistrates' courts were packed with policemen waiting for their cases to be heard, but there are fewer nowadays since their attendance is not required in trivial cases. Brief details are passed on to the court inspector who, providing the defendant pleads guilty, will pass them on to any magistrate who requires them. Thus the court inspector, who in practice holds the rank of either police inspector or sergeant, can appear a mildly curious figure when, in answer to an enquiring look or remark from the bench, he bobs ups and barks, "Fluffy toys, Your Worship," or "Hot Dogs, sir." These are, of course, brief details of the street trader's goods. A drunk-and-disorderly might warrant a quick "Singing and shouting, Your Worship", or "Urinating against a wall, sir." There is a Brecht play in there somewhere.

If the defendant pleads 'not guilty', the case is remanded for the arresting PC to attend and give evidence. This does save a lot of police time (thought it wastes some of the defendants') but has the disadvantage of depriving them of familiarity with court procedure. They are, of course, taught this in training-school and also attend their local magistrates' court as onlookers during their first few weeks out on division, when they are still being 'carried' by their 'parent constable', but there can be long gaps after that if none of their charges requires their attendance at court.

One young PC, on his first day out of training-school, was sitting in Marlborough Street as a learner when he observed something he thought was not part of normal procedure: a man in the public gallery picking up a coat which a defendant had left draped over the partition when he went into dock, and quietly exiting with it while the eyes of the court were elsewhere. The rookie acted with alacrity, hared out of the room and made his first arrest.

One has to admire the death-wish audacity of some criminals. Another had the dastardly cheek to steal a bottle of milk from the court doorstep. "What an impudent theft!" exclaimed Mr Harmsworth before Exhibit A was whipped away to matron's office to put in the gaoler's tea.

Women police still attract more attention in the witness-box than policemen, but these days they are treated in the same way. No longer do they have to put up with cross-questioning about the legality of their position as they did from Mr Mead (he had something of a case at first since it was pretty anomalous), nor are they accused of lacking moral perception when they get mixed up in cases "repugnant to any person of average decent ideas". By the time I became a policewoman, they were always treated with consideration and dignity – more consideration often than the men received. We needed it too, still harbouring as we did our inbred feelings of inadequacy and being so much more in the spotlight, since women in authority were still rare in the fifties. Any case we were involved in was much more likely to receive Press attention. One can imagine how WPC Lightfoot, who chased and caught a fleet-footed flasher in Hyde Park, did not stand a chance of staying out of the papers.

Other professional witnesses are store detectives, some of whom are excellent and more practised in giving evidence than many police-officers, and social workers and probation-officers. The two latter vary from the excellent, who really help their clients by being fair and realistic, to the pathetically silly, who want you to believe that their clients have no faults whatsoever and that all their troubles have been brought upon them by their parents and/or the police. As one once-hardened criminal, who is now a friend of mine, remarks, "It's pretty insulting of them making out we're not responsible for ourselves like that." No one pretends that deprivation does not play a part in crime, but this self-glorying, "I'm the only one who understands them – the prosecution are the dirty enemy", attitude of some is hard to take and, of course, useless to the people they are purporting to help.

Fortunately there are still a good number of sensible adult people in these services, and their introduction into the system was an important part of the humanizing of the courts in this century. Herbert Anders, Court Reporter at Marylebone from 1893 to 1956, thought them the most beneficial innovation for the defendants he had seen during his working life. Of course, before the Probation Service became official, some similar work was done by court missionaries and welfare-workers, usually in a voluntary and unofficial capacity. Sandbach claims that Frederick Mead was the "real originator" of the probation system and that, long before it was thought of by the legislature, he had evolved a system whereby he remanded young offenders on bail for a while and asked the court missionary to keep an eye on them during that time. When the offender came up again, the missionary gave a report which often saved the necessity of a prison sentence.

When it comes to non-professional witnesses who are usually unfamiliar with the surroundings and their present role, they mostly tend to reticent behaviour. Occasionally comes one who has been waiting for this chance to say just what he thinks and to give a highly-coloured, dramatic and opinionated version of what he saw – or even what he did not see.

I had personal experience of such a blood-and-thunder witness. A man, who had seen me and my husband flying through the air after being knocked off our motorbike by a traffic-light-jumping van, could not wait to tell the court how disgraceful it all was. He had never seen such a violation of the law. The van had flashed past; he had heard a dreadful piercing scream which had cut through him like a knife (mine – boy, can I scream) etc. He almost lost us what was a stonewall case. Fortunately the day was saved by his opposite, a witness who stuck solely and unemotionally to the facts and what he actually saw. He was a monosyllabic taxi-driver who, despite being continuously cajoled by soft-voiced defence counsel into admitting that he could easily be mistaken about the light, kept repeating unequivocally, "It was red."

It would have been a shame if the offender in that case had not received a sharp lesson, if only for the sake of other road-users, but it would not have been catastrophic. In something more important, such as a murder trial, the over-dramatic witness can be a serious menace, particularly if they are essential to the prosecution.

One who really went over the top (in more ways than one) in Marlborough Street, was a deaf and dumb man who was a witness in a murder charge brought about by the use of a shot-gun in a jewellery-shop raid. The witness was said to have been the purchaser of the shot-gun, but he refused to co-operate with the sign-language interpreter (insisting, it is reported, on using the Irish sign-language which the interpreter did not understand), pounding on the woodwork, throwing the New Testament out of the box and attempting to climb out himself. What the interpreter did understand of his testimony amounted to swearing, threats and offers to take on everyone in court. Finally Mr Harmsworth ordered that he be removed, adding that it was frightening that someone like him could obtain a shotgun by post.

Some of the non-professional witnesses are well able to handle the limelight. One day in the early fifties a virtual cavalcade of war-time talent stepped in and out of Marlborough Street box: Max Miller, Sandy Macpherson, Peter Kavanagh and George Mitchell (of the George Mitchell singers), there to assure the magistrate that they had not agreed to appear in an Albert Hall concert which the accused was touting. Sandy Macpherson pointed out that he was not, as had been suggested, "a variety artist" but "a broadcasting performer". "They are a different class, are they?" enquired the magistrate. "A little bit, sir," he agreed amid court laughter.

Many of the rich and/or famous appear as owners of minks or trinkets stolen by the accused (though it was merely a woollen coat which Peter Ustinov had had appropriated by a passing Pole), but some arrive there as a last resort in an attempt to keep a particular fan at bay. 'Diddy' David Hamilton, the disc-jockey, was nearly driven to distraction by a young lady who continuously rang his doorbell ("ANITA HITS A WRONG NOTE WITH DJ DAVID"), and another man (nameless) felt it necessary to keep his old *amour* from threatening his new young wife.

Several princes have put in an appearance, but, to my knowledge, only one budding emperor. In 1847 Prince Louis Napoleon Bonaparte called in during a lull between his attempts to establish the Second Empire in France. He had already had two shots at it, in 1836 and 1840, and after the last had been imprisoned in perpetuity but had eventually escaped in May 1846 and returned to Britain, where he was seen about in society, a not too surprisingly brooding and aloof figure. His greatest supporter in Britain was Count Alfred d'Orsay, a great dandy whose appearance was emulated by Charles Dickens and who helped guide the then young writer into a richer world.

In 1847 Prince Napoleon found himself short of cash, or "in temporary want of £2,000 from delay in the transmission of his customary remission from his estates in Italy". One Charles Pollard became "acquainted with this fact" and wrote to the Prince, offering to lend him the money for two months at an interest rate of five per cent, on the receipt of two bills of exchange. Unfortunately, the Prince, though considering himself fit to rule millions, was not smart enough to handle this little transaction and handed over the bills before getting the money which Mr Pollard promised to return with the following day. Of course he never did. He did try to make use of the bills, however, declaring them as good as Bank of England notes. He had got as far as an offer of £750 plus two hogsheads of wine from a wine-merchant when things began to go wrong and the police were called in.

Everyone ended up at Marlborough Street. There the Prince said his piece, and PC West told the court that, when he had searched Mr Pollard's lodgings in Essex Street, he had found "a quantity of papers, principally relating to money-lending advertisements, taken from the morning papers". So it was quite possible that the Prince had advertised for a loan, though he claimed not to know how Mr Pollard had got wind of his dilemma. (At one point he had proposed to the incredibly wealthy Miss Burdett-Coutts, but she had decided that her philanthropy could be put to better purpose elsewhere.)

The defence counsel, Mr Hawkins, acted rather strangely, asking Mr Hardwick at the second hearing if he was still determined to send the case before a jury, for, if so, he (Hawkins) would reserve the defence in the interests of his client. It was odd because the defence, which was that there was no case to answer, was a good one and could have stopped the case going 'up the road'. But then, of course, Mr Hawkins would not have made so much money out of it; some things never change.

There was no case to answer, Mr Hawkins claimed, because the accused had been charged with stealing the two bills of exchange. Now the paper used and the stamp had belonged to the defendant, and the right he had to use the bills had been conferred upon him by the Prince, who intended to part with the bill and never wished to see it again. The judge agreed and, though he "greatly regretted it", was forced to direct the jury to acquit. In fact the wrong charge had been made: an indictment for fraud would have covered the case much better.

The Prince's next public appearance was in Paris, during the revolution of the following year. Soon he had power which he used to both good and ill but eventually overstepped. He was defeated by Prussia in 1870 and came back to Britain to plan his next attempt from a house in Chislehurst which had the dual advantages of being not very far from London but also on the road to France. However, three months before his next sortie was scheduled to take place, he died, following a gall-bladder operation.

11

The Street Tea-leaves

Among the best places in London to get your pocket (or handbag) picked are the underground, bus-stops, Oxford Street and other main tourist shopping-areas. According to Mayhew, it was just the same in 1862. True, the *modus operandi* of his "railway and omnibus pickpockets" differed slightly in that they confined their attentions mainly to those sitting down alongside them, the voluminous clothes of the period being of great assistance in covering their activities. Nowadays pickpockets are more likely to relieve you of your purse or wallet when pushing on and off the bus or train or while standing in the queue. However, now, as then, working mob-handed is still considered more efficient and safer. Three is acknowledged to be the best number. One distracts the 'mark' by bumping or blocking; the second makes the dip and passes to the third, who makes his escape. Thus, should the first two be caught, the evidence of the property has gone.

Despite the present spate of activity, the offence has not been consistently popular since Mayhew – spasmodic rather. Certainly during my service in the 1950s, pickpocketing was relatively rare and always considered to be a rather un-British crime. But Mayhew noted few foreign practitioners, apart from several Germans and rather more French, the bulk being home-grown and the most prolific of these being "the Irish Cockneys", whom he called "the cleverest of the native London thieves". When describing the methods of pickpockets, he waxes quite poetic:

A young lady may be standing by a window in Cheapside, Fleet Street, Oxford Street or the Strand, admiring some beautiful engraving. Meantime a handsomely dressed young man, with gold chain and moustache, also takes his station at the window beside her, apparently admiring the same engraving. The young lady stands gazing on the beautiful picture, with her countenance glowing with sentiment, which may be enhanced by the sympathetic presence of the nice-looking young man by her side, and while her bosom is thus throbbing with romantic emotion, her purse, meanwhile, is being quietly transferred to the pocket of this elegantly attired young man, whom she might find in the evening dressed as a rough costermonger, mingling among the low ruffians at the Seven Dials or Whitechapel or possibly lounging in some low beershop in the Borough.

Our current pickpockets fall into two main groups: the foreign professionals and the young native-born, some amateur and some very professional. The former hail largely from South America and Algeria. Often they operate in large, highly-organized gangs which move about from country to country to wherever the best pickings are most likely to be – International Fairs, Carnivals, Olympic Games etc. They honour London with their presence during the summer tourist-season and the Christmas shopping-rush, should there be nothing more lucrative elsewhere. Tourists are by far the best prey, since they are usually distracted by new sights and sounds and finding their way around – and they carry large sums of money. It is due mainly to the increase in tourism that this crime has grown again in London.

Fortunately, present pickpocket arrest-rates are good, and although we cannot always keep out the foreign gangs even if we are aware of them, their arrival does not always go unnoticed. One large Chilean group stayed in a good London hotel, to which they returned nightly with the booty. They had sophisticated contingency-plans to be put into operation should any member be caught, and these included having the name of a London solicitor should one be needed and methods by which they would not implicate the rest of the gang. However, the Yard had known about them from the moment they stepped off the plane and had kept tabs on them ever since, and within two weeks ten out of fifteen had been caught red-handed. All such professionals, when arrested, are found to have large sums of foreign currencies and travellers' cheques and large-denomination British notes on them, testifying to heaven-knows-how-many spoiled holidays and to the true meanness of this nasty crime.

London-born pickpockets who frequent the West End are almost entirely second-generation immigrants, usually of Jamaican or West Indian parentage. Most come from South London and are loosely known as 'the South London Mob'. Very useful in catching them are the one or two police-officers who look unnervingly (for them) like them, even down to the current Rastafarian hat-style, be it woolly beret, cord cap or whatever. Keeping away from Oxford Street is sometimes a condition of bail for these youths, and on one occasion the 'dip squad' spotted a boy whom they knew to be under just such a ban, as he alighted from a bus in Oxford Street. They fingered his collar before, they thought, he could start his happy hunting, but as they were addressing themselves to him, a woman ran up and told them she had just watched him trying to pick pockets on the bus and had not known what to do about it.

One can understand her reluctance to take action herself. Only a few years before, a fourteen-year-old schoolgirl named Patricia had seen a well-built, athletic-looking Jamaican stealing from her mother's handbag while they were standing on a bus in Oxford Street. Not waiting to be told what to do, Patricia, who wanted to be a policewoman and had just begun judo classes, floored him and sat on him to hold him down. While struggling, he kicked and punched her. Other passengers, including two men, and the bus-conductor declined to assist and merely looked on. However, the conductor *was* persuaded to fetch the police, and next day a bruised and limping Patricia was congratulated and thanked by Mr Harmsworth, after the man, who had fourteen previous convictions, had been given twelve months inside.

Apparently the trade was a little less seasonal in Mayhew's time, since, "when the gentry and nobility have retired to their country seats in the provinces, crowds of strangers and tourists are pouring into the metropolis every day". But big events have always been favoured: he mentions the popularity of the Chartist gatherings, the Great Exhibition and the occasion when crowds formed to watch a female Blondin crossing a rope over the Thames. And *Cobbett's Evening Post* of 1st March 1820 printed the following scurrilous warning regarding a meeting of one of the current minority groups: "Monday, according to annual custom, the Jews' Fair commenced in Duke's Place, and it is to continue for three days. At an early hour a motley group of Hebrews, of the very lowest description, assembled on the spot, gambling, sausage-frying, fryed-fish, together with confectionery, were very abundant, and it seemed to be a scene of attraction at that end of town, and persons passing by found it prudent to take particular care of their pockets."

Unsurprisingly, pickpocketing seems always to have been

associated with immigrant and underprivileged minorities, though with regard to the Jews it is hard to know how much actual crime they did commit and how much was prejudicially laid at their door. They were also rather despised for their role as 'fences' because that was held to be a way of gaining from crime without much risk.

The big fairs and other events still attract the light-fingered, but fortunately the police are not unaware of this. On the Monday morning after the big switch-on of the Oxford Street laser-beams, at Christmas 1978, the lists at both Marlborough Street and Wells Street were heavy with 'dips', since the dip-squad, only too well aware how irresistible all those upward-gaping crowds would be, had been out in force too.

Some types of nineteenth-century street theft such as horse-stealing and child-stripping are no longer part of the Marlborough Street scene, though dog-stealing still comes up now and then. It was still quite prevalent earlier this century, as the court's records show, with regular entries such as: "Stealing a Pekinese dog value £30. Further stealing dog's collar value 2s 6d.

Receiving a Cairn Terrier, knowing same to have been stolen, value £60." The man who stole the Pekinese got three months' hard labour.

The West End suffered particularly from this offence during the nineteenth century, ladies' pets and gentlemen's sporting-dogs being the favourite targets. Not only were they worth something in their own right, but as objects of affection to the idle rich they could be held for ransom; so the thieves could not lose. They would wait for a plea for their return in *The Times* or on a handbill, then get a dog-receiver or 'fancier' to negotiate terms, sometimes having him pass on the message that, should the terms not be met, the animal would be killed. This was unlikely, however, since good prices could be got for British dogs on the Continent, especially in Germany, if the home market were felt to be too risky.

Also common to the West End, mainly in the earlier part of the nineteenth century, was the crime of child-stripping. It was committed, held Mayhew, largely by debauched drunken old hags who tempted well-dressed children into some quiet mews and there relieved them of some of their expensive attire, particularly their covetable boots. The hags then told the children to wait where they were and left on some pretext, saying they would be back soon. Dusk on winter evenings was the favoured time for this offence.

One method of street theft seems to have been going on ever since shops had windows: making a hole in the glass and haring off with some of the contents. Glass-cutting implements were easily carried and it was a crime which youngsters could be easily trained to execute – they were less likely to arouse suspicion when just hanging around. The *Hue and Cry and Police Gazette* of 21st March 1818 describes just such a case: "A boy named Robertshaw, aged fourteen, and another named Fisher, were charged at the Marlborough Street Office with cutting various shop-windows and stealing articles through the apertures they made. Robertshaw was committed for trial and the other detained for further examination. It was found that they are connected with a regular organized gang of young depredators [plunderers]."

When, during my service a man was caught in the act of cutting into the shop-window of a Regent Street jeweller, an officer gave long and exhausting chase only to find at the end of it that the potential thief was not only a fellow police-officer (off sick) but a colleague from the Section House. The culprit went to prison for this escapade.

In the days when shops had lavish displays of goods outside on the street, snatching from them and running was a common offence. The end of the Second World War saw the beginnings of a more sinister variant: the armed shop-raid. Such a raid, in 1947, produced one of the most publicized murders of the post-war years which thus entered the ranks of the crimes which can be identified in a couple of words (usually the name of a participant, premises or venue) by those around at the time. This was 'the de Antiquis murder'.

The lead-up to the crime began at about two-thirty on the afternoon of 29th April 1947, when three men, Charles Henry Jenkins, a twenty-three-year-old lighterman, seventeen-year-old Peter Rolt, a warehouseman, both from Bermondsey in the East End, and Christopher James Geraghty, a twenty-year-old labourer from Liverpool Road, near King's Cross, drove up to Jay's, a jeweller's shop in Charlotte Street, just north of Oxford Street in the West End. Pulling up face-masks, they entered, drawing out pistols as they did so, and proceeded to hold up the manager, Mr Ernest Stock, and his staff of six. Or at least they tried to, for the public were braver then, probably because fewer of them had been shot.

An elderly assistant threw a chair at one of the raiders, and the manager tackled another but was struck on the head with a pistol-butt for his pains. During this mêlée a shot was fired by Geraghty, a 'warning shot', but no one was hurt, and the gunmen ran, empty-handed, out into the street, hotly pursued by a young assistant shouting, "Police! Police! Stop them!"

Jumping into their car, the desperate, failed thieves found their escape blocked by a lorry, so they promptly jumped out again and made off down the street. They were seen by an approaching motorcyclist, thirty-four-year-old father-of-six Alec de Antiquis, who swung his bike round and put his foot down as though to stop in their path before toppling over with a bullet in his head. He died soon afterwards of brain-haemorrhage. But public resistance was not yet over. Another passer-by, an accountant named Charles Herbert Grimshaw, trip-kicked one of the gunmen and jumped on him as he fell but had to release him when he received a kick to the head which dazed him; then he found himself staring down the barrel of a ·320 revolver.

Losing their pursuers, the three men ran on up Tottenham Court Road and turned into Torrington Place, where one of them jumped onto the running-board of a passing cab but was brushed off by the driver. Then he and one of the others ran into a nearby block of offices to rest. There they compounded the stupidity of leaving their (stolen) car outside the premises they were raiding and without a driver *in situ*, by divesting themselves of raincoat, gloves and tell-tale white scarves which had been used as masks and tucking them away behind an old, disused counter before re-entering the street and disappearing from view.

Most murders become famous because they are mysterious or involve deep, forbidden passions, but the reason the de Antiquis murder so hit the headlines was because firearms had been used and a man killed while bravely 'having a go', as it used to be called. In fact there had already been a burglary in the area that day in which an escaping thief had fired several shots at a policeman, and thus the two cases were headlined "FIREARMS USED IN SHOP-RAIDS" in *The Times* the next day.

Three days later a foreman painter in the office-block found a raincoat tucked away behind the disused counter, and when he picked it up, a white scarf dropped out of the bundle. In the pockets were a cap and a pair of gloves. The raincoat was traced to the brother-in-law of one Charles Henry Jenkins, but it had been lent to the raider by his sister. Fifty yards from his home two pistols were found dumped in the Thames, one of which was of the same calibre as the bullet-hole in the victim. Evidence came to light that Geraghty had been one of the raiders involved in a similar but successful raid on a jewellers in Queensway only a few days before the Charlotte Street débâcle, and, as the witnesses and evidence began to pile up in the glare of publicity, Rolt and Geraghty eventually made confessions but declared that Geraghty, who fired the shot, had meant only to frighten de Antiquis. This was probably so, since they had not used their guns on the shop staff when provoked. However, this did not save Geraghty or Jenkins, who were hanged on 19th September that year. Nor should it have done: if you hold someone else's life so cheap that you carelessly run the risk of killing them, you should be prepared to forfeit your own. Rolt, who was under eighteen, was detained till His Majesty's Pleasure would be known, with a recommendation that his sentence be not less than five years' imprisonment.

Before going to the Old Bailey, the whole story, as was then the requirement in law, was first unfolded before Mr Sandbach at Marlborough Street. Pathology evidence was given by the famous, but by then failing, Sir Bernard Spilsbury. Superintendent Robert Fabian, who was present at the post-mortem, had been shocked by the "sudden declension of sureness and perception" in the great pathologist, the authors of *Sir Bernard Spilsbury* relate. He had been "sadly puzzled" when unable to find the exit-wound, when, in fact, the bullet was still in the head. It dropped out during the search, to be picked up by Fabian, who handed it to Spilsbury, "reminding him he had found it. But Spilsbury knew he had not found it".

Sir Bernard, who had appeared as prosecution witness many times at Marlborough Street, was soon to have a post-mortem performed on himself after his suicide in his gas-filled laboratory three months later. The de Antiquis murder was his last big case, and he also performed the post-mortem on the bodies of Geraghty and Jenkins, as he often did on murderers he had helped to convict.

12

The Mary Annes

A Marlborough Street magistrate who succumbed to pressure from above, such as the court has so often had to endure, was James Lennox Hannay. One can scarcely blame him, since he was the latest in a long chain of men who had done so, from the Home Secretary and Lord Chancellor to the Attorney General, who had, in turn, also applied it downwards. The pressure – or, in fact, direct interference – came from the Prime Minister and, it is now thought, the Prince of Wales (the future King Edward VII), all of them conspiring to pervert the course of justice in covering up the Cleveland Street Affair of 1889.

It began in July of that year when Post Office police, in the course of a routine investigation of a suspected theft, uncovered the fact that several of their young messenger-lads (fifteen- to seventeen-years-old) were regularly attending a male brothel at 19 Cleveland Street, for the delectation of visiting gentlemen. They quickly informed the Metropolitan Police, who arranged for a special Saturday-morning sitting at Marlborough Street, where warrants were issued for the arrest of the brothel-keeper, Charles Hammond, and a post-office clerk (ex-messenger boy) who had recruited them, Henry Newlove.

Hammond fled the country before the warrant could be executed, Newlove, caught, began to talk. He talked about the regular customers, including Lord Arthur Somerset and the Earl of Euston. Thirty-eight-year-old Lord Arthur, a cavalry officer, was superintendent of the royal stables and a very good friend and extra equerry to the Prince of Wales. The ranks closed. The Prime Minister, Lord Salisbury, personally blocked the extradition of Hammond from France, much to the fury of the police. However, despite lack of encouragement, they soon had enough evidence for a warrant against Lord Arthur. Again the Prime Minister intervened in something which had nothing whatsoever to do with him in the normal course of events.

The Home Secretary was soon instructing the frustrated Director of Public Prosecutions not to proceed since there was 'insufficient evidence' and to remand Newlove for a third time at Marlborough Street since there was an expectation of bringing Hammond before the court – this when he had already blocked Hammond's extradition. However, George Veck, an ex-telegraphist who had aided Hammond's escape, could be arrested – a foolish move this, since when arrested he had on him correspondence regarding a Mr Brown, a pseudonym for Lord Arthur, and a young man named Algernon Allies. The police tracked down the nineteen-year-old, curly-haired, good-looking Allies, and he admitted knowing Lord Arthur most intimately and being, in fact, kept by him. Still, although what Allies admitted he had done with Lord Arthur was a criminal offence, and although the others had been charged with similar crimes as well as with procuring, it was considered 'that there was insufficient "untainted evidence" against him, despite the fact that the DPP thought the evidence against Lord Arthur stronger than that against Veck. (There was, in fact, some police evidence against the equerry.)

Soldiering on, the police found a flamboyant male prostitute, John Saul, who knew Cleveland Street well and produced more respectable names, including that of the Earl of Euston, but they knew that his very appearance and way of life would make his evidence unacceptable.

When it could be held back no longer, the case against Newlove and Veck came up for committal hearing at Marlborough Street, on Monday 2nd September 1889. Meanwhile Lord Arthur Somerset took four months' leave and left for a holiday on the Continent. The problem about the hearing was, of course, that since all the 'customers' were committing offences, their names should be disclosed, and normally would be. Prosecuting solicitors were instructed that in this case they should ask only for descriptions, even pseudonyms, but not names.

It was a strategy [say the authors of *The Cleveland Street Affair*] that appeared to salve their consciences, but only, as it turned out, by imposing a frightful burden on that of the magistrate, Mr Hannay. On Wednesday 4th September, after the third day of the committal hearing involving Veck and Newlove, a worried Mr Hannay buttonholed Sir Augustus Stephenson [the DPP] and voiced his qualms. Sir Augustus mentioned the meeting in a memorandum to the Attorney General on the following day:

"After case was over yesterday Mr Hannay the magistrate came to speak with me privately – said that in an ordinary case, i.e. one that did not concern the Treasury [the DPP was part of the Treasury], he would have felt it his duty to call for disclosures of the names and then had it brought before him, by warrant and included in the charge ... he wished the Attorney General to bear in mind his position".

The next problem was the trial. If the defendants pleaded 'not guilty', there was a big risk that the names would slip out. A compromise was reached. The defence counsel, realizing the strength of their position, said Veck and Newlove would plead 'guilty' to the less serious charges against them, if the others were dropped. They were, and the pair received, for the time and the offences, very light sentences, of four months (Newlove) and nine months (Veck). There were no reporters in court at the time since the case had not been set down on the official court list. It had been noticed however, by W.T. Stead of anti-white slave traffic fame, whose magazine, the *Pall Mall Gazette*, commented:

We are glad to see that Sir Augustus Stephenson, Solicitor to the Treasury, was present at the Marlborough Street police court yesterday, when two prisoners were committed for their trial in connection with a criminal charge of a disagreeable nature ... the question Sir Augustus Stephenson will have to answer is whether the two noble Lords and other notable persons in society who were accused by the witnesses of having been principals in the crime for which the man Veck was committed to trial are to be allowed to escape scot free. There has been too much of this kind of thing in the past. The wretched agents are run in and sent to penal servitude: the lords and gentlemen who employ them swagger at large and are even welcomed as valuable allies of the Administration of the day.

Newlove and Veck were two weeks into their penal servitude when Lord Arthur Somerset returned from abroad to attend his mother's funeral at Badminton. Police, feeling their case even stronger now, sought to arrest him and even followed him to his mother's graveside, but the decision was passed around long enough (even distinguished royal courtiers making direct representations) for him to leave again quite openly two weeks later. A month later a warrant for his arrest was applied for at Marlborough Street. It was still in existence, unexecuted, at his death in exile in the South of France in May 1926.

More people were to go to gaol over the affair, though not, of course, the aristocratic offenders. A journalist named Ernest Parke got a year for libel against Lord Euston in attempting to expose the affair, and Arthur Newton, Veck and Newlove's defence solicitor, six weeks for attempting to spirit some of the boys out of the country.

The writers of *The Cleveland Street Affair* suggest that the whole cover-up was in aid not only of Lord Arthur Somerset but also of the problem prince Albert Victor (Eddy), who was the victim of rumours that he was Jack the Ripper but was known to be a regular guest of the 100 Guineas Club, the most luxurious of the male brothels of the time which featured young men dressed as women.

Only one real effort was made to expose the affair, this by the well-known Liberal MP Labouchère, who was, in fact, largely responsible for the then current problems of homosexuals, since he had introduced the amendment to the 1885 Criminal Law Amendment Act which made gross indecency between males an offence punishable by up to two years' hard labour. It became known as 'the Blackmailers Charter' and caused a great deal of suffering but, at least in part, was introduced in the name of some parity in the handling of male and female prostitution. Before this, male prostitutes had been largely left alone, though there were plenty of them about. It also, like the female-suffrage drive later, put a little social equality into the system, bringing, as it did, the rich and influential into conflict with the law – a law so harsh to the poor – for the first time. They did not, of course, usually end up in prison, but many were driven into exile, which is punishment too.

By the time I came to the Marlborough Street area, homosexuals brought in for offences relating to their homosexuality were few: the occasional enactors of gross indecency from Hyde Park – in other words doing it in the open, for which heterosexuals were also charged; a few male prostitutes for importuning, and those caught by the 'lavatory patrol'.

The patrol was necessary because certain West End toilets were plagued with predatory homosexuals who would importune while at the stalls, gazing meaningfully down at the adjacent male's penis then tracking up to his face – which is all very well if that is what you went there for, but something of a menace if all you want is a quiet pee. If the importunee responded, they would couple, sometimes elsewhere but frequently in the nearby closet.

The police would arrest them, but only after long, continuous observation by two officers, who often trailed the man from toilet to toilet. One toilet and one importune was not enough in order to prove the crime 'persistent': it had to be several. Evidence had to be stonewall, partly because it was difficult to prove in court. "He has a bladder complaint," the Harley Street doctor would say in evidence, partly because, though it was a charge naturally dealt with lightly, no one underestimated the seriousness of it, and partly because the police never knew who they were getting. It could be a rich and influential businessman, an orchestra conductor, a Peer of the Realm or an MP. The risk of pressure was, I believe, much less by then, but the influential could often afford the best counsel, gracing even Marlborough Street with 'top silk'.

These days not so much 'vice' of either kind is seen there, though homosexuality is sometimes pertinent to the offence – the female prostitute who turns out to be male, or undergoing the change from male to female, for example. However, the only real effect of this is to change the charge from soliciting to importuning and throw the police-station and/or court into a bit of a flurry about which cells to put them in. Some have been charged several times before their true sex is discovered, and one had even been on remand in a woman's prison without, apparently, anyone noticing 'her' penis. The only thing that bothers me about these cases is: do the customers know what they are getting beforehand? A prosecution under the Trades Description Act would sometimes seem more appropriate.

Recently an unhappy person, in the middle of the tough road from male to female, was charged with shoplifting a suit. "A man's or a woman's suit?" the magistrate asked gently. "Oh, a woman's!" was the quick response. He wanted it so as to look smart for a job interview. What kind of job? With an escort agency.

Female homosexuals rarely appear, but this is not really so strange since women in general commit so much less crime than men. However, it is interesting that this person, changing into a woman, should then commit the predominantly female crime – shoplifting.

13

Solicitors and Counsel

"There are one or two legal gentlemen who seem to have the principal part of Great Marlborough Street cases in their hands," commented *The Graphic* in 1887, and that has not changed much. In fact, every court has its regular local solicitors, and, hearteningly, they are usually among the most honest and the best of their kind.

Situated in the street itself, just opposite the court, is the court's longest-serving and most respected firm, Claude Hornby & Cox. The wealthy Claude Hornby, who practised for the love of it, began the firm in the mid-1920s and was joined in 1946 by A.E.Cox.

Claude Hornby always felt that the best thing one could do for a client was to get him to tell the truth, and he would sit them down and ask them to do just that. A secretary would sit by, taking notes, but, when they had finished, like as not he would say, "That was a pack of lies. Now tell me the *real* truth," and they would.

"You could always rely on him not to ask you to tell outrageous lies for someone who was obviously guilty," Lord Justice Lawton recalls. He also remembers his knack for keeping the well-known out of the limelight during their court appearance, and thus out of the newspapers. "What do you do for a living?" a magistrate asked idly of one shabbily-dressed client. "A musician, sir," he replied. "Oh, a street musician, I suppose," murmured the magistrate and dismissed him without further comment and a nominal fine. In fact he was a world-famous concert-artist.

Claude Hornby died in the early 1950s. "He was quite well off," says his former partner, now Judge Edward Cox, "and was one of those people who seemed to keep on inheriting money, but he just *loved* being an advocate, and as long as he could get enough time off to watch Middlesex play, he was happy." The firm still continues in the expert hands of Timothy Lawrence, Chris Green and John Howard, three most competent solicitors who are trusted implicitly by the magistrates 'across the road' and who are frequently called upon at a moment's notice to assist in a difficult situation. Tim Lawrence is also Secretary of the London Criminal Courts Solicitors Association.

There are several other intermittent regulars who are very much respected by the court staff – and one or two who are not. Those who are not are inefficient, arrogant (though often both since the traits seem to go together) or bent.

Strangely enough, the inefficient can often cause more pain to their colleagues, the police and the magistrates, who hate to see someone badly prosecuted or defended. It is small wonder that some hoot with laughter when they hear certain legal gentlemen spouting that legal aid is everyone's right, when they know that, if any member of the public acquires the right to that particular lawyer's services, he will be worse off than if he says to the magistrate, with his own voice, "I am sorry. I did it. I won't do it again."

Sometimes, even wily criminals are encumbered with one of the arrogant inefficents. One apologized to Bob for his: "Sorry about that rude ****. Don't know what he's bleedin' doing. Wait till I catch the bastard who put me onto 'im."

Stanley French tells how he would curse the presence of such men and wish that the magistrates had been left to get on with the case unaided instead of having to waste time, particularly if they had to protect the defendant "from the incapacity of his legal representative". He remembers J.B. Sandbach's telling a defendant; "Well, Mr So-and-So, your learned counsel has done his best to get you convicted, but I find you 'not guilty'."

Of course everyone has to learn, but it seems a little hard on defendants who have no idea what they are getting. What is needed is a *Which* on legal men.

As for the bent ones, what really outrages those who know what is going on is not the way they are prepared to weave such wicked webs of lies but the way they so often take cases 'up the road' to Crown Court when it is not necessary. They are doing it either with rich people they want to milk or with legal aid for which we are paying. To add insult to injury, they often also parade as the conscience of the legal profession: only they care, are liberal and enlightened – they are also making a fortune. Mr Robey, to his credit, had a go at these men in court once. He told a woman defendant he would not allow her to be prejudiced by one of these solicitors (dragging the whole thing on is often a nightmare for the defendant, of course) and would grant legal aid to her *after* she had made the decision about which court she wished to attend, since "It does happen that some firms of solicitors, not in the interests of their clients but in the interests of their own pockets, will advise election for trial in quite a trivial case."

In days past, the peculiarities of Marlborough Street cases and clients have proved stumbling-blocks for solicitors as well as magistrates and police. One such was Arthur Newton, who was featured in the *Vanity Fair* 'Men of the Day' series on 21st September 1893 as "The Marlborough Street Solicitor". Then thirty-three years old, he had been qualified for nine years but had not practised all that time "for he was not poor enough", the magazine claimed; his father was actuary and manager of the Legal and General Life Association.

Yet, in the last seven or eight years [*Vanity Fair* continued], he has come to employ a considerable staff in Great Marlborough Street, and to be employed by most of the persons of any note who may succeed, either by mischief or ill-luck, in getting an introduction to that other Mr Newton who, with Mr Hannay, presides over the Great Marlborough Street Police Court ... There he once got himself into trouble by too zealous defence of an undeserving client. He was not a man of great influence, and therefore his success is mainly due to himself; yet he has the great advantage of a good appearance which contrasts strangely with that of the ordinary type of Police Court advocate. He is not eloquent, but he is lucid; and though he is strong yet he is courteous. He misses few points, and it is the common opinion that he has deserved his success.

He claims descent from that Sir Isaac Newton who was supposed to have been the only man since Adam to connect an apple with the fall ... With the exception of the Knight of Ely Place and of perhaps one other, he is the most widely known criminal solicitor in London.

He can swim, and he has more than once been found guilty of giving a conjuring entertainment.

JEHU JUNIOR

He needed to be good at sleight of hand since 'embarrassing cases' were his speciality. The first to bring him to prominence was 'The Cleveland Street Affair' (see pages 100-103).

Before Veck was arrested, he told Henry Newlove's mother not to worry about money, since he would instruct a solicitor to defend the young procurer. That solicitor turned out to be Arthur Newton, whose services, the police knew, neither Veck nor Newlove could afford and for which, they surmised, Lord Arthur Somerset was paying.

Newton often employed Augustus de Gallo, a Marlborough Street interpreter, as a part-time enquiry-agent. The day after the police had traced Allies, Lord Arthur's more permanent *amour*, de Gallo appeared at the boy's home in Suffolk and seemed upset to find that he had gone off with police. Had he left any letters behind? the interpreter enquired. He had not.

Arthur Newton saw Newlove and Veck through their subsequent trial, letting it out that if the police did not leave this thing alone, "a very distinguished person" would be involved. He was referring to Prince Albert Victor.

However, though Algernon Allies was still a threat to the uncharged Lord Arthur, the police were guarding the boy very carefully, but not carefully enough to prevent someone's getting to him with a very good proposition: a trip to America, all expenses paid and money for him to live there – permanently.

Allies agreed, and an arrangement was made for him to meet the agent again that evening at the corner of Tottenham Court Road, from whence he would be whipped away to Liverpool to leave for the New World the next day. However, Allies told the police, who also kept the appointment. They watched the boy and the agent board a hansom cab and followed it back to Marlborough Street. There the couple entered the 'Marlborough Head' public house situated directly opposite the court. Inside was de Gallo. The police stepped in and found the agent to be Henry Taylerson, managing clerk to Arthur Newton, who refused to answer any more questions until he had seen his solicitor.

The police requested permission of their bosses to arrest the trio for conspiracy to pervert the course of justice, but the usual procrastination followed, allowing Newton time for a cheeky but clever counter-attack. Two days after the incident he sent an indignant letter to the DPP, complaining about disgraceful police behaviour. This poor boy Allies was being hounded and threatened by them, and now they were interfering with his, Newton's, managing clerk.

He then played the old but effective trick of agreeing with the obvious, irrefutable facts of the case but putting an entirely different interpretation on them. Newton, his clerk and the interpreter had been acting on instructions from the father of Allies, who wished to remove his son from "objectionable associations" by means of a new life abroad. The boy was perfectly willing to go along with this but was in a state of terror due to police threats.

The DPP responded to Newton's letter by saying that the police were well aware that Allies's father had no money to send his son anywhere and warned him that the boy was still a potential witness against Hammond (he could not say Lord Arthur, since the latter had not yet been charged), and anyone being party to his leaving the country could be charged; but none of them was.

It was small wonder that Newton was undaunted. His next move was over to Belgium, where he saw Hammond off to the United States from under the noses of the British police who had him under observation over there. They were particularly angry about this since they felt that their pressure to have Hammond extradited was about to succeed.

In December, after the warrant for the arrest of Lord Arthur Somerset had at last been issued, the post-office boys were formally dismissed from their jobs. Looking around for something else, they consulted one of the police constables who had guarded them for so long. He told them that someone had asked him to let them know when they were dismissed. That someone was, of course, Arthur Newton.

The solicitor offered them a lovely new life in Australia, a new outfit of clothes, £50 to spend and so on. They accepted and were to leave for Dover on the following day when one of the boys' mothers got wind of it and went to the police and asked them what was going on.

This time the police were allowed to act, but for the first time in this case they were involved in a little covering-up themselves by not divulging the complicity of one of their own men. Perhaps for this reason the case against de Gallo was dropped, and at the trial no evidence was offered against Taylerson. The case against Newton was, however, proceeded with, albeit in a half-hearted manner.

The very mild prosecution was conducted by the Attorney General in person. He readily agreed with the defence that Newton was obviously acting only in an excess of zeal to protect his clients from blackmail. The judge was not quite so easily won over and gave the solicitor six weeks in prison. However, the Law Society did not feel that a prison record should be any bar to his continuing as a solicitor, and when he came out, he took up where he had left off and prospered for the next twenty years. Then his excess of zeal overtook him again.

Having acted as solicitor to Crippen, he promptly sold the murderer's death-cell confession to *John Bull* magazine. This time the Law Society did not approve. Not only was he breaching the confidence of his client, he had made up the confession. They suspended him for one year.

A year after his re-instatement he was back in the dock again, accused with two others of conspiracy to defraud a rich young Austrian of £13,000 for land in Canada which they did not own. Newton conducted his own defence, using his middle-age and now poor health as mitigating circumstances; but it availed him nothing. This time he got three years' penal servitude and was debarred.

When I speak of lawyers, I am, of course, referring to both solicitors and barristers, both of whom can act in magistrates' courts. Barristers who attend are instructed by the solicitors, who may feel they need to bring in the 'big guns'.

The big Oxford Street stores have such constant need of prosecution counsel in their shoplifting cases that many of them retain the permanent services of one barrister, James Bullen of the deceptively quiet voice and soft approach. An excellent and totally honest counsel, he will bend his head slightly forward as he puts the mild, innocuous question that cuts the ground from under a defendant before he has even noticed it trembling. James hones up his brain, between times, by taking on highly complex industrial-tribunal cases or those involving international law, shipping, etc.

Despite the impression given, most barristers and solicitors dealing with criminal cases are competent and honest – and usually good company, talking being their job. Someone who was particularly grateful for this attribute in a barrister was the writer Nicholas Monsarrat, when, during the last war, he was aboard a corvette on bleak duties among shipmates who disapproved of him, since he was from the Royal Naval Volunteer Reserve and therefore regarded as a "pink-cheeked amateur" and playboy. His gloom was lifted by the arrival of someone not only in similar circumstances but who could talk. "Instead of the zoo-like grunting and snuffling which had ruled us so far, actual sentences were now to be heard, with verbs and all." It was Jim Harmsworth, Monsarrat reports in his autobiography *Life is a Four-Letter Word*, who had been a barrister in civvy street and hoped one day to return to practise "when all this inconvenience is over".

Lieutenant St J.B.V. Harmsworth RNVR was not only interestingly connected, his cousin Esmond being Lord Rothermere of Fleet Street and *Daily Mail* fame; he had also "the added glamour" of having been torpedoed, in an armed merchant-cruiser called *Patroclus*, which went to the bottom off Bloody Foreland in November 1940.

When asked about the incident by the curious fellow-lieutenant, St John said: "Oh, I simply swam about a bit. There were various people looking after us, and they came round to me before too long. But I must say that Bloody Foreland was christened with tolerable accuracy. Quite apart from the snow, the water was *extremely* cold." He admitted that when he heard that the captain of the ace U-boat which sank them had finally lost *his* craft and had been taken prisoner, he "opened a bottle of fizz".

All of this sounds authentic to anyone who has heard Mr Harmsworth in his latest role as magistrate at Marlborough Street.

14

Regular Game-chicken

"The habitués of Marlborough Street comparatively seldom see great hulking animals with broken noses and dislocated jawbones and hair still clotted with their blood ..." So wrote the correspondent of *The Illustrated London News* in the issue of 9th October 1847. However, Marlborough Street obviously did occasionally see the aftermath of punch-ups, as the same magazine colourfully reported on 28th March 1842:

A REGULAR GAME CHICKEN

Wednesday, at the Marlborough Street office, the business of the court was somewhat varied by the apparition of a cab-driver with a bloody nose, who had moreover contrived to render his appearance as appalling as Banquo's ghost by smearing the sanguinary stream over a considerable portion of his face. At the bar, the brawny frame of a well-known character, old Joe Arnold, the Piccadilly waterman, commonly called 'Thirsty Joe', was conspicuously visible. Something had evidently occurred out of the common way to ruffle his temper, and he stood rubbing his brass badge to restore its damaged resplendency, at the same time casting wrathful glances at the gore-bedabbled complainant. Though the snow of three-and-seventy winters was displayed on the remnant of bristly hair that still stuck on his head, time had so little impaired 'Old Joe's' enormous strength that he was even now more than a match for any rough and refractory cabman and quite as well able – at least so he boasts – to renew feats of his youth, namely taking the conceit out of two of the biggest coachmen in London and getting none the worst in a glove-fight with the unconquered 'Game-Chicken' [a well-known prize-fighter].

Mr Hardwicke (to the cabman): Who assaulted you?

Cabman: Vy, old Joe, the vaterman.

Joe: Served yer right.

Cabman: Ven I put on to the Piccadilly rank, old Joe vouldn't vorter my oss.

Joe: Because you never hacts hupright like a man. You never drops no penny, nor no hapenny, nor no nuthin.

Officer: Silence.

Cabman: Ve gets into a bit of hargument, and then Joe knocks me down.

A second cabman came forward as witness. He confirmed the story about the argument and the knock-down blow, and added, that, on going to help the other cabman, he was himself knocked down. A third cabman gave the same testimony, and he too had fallen beneath the victorious arm of Joe the waterman.

Mr Hardwicke: Well, what have you to say to this, Joe?

Joe: Sy? vy that the whole lot is the three werry worst wot puts on my rank; and any nobleman or gentleman wot I've a respect for never gets in their cabs without leaving their property with me, if I knows it. They owes me pounds and pounds, and they expects me to lend 'em my buckets, but I vont have that ere, at no price.

Mr Hardwicke: But why did you strike this man?

Joe: Cos he called me a name wot no Englishman will stand.

Officer: What?

Joe: Vy, a wagabone.

The cabman declared that the waterman had no ground to show sensitiveness at the term applied to him, for he had used the same epithet to them in the first instance; and that at all times the old waterman's vocabulary was more remarkable for energy than politeness.

Mr Hardwicke: You must pay 10s.

Old Joe turned rather glum at this decision, diving first into one pocket and then another. Upon finding his numismatic searches perfectly unavailing, he slipped his hand under his apron and, drawing forth his watch, whispered to a sympathizing friend certain instructions, of which the only part audible was, "Ax on it as much as vill kiver the fine and pay for a drop of summut for our two selves." The mission of the friend was so effectual that in five minutes old Joe was quenching his thirst at a favourite public house.

A couple of months later the same paper was reporting a much more typical Marlborough Street offence, involving the requisite gentlemen, honour, servants and a foreigner – or at least someone with a foreign name, Baron Osten, a colonel in the Hanoverian Hussars. The Baron, "a gentleman far advanced in years", appeared with his head bound up, the victim of "a very violent assault by Mr F. Pridham". The case excited so much interest, we are told, that the court was crowded with all kinds of personages, including a lord, an MP and one Sir Vincent Cotton, who turned out to be pertinent to the case.

Baron Osten told Mr Maltby that he had been in his room at 12 Dover Street, writing, when his servant had told him that a gentleman wished to see him. No sooner had he been advised of this than the said gentleman pushed past the servant and entered his room, "swaggering and stamping", and said, "Baron Osten I presume?" It appeared that the gentleman, Mr Pridham, had a bone to pick with the Baron. Had he not traduced the good name of Dr Pridham, his father, at Pratt's Billiard Hall, by saying he was a billiard-marker? The Baron denied this but said he thought it was probably true and rang for his servant and told him to stay close by. However, as soon as the servant closed the door behind him, Mr Pridham lashed out with his silver-topped stick across the Baron's chest and head, causing blood to flow freely. He attempted to reach the Turkish sabres on the wall, with which to defend himself, but Mr Pridham was too quick for him. Finally the servant rushed in, and the police were called.

Mr Pridham told a story slightly different to that of the Baron and his servant. With "an air of indifference", he said: "You have heard their version of the story, now hear mine." But there was something to clear up first: "I must, however, before entering upon my defence, contradict the statement made by the servant that he laid hold of my collar. He did no such thing. When the bell was rung by his master, he merely came into the room, danced a sort of hornpipe and then ran off. [Laughter.] Had he stopped, I might not have flogged the man as I did. I, however, was the first person assaulted." He then told how he and his father, Dr Pridham, had sought all over London, at various clubs, Crockford's, White's and so on, for the Baron, whom, they had heard, was spreading derogatory remarks about the elder man. They decided he had gone into hiding but tracked him down – having no intention of assaulting him. The servant, without waiting for Pridham's card, had skipped upstairs so fast he could scarcely catch up with him. (Pridham was playing the best defence game of agreeing with most of the evidence but putting a different interpretation on it.) When challenged, the Baron had "hemmed and hawed" then finally said that he was not the only one and mentioned, among others, Sir Vincent Cotton. Then the Baron asked him to leave. He, however, put a hand on his shoulder and asked for an answer, yes or no, whereupon the Baron pushed him away. Was this the assault he complained of? asked Mr Maltby. He answered that it was and that he considered it an insult which no gentleman could brook. Mr Maltby observed that Pridham's laying his hands on the Baron constituted the first assault, but the defendant, now in full flood, was unabashed:

"I then struck him with my stick on his shoulder. He then attempted to seize a sabre which lay on the sofa, and had he got hold of it, murder might have been committed, as I am so expert a swordsman that I should have wrested it from him and perhaps cut him to pieces. [Great laughter.] He then rang again, and the servant came in, danced a hornpipe and went out. I then laid my stick about the fellow's head, who howled most lustily. At length, having beaten him to my heart's content, I went out of the room. At the door I was met by some females who came running up stairs, some, I suppose, of the landlord's family. One of them put her apron to her eyes and, whining, said, 'Oh! the poor baron's murdered' and squatted down and seized me by the legs, while a fat man, having toiled up the stairs laid hold of me by the collar." (Roars of laughter.)

Mr Clarkson (for the Baron) said that he had to remind the prisoner that he had alluded to a gentleman of rank and that he thought it only fair to tell him that that gentleman was now present. The defendant apologized for making use of any name, it had slipped from him accidentally in the heat of the moment.

Mr Maltby committed Pridham to Newgate for trial, an action to which he responded with a careless, "Very well, sir." Sir Vincent Cotton then piped up that, as he had been alluded to, he would merely say that he wished to state publicly that he believed the report to be true and that he had been similarly served by the same party ten years before.

Walking-sticks and umbrellas have always been among Marlborough Street's favourite weapons. A typical entry in the court's records of 1917 reads: "Assaulting Robert McFarlane by striking him on the face with an umbrella." Also typical is the accompanying charge, subsequent to the original: "Assaulting PC 383 D.Wm.Rose by striking him on the face with his fist." Umbrellas were still going strong in my day (Bob's pocketbook for 1960 tells of a gentleman's using an umbrella in an increasingly familiar manner – for striking a car roof in a fury), but walking-sticks were losing ground.

Assaults brought on by the use of motor vehicles are commonplace now and increasingly serious. Popular opinion has it that this is an offence that anyone is liable to commit, but, in fact, a great many brought before the courts for it turn out to have criminal records. The parking hassle is not however, new. *The Illustrated London News* of 1842 tells one such tale, giving it, in the manner of the telling, a little more dignity than it deserves: "MARLBOROUGH STREET – Mr White, surgeon of Aldersgate Street, was convicted before Mr

Hardwick, of an aggravated assault on Thomas Davis, groom to Mr Pettigrew, surgeon, Savile Row, and fined £3 and costs. The affray grew out of a contention for precedence in a carriage rank between the rival Galens*; and the result sets at rest the hitherto unsettled question – 'Who can decide when doctors disagree?' Answer – Mr Hardwick.''

The earliest buses were also a cause of much violence. The first of the new omnibuses were brought onto the streets of London by George Shillibeer in July 1829 and ran from Paddington to the Bank. They were advertised as being particularly suitable for the transportation of women and children, which the short-stage coaches were not felt to be. Hammersmith/Hyde Park Corner/St Paul's was the next route to be opened up, in 1830, but by then everyone who could get together a vehicle and horses was starting to get in on the act. There were no regulations to speak of, and competition was fierce (Shillibeer quickly went bankrupt) and rough. Drivers and conductors had no training and no tests to pass and were often shabby and uncouth, unlike the Shillibeer originals who were held to be vastly superior to the rude ruffians on the short-stage coaches, especially those on the Paddington route. Of course there were two sides: many of the passengers were 'gentlemen', and gentlemen were used to getting their own way.

Thus a typical Marlborough Street bus-case related by the conservative Press in 1842 told of "a ruffian" (the conductor) and "a gentleman" (the passenger) travelling on one of Powell's Brentford Omnibuses. When "a lady" alighted from the bus in Coventry Street, she tendered the conductor the fare of sixpence. He asked for a shilling, and an altercation ensued. The gentleman, overhearing, also tendered sixpence, since that was what he always paid to and from Hammersmith. The conductor, named, almost unbelievably, William Wheels, insisted that his was "not a sixpenny bus" – stalemate, but not for long. "Bill, you tackle the lady, and I'll have it out of him!" the ruffianly conductor was alleged to have called out to a friend standing nearby, before assaulting said gentleman. Another passing gentleman verified this, telling the court he had never seen a more ruffianly assault. We are not enlightened as to what Mr Wheels said in answer to the charge, but Mr Maltby, we are told, observed "in a very indignant tone" that it was necessary to protect the public, and

* Second-century Greek physician.

females in particular, against ruffianly conduct from omnibus-drivers and conductors, and, as a warning, he would impose the highest penalty: 5 shillings' fine or two months' imprisonment. "The fine", it was reported, "was immediately paid."

While the result of petty squabbles outside clubs and pubs are the most frequent assault-cases to come up in Marlborough Street and many other courts, the area occasionally throws up something a little more colourful, such as "The Battle of the Bolognese" or the fracas in the old people's home.

In places such as the latter, passions often run high. Earlier in the century a workhouse in Poland Street, very near the court, threw up the occasional violent assault. But life was better and more leisured by the 1960s, and Sadie, a slim sixty-one-year-old, wanted to take advantage of this by doing a spot of sunbathing in the garden of the Home which also acted as a refuge for the destitute. However, she later told Paul Bennett, the assistant matron did not approve and told her: "If you want to sunbathe like that, go to the Lido in Hyde Park; then the police will pick you up." She was showing too much, the assistant matron had continued, but Sadie had not time to listen further, so she walked away, whereupon, she alleged, the assistant matron dragged her back by the hair, struck her and banged her head against the bathroom wall. Sadie, being by her own account a very restrained lady, did not strike her back but merely grabbed her starched cap and crumpled it (almost as bad, in my book, speaking as an ex-nurse!), then telephoned Scotland Yard. Later she summoned the assistant matron for assault, obviously having been told that this was her best means of redress should she wish to exercise it. And Sadie did.

No, no one had complained about her sunbathing, though possibly some of the other women who had been showing more than she had might have caused comment, she told the defence counsel.

"I had only my shoulders exposed. I can show you the mark if you like, sir," she offered Mr Bennett. "I am quite willing to take my blouse off."

Mr Bennett thought that would not be necessary.

No, a crowd had not gathered in the street to watch her, she further answered counsel; if they had, she would have put her blouse back on, since she was shy. No, she had not told the assistant matron to shut up, nor had she threatened to bash in her face with a cup. She had thrown the cup down in anger when the woman had called her a prostitute, since, if she had been one of those, she would be living in luxury today, not in the Home.

The assistant matron, who denied the charge, told the court that Sadie had been sunbathing "rather outrageously" on the grass, with her dress off and sometimes also her brassière removed. She had previously requested her not to sunbathe "in that manner", as she had been getting complaints from the residents and staff. When she again requested that she desist, Sadie had shouted, threatened her, thrown the cup and pushed her into the bathroom and slammed the door. Mr Bennett, faced with the two stories – not to mention an offer of a minor striptease, finally dismissed the case.

"The Battle of the Bolognese" took place around the same time and in another venue given to a build-up of 'feelings', a restaurant kitchen. In ingredients, the crime could be said to be typically Soho in that it involved foreigners, food and an element of the bizarre. It was, the detective sergeant who unravelled it told Mr Wilson, the outcome of opposing factions of Greek and Spaniard in a well-known Jewish restaurant.

The Greek had obviously acquired one or two British habits, since, when a Spanish waiter had poured some bolognese sauce over a plate of spaghetti, he had objected, telling him it was not his job. The waiter threatened to pour it over his head instead, and the chef dared him to do so – not a wise move, for Carlos promptly smashed the whole plate over his skull, then weighed in with a silver dish, causing cuts which required seventeen stitches.

The Spaniard, now standing charged with causing the chef grievous bodily harm, admitted the assault but pleaded constant provocation. The chef, a much bigger man than he, had kept pushing him around, calling him stupid when he touched a sideboard with a trolley and even threatening to kill him before the day was out. Finally he had made him lose his temper by trying to trip him as he left the kitchen with the spaghetti, nearly causing his face to touch the hotplate. That was when he had clouted him with the pasta, plate and all.

Magistrates really do need the wisdom of Solomon at times. However, the waiter had pleaded guilty, so Mr Wilson conditionally discharged him – which meant that he could go but if he misbehaved again he would also have to settle this account. "There must be no more violence, whatever the provocation," Mr Wilson insisted.

Provocation is a difficult thing to avoid in a restaurant kitchen, as

Arnold Wesker illustrated in his play *The Kitchen*, written after personal experience of working in a large restaurant with a mixture of the more volatile races. Incidentally, Mr Wesker also had an appointment with the 'beak' at Marlborough Street at about that time, on a trivial parking-meter offence. He pleaded 'guilty' by post and was fined 30 shillings. He could not appear personally since he was in New York for the opening of his hit play *Chips with Everything*.

15

Press and Public

The public were not officially allowed into Marlborough Street Court (nor any other public office or police court) during the first fifty years of its operation. Consequently, often the only non-involved, unbiased persons present were the Press reporters, so, not unnaturally, they soon began to regard themselves as the watchdogs of justice.

But even they had to fight to safeguard their right of entry. From the beginning editors were aware of public interest in London's new police courts and began regular reports of the more interesting cases from each. Several attempts were made to curtail this by way of libel-suits brought by magistrates and defendants, and by pronouncements, on the advisability of such reporting, from judges.

In 1819 Birmingham magistrates decided to ban reporters from their courts, on the grounds that their activities were unfair to the defendants. In London, John Black, from 1817-43 editor of the *Morning Chronicle* (for which Dickens became a reporter) is credited with leading the fight for freedom of the Press to report police-court cases (reports from assizes and Quarter Sessions had long been a feature of most newspapers), but others participated, not least that extraordinary Tory-turned-militant-reformer William Cobbett.

Born a peasant in 1742 and self-educated, he was at times a soldier, farmer, newspaper proprietor, indefatigable pamphleteer and tractist and the introducer of the forerunner to Hansard. By 1820 he had been sued for libel several times (once for ridiculing a doctor who bled and purged his patients during a yellow fever epidemic in America, where Cobbett was living) and served two years in prison for an article criticizing military flogging. A pugnacious, inconsistent man with some dubious ideas, he did care about social justice and the poor and reduced the price of his newspaper, *Cobbett's Weekly Political Register* (much respected for its accuracy and intelligence), so they could buy it.

In January 1820 he launched *Cobbett's Evening Post*. It was to last only until March, but the issue of 16th February had a little go at Marlborough Street:

MARLBOROUGH STREET – SERIOUS CHARGE AGAINST A LADY IN HIGH LIFE.

Yesterday a case which, we understand was of great interest to the public, came on at this office, and we regret much that, in consequence of our exclusion, we are not able to lay the full particulars before them. The case was heard in a room, at the above office, entitled, 'The Justices' Private Room'. It was hinted to us that the daughter of a Peer was charged with a robbery; the parties inquired whether any strangers were in the room, and the Reporters were ordered to leave, which was acceded with great reluctance on their parts. The writer of this article spoke to the Magistrate, and was informed that it was a *family concern*: and on intimating that he always understood that a Police Office was a public Court of Justice (and his professional avocation called him there), he was answered "That he was very much mistaken". With due deference to the superior judgement of the Worthy Magistrate, he then quitted the office and in vain endeavoured to gain further particulars than that a lady of consequence, moving in fashionable circles, was charged as before mentioned. The office was crowded by fashionably-dressed persons, whose mourning* gave the office a sombre appearance. The lady charged was intimately acquainted with a gallant Captain in the Navy, whose losses, in consequence of a shipwreck on a last voyage, amounted to £80,000, and on his return to England, the fear of becoming insolvent induced him to place his trunk in the lady's possession, when, on receiving it back, he ascertained that it had been robbed to a great amount. From the exertions of the officer several hundred pawnbrokers' duplicates were traced to the prisoner. A numerous train of pawnbrokers attended, and we understand that the lady, on condition of arranging matters privately, was liberated.

Newspapers really developed in the nineteenth century, the variety of publications multiplying rapidly and the Sunday newspapers coming into being. Police court reports were meat to all of these and became increasingly sensational. Told in narrative form, to which as much colour as possible was added, since the reporters were paid by the line (the famous 'penny a line'), many of the descriptions were what would now be considered libellous. As you will have noticed among some already-quoted excerpts, defendants might be described as 'foreign swindlers', 'low ruffians' or 'gentlemen of fortune', their

---

* George III had died on 29th January, and the funeral was on the day of publication.

manner 'plausible' and their appearance 'wild' and 'excited'. Prosecutions were referred to as of 'disgusting cases' or were said to relate to 'a desperate attempt at murder', even before conviction. And, while 'foreign' was meant as a term of deprecation, 'Jewish' was much more so, and reports concerning defendants who were of this religion were sometimes accompanied by sketches of ugly, long-haired, hook-nosed cringing and oily-looking Fagins about to leap on some poor, unsuspecting Englishman.

Magistrates' decisions were sometimes criticized for their harshness by the radical Press and their leniency by the establishment, some of whose deliberately vague and biased reporting makes chilling reading. For example, the following appeared in *The Illustrated London News* of 27 August 1842: "MR CHURCHILL'S CASE – A base conspiracy to extort money from a gentleman named Churchill, was fully exposed on Monday at Marlborough Street through the zeal and activity of the police. A charge of a very gross nature was made against Mr Churchill by two ruffians in Hyde Park, who are now in the course of being punished for their infamous conduct." There was not, as you will notice, a fact in sight, though, granted, only the gentleman had his name mentioned.

After *Pickwick Papers* was published (1836-7), there was a tendency to report all Cockney and Jewish speech phonetically (as in 'A Regular Game-Chicken'), but somehow this often resulted in making both manners of speech sound the same: lisping Welleranian. In 1835 Dickens had become a reporter for the *Morning Chronicle*, and he occasionally did police-court reporting. The following two reports are rather different from the norm and were published in that year, so there is always the possibility ...

MARLBOROUGH STREET – A LEGAL LUMINARY – John Brown, a chimney-sweep, better known amongst his fraternity as the 'Chummy's Chancellor', was yesterday brought before Mr Chambers, charged by the police with having grievously infringed a certain statute [the New Street Act] by bawling aloud in the public streets the words, "Sweep, soot ho!"

The capture of the culprit having occurred under circumstances of vast importance to chimney-sweeps in general, the defendant having in full meeting intimated that he had discovered that the Hact was a vile himposition, and that he was ready to volunteer and put his discovery to the proof; he was escorted to this office by several professors of the sable science, all anxious to learn the result of the experiment. As a preliminary step the defendant had in the early part of the morning placed himself within sight and hearing of a policeman in Berwick Street, uplifting his voice and singing out, "Soot ho!" with all his might. He was desired to desist, but he set the policeman at defiance, consequently it was found necessary to take him to the station-house. The inspector, unwilling to detain him, said he had no wish to press the charge, if he would promise not to offend again; but the sooty here resolutely declared he was determined to "try the question", and in order to give him the opportunity he was brought to the office.

The charge having been stated, Mr CHAMBERS asked the defendant how he came to conduct himself in the manner he had done?

Brown: Vy, your Lordship, cause I knows the Hact.

Mr CHAMBERS: Then you must know that you are subject to a penalty every time you call out?

Brown (winking to his comrades): Walker! The Hact, vich I always carries in my pocket, perwides that no policeman can't take no chimbley sveep vithout a varrant or summons, or summut of that ere sort. If so that he has done sich transgression, vy it's a reglar breach of priwilege, and a unlegal violation of that constitution which every Englishman is born with. Vere's the policeman's varrant, I axes you?

Mr CHAMBERS: Why, you appear to be quite a lawyer.

Brown: I should think so. I knows that ere Hact from top to bottom. There aint no clause whatever in it vich allows policemen to take sich a summary course as vot he has done. He's got first to find out his address, that's the reglar vay, and then proceed with a varrant or a summons. Now, I'm blowed if he nor anybody else knows ver I lives.

Mr CHAMBERS: I can tell you if you are brought here again I will soon settle the question. You must not cry "Sweep" in the streets.

Brown: Praps I vont and praps I vill; howsomhever, I knows the Hact.

Mr CHAMBERS ordered him to be discharged: and the 'fraternity', who looked upon this as a kind of triumph, evinced their gratitude by adjourning to a neighbouring public house and treating their Chancellor with a double pot of heavy.

The second report, published a month later, on 22nd September 1835, is much more ambitious in that the speech reported in it is Scottish:

MARLBOROUGH STREET − A VISITOR FROM MODERN ATHENS − Davie Morrison, a 'wee man' in a pair of Highland 'breeks', and without a shirt, was brought before Mr CHAMBERS yesterday, charged by the police with having been found in Leicester Square, at 'ae wee short hour ayont the twal', lying on his back snoring from the effects of prolonged potations of 'barley-bree'.

Mr CHAMBERS: How came you to get drunk, Mr Morrison?

Davie: I dinna think I was just preceesely what ye wad ca' drunk: but there's na' doot I was a wee bit waur o'liquor.

Mr CHAMBERS: Was it whiskey you got drunk on?

Davie: Whesky; no, na – it's no vary often a puir boddy lik mysel get ony thing stronger than pumo-water, or may be sma' beer.

Mr Chambers did not think it was likely that small beer had made Davie so drunk, and Davie did admit to him that two 'Glasgy' lads he had met had given him a drink of ale with a taste of rum in it. He was down south, he informed Mr Chambers, because his doctor had told him a change of air would do him good since he was "no very weel" but he was going back to "Auld reekie" as soon as he got oot of his trouble. What, Mr Chambers asked, had he done with his shirt? It was safe in his parcel here, Davie assured him. Then why did he not wear it? the puzzled magistrate wanted to know. "Davie: 'Wear it! Eh, mon! Do you no ken that's just the vary way to dirt the linen and to gar it wear oot!' "

One gets the feeling that Davie was having Mr Chambers on. The magistrate discharged him on this occasion but warned him that if, on his next visit south, he was brought before him, he would not be so lenient. With this, the *Morning Chronicle* reporter noted, "The 'Modern Athenian' shouldered his bundle and walked away, apparently well pleased at the issue of the interview."

In 1847 *The Illustrated London News* described the inner workings of Marlborough Street Court, inner workings that the public (at least the unfashionable public) could not always see. However, with the passing of the Jervis Act the following year, the public acquired the right, in theory at least, to witness police-court proceedings. It was an innovation which has been likened in importance to recognition of the rights of the common man, as significant as the signing of Magna Carta. Nonetheless, there were still occasional private sessions, particularly in the provinces, since magistrates had been put under no obligation to announce their every special sitting.

However, the removal of the stamp tax in 1855 heralded an even greater growth in the number of newspapers, and, since reporters needed the news, they made an effort to be well-informed about sittings or acquired contacts who would keep them informed.

Possibly because of the coverage magistrates' courts received in the Press, attendance in the public galleries grew and became an excuse for an outing. What with the sightseers and what *The Graphic* of 20th August 1887 termed the typical "broken-hearted mother" and "sobbing sisters", praying for a light sentence on their erring young relative, the galleries were often packed. Their decline in popularity began during the First World War, and today there are few objective onlookers − perhaps two or three at a time, and most people are woefully ignorant about the scope and workings of magistrates' courts.

Incidentally, the 1887 series on Marlborough Street, Bow Street and Thames Courts in *The Graphic* concluded with a last few remarks about Marlborough Street, although they had already expended half their coverage on that court. Marlborough Street collected most money, they commented, because most people who appeared there opted for a fine rather than a prison sentence, but this was only a small help in the cost of maintaining the Metropolitan Police, who were not so bad really.

The reason for this sudden defence of the Peeler was that the paper had printed its first, rather glowing report on Marlborough Street when the Case of Miss Cass broke and shed a much more critical and searching light on that court. Obviously their faces were a little red as they had given little hint of the possibility of deviance from truth on the part of the police though had admitted there were some "erring mortals" in their midst in relation to bribery. Since the first article had been printed, *The Graphic* commented, the police force had been under attack, "and has been exposed here and there to as much obloquy as though the whole force of nearly fourteen thousand men were an army of black sheep, of which the public should be wary and distrustful". They admitted that the police were exposed to much temptation, particularly since they were not very well paid, but, "by and large, Robert is an honest, civil, patient, faithful servant of the public". Indeed, the writer of the articles declared, he had thirty years' experience of meeting the police, on and off guard, in all sorts of circumstances and during "much slumming before slumming became safe and fashionable" and had found that the public could trust their police and "it may be kind to say so at this little crisis".

Two years later, in 1889, came 'The Cleveland Street Affair', which *should* have been treated to the full glare of publicity but was not, due to the influence of those involved. However, one editor did try to break this silence − a gesture which cost him dear.

On the day that a warrant for the arrest of Lord Arthur Somerset was at last applied for at Marlborough Street, Ernest Parke, the twenty-nine-year-old radical editor of the *North London Press*, published the following story:

THE WEST END SCANDALS – NAMES OF SOME OF THE DISTINGUISHED CRIMINALS WHO HAVE ESCAPED.

In an issue of 28th September we stated that among the number of aristocrats who were mixed up in an indescribably loathsome scandal in Cleveland Street, Tottenham Court Road, were the heir to a duke and the younger son of a duke. The men to whom we thus referred were the Earl of Euston, eldest son of the Duke of Grafton, and Lord H. Arthur G. Somerset, a younger son of the Duke of Beaufort. The former, we believe, has departed for Peru. The latter, having resigned his commission and his office of Assistant Equerry to the Prince of Wales, has gone too.

These men have been allowed to leave the country and thus defeat the ends of justice, because their prosecution would disclose the fact that a far more distinguished and more highly-placed personage than themselves was inculpated in these disgusting crimes. The criminals in this case are to be numbered by the score. They include two or three members of Parliament, one of them a popular Liberal.

Unfortunately, although Ernest Parke was right to attack the cover-up, he had not checked his facts properly first. Not only had the Earl of Euston not gone to Peru, he had not even left the country, and Parke was unable to prove that he had been involved with the young post-office boys. True, he did admit to having once gone to the Cleveland Street premises (he could not deny it, since he had been seen), but he gave a different interpretation of the visit. He had gone there to watch *poses plastiques* (still nudes).

Ernest Parke was found guilty of libel and given twelve months in prison.

Five years later Oscar Wilde was prosecuted, and there was no cover-up. In fact, the nadir of court reporting was reached, the newspapers crucifying him before even the judge got to work.

Newsworthy magistrates' courts which sat daily began to acquire regular, permanent reporters. Eventually independent agencies evolved around certain courts, regularly supplying newspapers and large Press-agencies with details of anything of note happening in their particular area. This suits the papers very well, since it is now necessary to send a reporter to a court only when a special case arises, when in-depth, exclusive material is wanted.

Subsequent to this development, it began to be the case in some courts that the reporter had been around longer than anyone else, police, magistrates or civil staff. For example, Herbert Anders was introduced by his father to the trade at Marylebone Court in 1893. He remained there for sixty-three years, also taking over the Marlborough Street agency in 1921. In 1926 he was joined by Len Almand, who in turn stayed (reporting for both courts) for fifty years, excluding a short break for World War Two. After that war, Len took over the agency from Herbert Anders and ran it, from Marlborough Street, until 1976. Both these men became liked and respected and very much part of their court 'families', and I am extremely indebted to Len for loaning me his precious Press-cuttings for this book.

Of course, the agency-owners needed assistance, and a stream of young men and women have had their first taste of journalism with Herbert and Len. In 1976 Len handed over to just one such a young man, Tony Asiak, who has run it successfully since.

In 1925 it became an offence to sketch or take photographs in court, and in 1967 the reporting of committal proceedings in magistrates' courts became restricted. It is now illegal to report more than the briefest facts of cases going on to higher courts – facts such as the names, addresses, ages and occupations of those concerned, plus the charges and the court's decision.

The Law of Libel Amendment in 1888 had declared that reporting of court cases was privileged and not generally open to libel proceedings. However, the doubt about the fairness of such reporting had grown. It did not seem fair that potential jury-members should read all the evidence before they began to sit in judgment. Nonetheless the new ban in 1957 was greeted with 'grave misgivings' from the Metropolitan Court Reporters Association, and Len, whose views were solicited by one newspaper, while admitting he had an axe to grind, pointed out: "By and large, a reporter plays a very large part in a court in that he does represent the outside world. The magistrate, even in these lower courts, is very much his own boss, and the fact that there is somebody on the sidelines who represents outside opinion, however poor an instrument he may be, is salutary. In the past, I have been the means of exposing, in my small way, a number of inaccuracies."

The legislation went through nonetheless. Herbert Anders had once likened the reporter of committal proceedings in magistrates' courts to a theatre-critic who sees and reports only on the first act. Now they were not even allowed to do that.

Since the Second World War there had been several attempts to get cases either held *in camera* or with reporting of them restricted. The Dowdall case was one such, in which Clyde Wilson, cited the demise of the Hungarian Premier Nagy as an example of what could happen if justice *in camera* became a habit.

There was also much Press attention given to a defendant's (also Hungarian, as it happens) objections to the withholding of the name of his accuser, from whom he was said to have stolen after being invited to his home. The name was being withheld, the Hungarian claimed, merely because the man was a barrister. However, it had by then become common practice to withhold the names of the victims of sexual assaults, especially children, and this may have seemed a similar case to the police, who themselves had suggested that the name should not be given. In the event, Mr J. Aubrey Fletcher, the magistrate, went along with them, but when subsequently witnesses in another case asked to write down their names and addresses, Leo Gradwell called a halt.

"This seems to be happening in every case nowadays," he said. "I expect soon to have a police-officer turn up in a drunk case and ask for his name and number to be withheld."

Later, when counsel in a drugs case concerning some very well-known people asked for it to be held *in camera*, adding that in four weeks' time the new restrictions on committal proceedings reporting would be coming into force, Mr Robey refused. Of course some cases must be so held – those concerning national security, for example, or when juveniles or seriously ill persons are giving evidence.

The arguments for both sides are good. There is no doubt that the public figure suffers more publicity than does the undistinguished, though, if they are very rich, this may be the only effective punishment, since a fine will not move them. Those in positions of expected propriety, such as MPs, doctors, lawyers and clergymen, are picked out too. Broadcasting House and, more to the point, the BBC Club are near Marlborough Street, and with the growth of broadcasting 'the BBC man' was added to that list. "BBC MAN ON DRINKS CHARGE" and "BBC MAN STOLE" were typical headlines. The 'men' could be anything from announcers to storemen in 'Aunty's' employ and could sometimes feature also as the goodies: "CHASE BY A BBC MAN", said a headline about the capture of a handbag-thief.

Aristocrats were always good news, especially in those deb-ridden, glamourless post-war days: "DEBUTANTE LAVINIA FINDS ADVENTURE AT THE FRONT DOOR", "THE DUCHESS LOST HER TEMPER", "HEIRESS DRAGGED FROM HOTEL BY UPPER BRACKET TEDDIES" and "WHY I STOLE, by the wife of a baronet," were typical proclamations.

But apart from the famous, vicars and nuns are, perhaps, the chief attention-catchers, so much so that anticipatory groans emit from police-officers on discovering that they have unknowingly arrested one of these limelight-drawing creatures. Sometimes they already know and have been forced into action nonetheless, and their colleagues, sensing trouble, steer clear. "I've never seen West End Central charge-room clear so fast," a PC told me, "as when the word went round that Pete had arrested a nun." No one wanted to get involved, especially the senior officer taking the charge. Pete was a mild, good-humoured fellow who had been forced into it. He still remembers it wide-eyed, (as Bob does his bus) mainly for the incredible lies he claims the sacred lady uttered in the box. These days they are not quite such an unusual sight at Marlborough Street, since every now and then an Italian or Spanish nun is brought in for shoplifting.

If you are brought to court, how best can you curtail personal publicity? First, plead 'guilty' (presuming you are, that is), which will prevent too many colour-adding 'details' leaking out. Next, make sure you have a fairly commonplace job for a firm which is not currently in the news. On arrest, while being charged or in court, say nothing interesting or provoking, apart from murmuring you are sorry – and that not too pathetically, and you will have to forgo the opportunity to bring up your dear old dying grandmother or this disease you are suffering from which caused you to do the deed. You may receive sympathetic publicity as a result, but it will still be publicity. However, if you are feeling a little impecunious, sympathetic publicity could be to your advantage.

In his book *This Old Wig*, J.B. Sandbach tells of an old mandolinist who had been written up in the touching-little-tale style which became popular in the 1930s. The street musician's mongrel dog, which held out his hat for him, had been in direct confrontation with a superior hound belonging to a lady. As a result the old man had sustained an injury from the lady's umbrella and had, in turn, assaulted her with his tongue, bringing into play words new to her. He was arrested for using abusive language likely to cause a breach of the peace, but Sandbach, it would appear rightly, dismissed the charge. The tale, most skilfully told, appeared in a newspaper, and money came pouring in, most of it anonymously. There was only one problem: the magistrate and the probation-officer, Charlie Morgan, found themselves elected as trustees of the money and had to be sure the musician received it. On the other hand, they knew the old mandolinist well, very well, and also what he would do with the money if he received it all at once. The resultant 'binge' might cause not only the cessation of his career but also that of his life. So they compromised. Every week Mr Morgan would seek out the old man on his patch and hand him some of his fortune, together with a little futile advice on how to spend it. But Charlie Morgan was a realist, so he would not expect much.

Mind you, even if you take all this advice on how to keep out of the papers, and as well as having behaved in a commonplace manner you have done something commonplace, it still might not work; you can never be sure what will take off. "I always tell new reporters not to dismiss a story too easily," said Len to Bob recently. "Sometimes the most humdrum occurrence can develop surprisingly. I well remember the time where a man jumped on a bus at the traffic-lights ..." "Don't go on," groaned Bob. "I was the arresting officer in that case."

It was, indeed, a very humdrum 'job'. A Nigerian gentleman had boarded a bus at the traffic-lights at the junction of Tottenham Court Road and Oxford Street. The conductor, knowing this to be an unsafe practice, to be discouraged, apart from being against regulations and unfair to the bus-queue waiting just around the corner, asked him to get off again. He refused. The bus-conductor refused to start the bus, and 'police', in the guise of Bob and his very young companion Terry, were called. However, even then the gentleman would not be persuaded. Impasse. Bob and Terry, having been taught at training-school that a bus-conductor is like the captain of a ship – in full charge, backed up the conductor. When reasoning failed, they eventually ejected the man, and when he refused to disappear quietly, they arrested him.

At Marlborough Street Paul Bennett obviously knew nothing about bus-conductors being like ships captains. They had no right, he said, to tell the man to get off; he could board at the lights if he wished. He dismissed the case and awarded £10 costs against the police. It was this decision (plus clever reporting, doubtless) which changed the case from the usual to the headliner. It hit the papers in a truly extraordinary fashion. "I still can't believe it," says Bob. "It seemed so ridiculous."

One London evening paper and a national daily gave it a front-page headline and all the others a great deal of space. Was the magistrate right or wrong? was the question now raging. Statements were issued by London Transport spokesmen, TUC legal experts and high-ups in the Ministry of Transport. Reporters sought the views of passengers, bus-conductors and drivers and even made test leaps onto running-boards at traffic-lights. Several leader-columns were given over to what the *Evening Standard* termed "the Bus-stop Battle". The decision is madness, said some; what about the rights of those waiting at the bus-stop; we must block this loophole in the law. Others said, great, glad we have *some* rights left, and began recalling officious bus-conductors they had known. Another leader began by suggesting that we leave off talking about NATO, SEATO and UNO for a minute and talk about freedom at home, as in the man on the bus case. The *Evening Standard* summed up the whole unreal affair thus: "Two days of controversy have not stilled the passions roused by Mr —. How could he have known, as he swung onto the bus standing at Tottenham Court Road traffic-lights, that this was the opening shot in an alarum that would take all London by the throat, split the capital into warring factions, make law, set light to feelings, provoke communiqués and drive all lesser intelligence from pride of place on the front page?" How indeed?

"What made it seem more unreal," says Bob, "was that nobody at the nick said anything to us about it. It was never mentioned. No reports called for, nothing." This was probably due to the fact that Paul Bennett had not criticized police action but blamed the bus-conductor and wished he could award costs against London Transport rather than the police. Bob did learn, however, that, no matter how innocuous a story may seem, if it comes up in a news-making court, before a good reporter, in the midst of the news-hungry silly season at mid-summer ... "I never realized that was your case," said Len, who later got to know Bob very well. "You know, I always use it as an example to trainee reporters."

These days the public gallery has a small, fairly regular flow of spectators, who mainly fall into three types: family and friends of the accused, the objectively interested (either regulars or occasional callers) and the educational group. The only ones that need any real watching (apart from the occasional 'nut' who might surface) are family and friends. The groups of students; law, sociology, nurses and, sometimes, foreigners learning English, often stay on afterwards and ask questions of the clerk of the court and the police staff. The questions are usually boringly predictable, particularly those from the propaganda-fed sociology students with their suggestion of "Why do they beat people up?" and "What makes them all such Fascist swine?"

Interruptions from family and friends during the proceedings can be amusing or even touching.

"Guilty! Mama! Guilty!" yelled one son whose shop-lifting mother hesitated when asked what she would plead.

"Her husband is in Leeds at present," said a barrister in another case.

"Oh no, I'm not, I'm here!" came an exclamation from the gallery.

"Of course," chipped in Rowland Thomas, "every man in Leeds comes down to Lords on a day like this if he possibly can."

Some domestic dramas are acted out via the public gallery.

"Oh no!" sobbed a girl when her fiancé got three months' imprisonment, which would take him well past their intended wedding date on Christmas Eve. And an Arab woman shoplifter was divorced by her husband as she stood in the dock. He stood in the gallery shouting, "I divorce thee. I divorce thee. I divorce thee," in that charming Muslim manner — though, the interpreter told us, he did agree to pay her fine before leaving her stranded. You cannot beat Middle-Eastern men for charm.

But it is the friends and sympathizers of the political demonstrators who are likely to cause the most disturbance, as this gives them an additional chance of publicity. When forty-two Greeks were brought into the dock in the mid-sixties (four at a time), their friends in the gallery immediately unfurled banners protesting at Fascism in Greece and Vietnam and began shouting slogans. Another time a bearded youth shouted at the magistrate, "You Fascist swine, Fletcher!" and "Long live Chairman Mao! Down with British Imperialism!" before vaulting over the barrier and lying down in the front of the dock.

It is not all one-sided though. Occasionally the magistrate peers at the spectators and takes exception to what he sees. Neil McElligott once did and sudden proclaimed loudly, and indignantly:

"There is a youth in the gallery *drinking from a tin*! This is not a picnic-place. Put him out."

16

The Case of the Missing Hands

At eight-thirty one November morning in 1917, Thomas George Henry, a resident of Regent Square, Bloomsbury, was setting off for his work as a packer when he spotted a bulky sackcloth parcel on the grass just inside the railings. Putting his hand through, he felt around the parcel and came to the conclusion that it contained half a sheep.

The railings were only 4 feet 6 inches high, so he climbed over, cut the parcel's string and removed the sacking. The 'sheep' had a second layer of wrapping, this time of sheeting, under which he found a woman's torso, clothed in chemise, vest and combinations. When he had recovered from the initial shock, Mr Henry blew the whistle which he happened to have about his person. This attracted the attention of many of the other residents of the square, and soon police were on the scene. However, Thomas George Henry was a glutton for punishment, and while he was awaiting the arrival of police, he examined another, smaller parcel about a yard away. This contained the legs. Fortunately none of the remains were bloody. They were surprisingly dry, in fact.

Further inspection by the experts revealed that the remains were of a thirty-year-old woman, about 5 feet tall, who had given birth and was healthy, well-nourished and of clean personal habits. That she was also of fairly comfortable circumstances "was indicated by the superior quality of her underclothing", *The Times* reported. On a piece of brown paper underneath her superior vest lay a note, on which was written, in angular writing of "distinctly foreign appearance", "BLODIE BELGIM". The dismemberment looked like a tidy and quite professional job, as the well-informed *Times* pointed out:

A doctor could not have done it with greater skill; a butcher might have done it with as much. Its purpose was twofold. The body was not disfigured out of sheer fiendishness, as in the case of the 'Ripper' murders, but was dismembered partly to make more easy the carrying and disposal of the burden and partly to conceal its identity. But, while this explains the absence of the head, it does not account for the removal of the hands at the wrist. The suggestions that this was intended to prevent identification by rings which could not be forced from the fingers is not convincing, for the severing of the fingers from the hands would have been simpler than the severing of the wrists. The reason for cutting off the hands, therefore, remains one of the minor mysteries of a baffling case.

Many Belgian refugees lived around Regent Square. This fact, coupled with the note, was felt to be significant. As the paper concluded blithely: "There is a strong belief locally that the crime may have been committed by a German, his victim being a Belgian woman, and his motive hatred of the people who stood in his country's way."

Dr Bernard Spilsbury, who had first come to notice in the Crippen dismemberment case seven years earlier, was called in to carry out the post-mortem, in company with Dr Gabe, who had first examined the unfortunate woman. They established the fact that "the death was caused by an injury to the head, which drained the blood from the body." "Probably the head was battered to pieces," *The Times* reported cheerfully, and went on, "or the throat was cut. Dismemberment of the body probably occurred after death," which seems a blessing.

More was revealed about the wrappings around the trunk and legs: some were pieces of white fabric as used by butchers to wrap meat, some were Joseph Rank flour-sacks, and there was a cotton sheet with a red mark, '11 11', thereon. A "laundry-keeper" soon recognized this mark as belonging to a Frenchwoman, Mme Gerard, of Munster Square, which is about a mile from Regent Square where the body had been found.

Since Mme Gerard was of the same height and build as the victim, had given birth to two children (both of whom had died) and had fair hair which Spilsbury had "concluded" from the trunk that the missing head would show, *The Times* now speculated that one vital part of the mystery was on its way to solution. Mme Gerard's husband was at the Front. Her neighbour, Mrs Adelaide Chester, was quick to describe the lady to the Press;

She could speak English slightly, but the French accent could always be detected, and she had the French way of gesticulation ... I do not think she was particularly happy. Sometimes she seemed to me as if she had been crying for hours. She had a most depressed, unhappy expression … Once or twice I have seen her in the company of a middle-aged man, who, she said, was a relative of hers. Once, when they passed me at the corner of Munster Square, they were quarrelling violently, speaking in French. I spoke to her, but she took no notice. I could hear her shrill voice a long way down the street, and she was gesticulating wildly.

Another neighbour, Mrs Barker, thought the French lady charming and pooh-poohed the suggestion that she was not dead but had left London to avoid the air-raids: "During a recent air-raid she was one of the calmest people in the Square, and she has never been known to leave the house to take cover. She said to me, 'Don't be scared. Your husband is going through much worse at the front than we are.' "

Mr Morgan, the local dairyman, had not found her the least bit depressed, quite the reverse – pretty and cheerful. She was often away and, when she came back, always said she had been visiting her husband in France. He also gave the Press their first hint as to why her hands might have been removed: "On several occasions she showed her hands to various people, including my wife. The hands were heavily scarred, apparently from burns, and the marks were so prominent as to amount to a disfigurement."

By Saturday afternoon a man was helping police with their enquiries, and by Monday morning a woman had joined him.

The following Thursday they stood side by side in the dock at Marlborough Street on a charge of murder. Thirty-eight-year-old Berthe Roche had on a black hat and a long grey cloak, and Louis Marie Joseph Voisin, a powerfully-built stableman, was wearing a long, light-coloured butcher's smock. Both were of French nationality and lived at 101 Charlotte Street – a street which has since been taken over by the London Greeks. Regent Square, Munster Square and Charlotte Street formed a rough triangle, each being about one mile from the others.

Chief Inspector Wensley, one of the greatest detectives of the late-Victorian age and early-twentieth century, who had been involved in the siege of Sidney Street seven years earlier, was in charge of the case. He told the magistrate, Mr Denman, how, in consequence of what the police had seen in Mme Gerard's room (a picture of Voisin and an IOU of his for £50), they had gone to Charlotte Street, where, somewhat later, they had found the head and hands hidden in a barrel of sawdust in the cellar. The head was badly lacerated, though an earring was still attached, and the be-ringed hands were scarred. Head and hands fitted the trunk perfectly.

On the same day as the first hearing at Marlborough Street, Paul Gerard, the murdered woman's husband, arrived in London and formally identified his wife's body. He was, the Press assured the public, "much affected" and "led weeping from the mortuary".

The next hearing was not until three weeks later, and then Voisin was dressed in a black Melton overcoat and "seemed cool and collected" though Mme Roche was "showing signs of sleeplessness, her eyes being very swollen and her face very pale".

Mr Henry retold the saga of finding the trunk in Regent Square. Police Constable Bendall, a rejoined pensioner, who knew Voisin, told how he had seen him driving a horse and trap from King's Cross (which is near Regent Square) toward Tottenham Court Road (Charlotte Street is beyond Tottenham Court Road) on the morning of 2nd November at 7.40 a.m.

Voisin asked what morning the 2nd was, and, on being told it was the pertinent Friday, he shook his head and said, "I did not use it that morning. I used it on Saturday to go to Surbiton" (he got his meat from Surbiton usually).

The concierge at Charlotte Street said she had seen Berthe Roche washing out a bloody shirt on the Friday morning and had been told by the accused that Voisin had, while killing a calf, hit it in the wrong place, causing blood to spurt about.

The concierge's daughter said that she had knocked on the door of Voisin and Roche the night the air-raid siren went, as she had been requested to do, but she had received no reply, though she had heard "women's voices" earlier.

Mme Gerard, it transpired, had been employed as a housekeeper by Voisin, who, as well as being a stableman, did a bit of free-lance butchering on the side. The police investigating the murder described how they had asked Voisin, through an interpreter, to write the words "Bloody Belgian" and how he had repeated the error found in the note on the body. Further, they had found a letter on Voisin which was addressed to Mme Gerard from her husband and which voiced his suspicions about her relationship with the stableman.

The evidence piled up and up. Police Constable Quantrell said that, almost before he had finished interpreting the charge, the woman Roche had turned to her fellow-prisoner and "apparently in a passion" said: "*Salaud, tu m'as trompé, salaud, salaud* ", to which Voisin had replied, "*C'est malheureux*," which the constable translated as "You nasty man, you have deceived me. You nasty man, you nasty man," and "It is unfortunate."

The daughter of Mme Gerard's landlady explained how Voisin had knocked on their door, on the Friday afternoon, and told them that Mme Gerard had gone to the country for a fortnight; also that she was expecting a sack of potatoes to be delivered and would they take them in? They had agreed.

When first tackled, Voisin had insisted that the missing woman had gone away, but after being charged, he made another statement. He had known Mme Gerard, he said, for about eighteen months and had met her while she was working at a nearby café. Twelve months earlier she had started working for him as his housekeeper but still kept on her own place. He had often visited her at her flat, even meeting her husband there when he was on leave. Roche had moved in a month before, while Madame was in France. Voisin insisted:

Mme Martin [Roche] is not connected with this crime at all. ... The crime was committed at Mme Gerard's place. I went to Mme Gerard's place last Thursday at 11 a.m., and when I arrived, the door was closed but not locked. The floor and carpet were full of blood. The head and hands were wrapped in a flannel jacket which is at my place now. They were on the kitchen table. That is all I could see. The rest of the body was not there. I was so astonished at such an affair that I did not know what to do. I go to Mme Gerard's every day. I thought a trap had been laid for me. I commenced to clean up the blood, and my clothes became smeared. I looked to see if anybody else was in the house, but they had all gone out. I left the head and hands in the thing they were wrapped up in and put the lot in the carpet. By the carpet I mean the small rug by the side of the bed. A pail was full of blood and water, and there were blood-stained finger-marks on the handle of the jug. I then went back into my house and had luncheon and later returned to Mme Gerard's and took the packet to my place. I was still thinking that this was a trap.

He went on to insist that he had no reason to kill the lady. He did know, however, that she was beginning to mix with bad associates and had taken people to her flat.

Dr Spilsbury did not go along with Voisin's tale. There was no doubt, he insisted, that the murder had not been committed at Munster Square but at Charlotte Street. The Munster Square flat simply did not have enough traces of human blood. The body had been remarkably bloodless, indicating that cause of death was probably from loss of blood and shock. Spilsbury estimated Mme Gerard had lost two or three pints before death. There was not that much at Charlotte Street either, but there was more than at Munster Square, and it was not animal blood, as Voisin claimed, but human, and it was most likely that the rest had ebbed away down a drain in the yard. She was killed, he thought, in the doorway of the yard.

Mr Denman found that there was enough evidence to commit the prisoners for trial, which began two weeks later at the Old Bailey. On committal Roche pleaded 'not guilty' and declared she knew nothing whatsoever about the case. Voisin repeated, "Mme Roche is entirely innocent. All that was found was taken from Mme Gerard's house to my house." There proved to be insufficient evidence against Roche, and the judge instructed the jury to find her 'not guilty'. Voisin, who persisted in his story, was found guilty and sentenced to death. However, the day before the sentence was scheduled to be carried out, there was a postponement for two weeks, so that he could be available for Roche's next trial, if necessary.

The couple had already, in fact, had three well publicized 'trials' – a long inquest hearing before the case came again to Marlborough Street, at which a verdict of murder had been brought against them; the Marlborough Street committal hearing, which those days was always in full; then the trial proper. These days the inquest would probably be postponed until afterwards, and the magistrates' court hearing could be completed quickly and mostly with statements.

In fact, it is very unlikely that Voisin killed Gerard. None of the blows (and there were many, the attack having been called 'ferocious') had penetrated the skull, and Voisin was a strong man. The point did come up once or twice. At Marlborough Street prosecuting counsel remarked, "It is a puzzling thing to know who it was who struck this large number of blows with so little strength, and with a weapon so inefficient as not even to fracture the woman's skull." It had been estimated that she probably took at least a half hour to die, through loss of blood, not brain-damage. He posed the question again at the trial and asked, "Was it a sudden meeting between these two women, jealousy, a quarrel and attack by one on the other with some weapon?" Mr L. Morgan May, Voisin's counsel, touched on the question in his closing address, but only just, when he suggested that his client had merely been forced, in a moment of panic, to conceal the crime and possibly to conceal 'someone else' but had not committed it himself.

When the judge summed up, he said that Mr Morgan May had defended Voisin with great ability, but there was a hint of criticism in his pointing out that, if Voisin had been called to give evidence himself, the discrepancies in his statements might have been cleared up and that Roche might also have been called to give evidence in his favour after the acquittal but had not been. Of course counsel may have thought them both better out of the witness-box, as they might only worsen the case – it is a chance you take. However, the crucial point, as far as the judge was concerned, was that made by Spilsbury's firm evidence: the murder was committed at Charlotte Street.

The trial left a lasting impression on one spectator, present on the final day. He was the seventeen-year-old Edward Robey, later a stipendiary magistrate at Marlborough Street. His father had been invited to lunch at the court that day with the Sheriff of the City of London and took him along. Since Edward had never seen a murder trial before, he sat in on the proceedings. He remembers being struck at the time by the medical evidence about the feeble blows to the head which made it improbable that Voisin was the assailant. As he says in his book *The Jester and the Court*,

> At his trial he never sought to put the blame on Roche, and he gave a ridiculous explanation about the presence of the deceased's head and hands at his place, which the jury obviously did not believe. ... When passing sentence, Mr Justice Darling, instead of leaving it to the interpreter to tell the accused what the judge was saying, himself uttered the statutory words in French and repeated them in English.
>
> Voisin gripped the front of the dock and leaned forward, obviously emotionally overcome by what he heard and understood.
>
> And he was not the only one in that Court; I was stunned and horrified ... When I came out of the Old Bailey and got on a bus, I was still dazed. I looked at the men and women in the city streets going about their ordinary affairs and unaware of what I had just witnessed – I thought how lucky they were – free to return to their homes; whereas that man ...!

Spilsbury's evidence proved even more crucial in the trial of Roche as an accessory, where it was even more necessary to prove that the killing had been in Charlotte Street. The expert witness accompanied the jury to premises where a ghoulish charade was played out when

Spilsbury demonstrated in dumb-show (as his biographers report in *Bernard Spilsbury: His Life and Cases*) "how the killing had been done", though I must say I would amend that to "how he thought the killing had been done". Although the doctor agreed that Voisin had not struck the blows, "It was when the victim cried out that he gripped her from behind, smothering her screams with the towel while his frenzied companion ... continued to rain down her savage blows." (There was some evidence of attempted suffocation due to the condition of her heart, but the factual way these statements are made is a little disturbing. No one knows what happened that night and never will.)

Roche was sentenced to seven years' penal servitude, during the serving of which she became insane and died shortly after.

17

"I'm the King of the Gypsies"

The most regular defendants at Marlborough Street Court have always been God and Jesus in, roughly, that order. Of course they make their appearance in contemporary human guise.

Those teetering on the edge of insanity often break the law and are brought before a court. Nowadays the magistrate is informed of doubts about the defendant's mental condition, and the latter may be remanded for a Medical and Mental Report (or, in police parlance, 'Nut and Gut') before any decision as to his culpability is made. Alternatively, just a mental report may be thought necessary. While this is being decided in court, the offender will, like as not, strengthen the evidence about his mental state by making an impromptu speech to the court and/or attacking the personal dignity of the magistrate, whose presence seems so often to inflame. His harangue, personal abuse and maybe threats of violence will, in many cases, be interspersed by general proclamations as to exactly who he is currently purporting to be.

"I am Jesus!" one fairly recent offender kept shouting. "And you!" he exclaimed, pointing the familiar accusatory finger at the 'beak', "are Pontius Pilate, and you want to wash your hands of me!" Possibly, very true. The magistrate in question was, however, one of the waggish variety and could not resist murmuring to his clerk, when they were sorting out what was to be done, that perhaps a crucifixion might be appropriate in this case?

In the days before medicals and mentals, the magistrates sometimes made the arbitrary diagnosis themselves. In 1842 Mr John Webb, a hosier and outfitter "carrying on an extensive business" in the Strand, was arrested after sauntering around auction-rooms in Leicester Street and pocketing whatever took his fancy, from an alabaster bird to a taper-stand. This predilection brought him before Mr Maltby, the learned magistrate at Marlborough Street. After the evidence about the auction-rooms, *The Illustrated London News* reported:

A communication was made to the bench, which caused doubt as to the prisoner's sanity. A person, said to be in the employ of the prisoner, made some statement which, if correct, would afford ground for the belief that the prisoner, at times, laboured under an aberration of intellect. Before the prisoner was sent off in the van, a clerk from Messrs Machin & Debenham's auction-rooms came to the court and said that the prisoner was a frequenter of the room and occasionally exhibited so much eccentricity in bidding that his offers were refused. That very morning he had been at the rooms to inspect the goods, and after he had left, a person from his house had brought back two billiard-balls which he had taken away. Mr Webb came again shortly afterwards, and he was seen to pocket four more balls. He was charged with the act, and the balls were restored. Mr Maltby said he could do nothing under such circumstances but recommend the friends of the prisoner to lay all these particulars before the judge when the prisoner appeared to take his trial.

Upon further examination on Wednesday, it was determined to give Mr Webb into the custody of his friends, a decided case of insanity being made out.

At least he was kindly treated and with some dignity.

However, magistrates were also used as judges as to whether people were insane even though they had committed no offence, and they could sign the committal order on the plea of any doctor without actually seeing the 'patient'. This led to some abuses, and to prevent these the law was amended, after a report by the Lunacy Commissioners in 1844, to the effect that magistrates (or clergymen, who also had the power) must see the person first. This, in turn, produced worse abuses and made a spectacle out of the mad – so much so that in August 1846 *The Times*' own Bow Street Court Reporter wrote to his editor in an effort to expose them. The letter was so humane and interesting that I feel justified in quoting from it at length:

You will imagine, Sir, a crowded court of gaping idlers, the associates chiefly of the thieves and vagabonds who are in custody, and all anxious for some excitement, which, perhaps, they have ceased to hope for in the frequently monotonous proceedings in the course of progress. A tremendous rush – a loud shrill scream, and then a fall and a scramble – a shout of laughter and an oath or two – some violent slamming of doors and stamping of feet; these, and similar noises, emanating from the passages and waiting-rooms outside; and seeming full of promise are heard in court. The mob within grow curious and impatient. There is what may be truly called a 'sensation'. You see them doubting whether it would be safe to step out and anticipate 'the fun' or best retain their places and wait the issue.

But amidst all these people you see a demure old gentleman, a stranger to such haunts, who – being himself as excited as the rest – is wondering how the magistrate, and the clerks, and the ushers, can remain so cool, taking no more notice of the piteous yells which drown their own voices, than of the striking of the clock – perhaps not so much even, for they have an interest in the latter. And then the reporters, too. Why are they not all bustle and agitation? Why doesn't that sedate-looking old gentleman in the corner put down his newspaper and prepare his manifold – his sheets of 'flimsy'. Why, Sir, I, who have sat and watched this 'motley group' and traced in their eyes all the various sensations, could tell him that such things are of almost daily occurrence and have long since ceased to move the officials of the court.

At length the 'night-charges' are over, and the excitement increases; and the overseer, who has been waiting one, two or three hours probably, good-humouredly begs his worship to take his 'lunacy cases'; his own time and the time of the surgeons in attendance being very precious. The court assents – the charge-room door is opened, and in rushes a poor frantic, half-strangled, half-naked woman, yelling and foaming, and almost exhausted by her efforts to elude the rough grasp of the workhouse porters and policemen who are called upon to assist. The overseer says she is the mother of a large family, has been well to do in the world, but generally very quiet. He attributes her violence to the strangeness of the place and all the people staring at her. The poor creature exclaims, "Why am I brought here?" "What have I done?" "Are you going to murder me?" "Release me, you villains!" The spectators laugh – the surgeon bows – the magistrate is satisfied – the order, which the clerk has already filled up, is duly signed; and this friendless, hapless woman is dragged away again back to the workhouse.

Sometimes cases are considered more doubtful, and the inquiry is of much longer duration. I recollect the case of one poor woman who, a few months ago, was brought before a magistrate not now upon the bench, and whose calm and rational appearance in court was such that his worship refused to sign the order. Some such scene as the following occurred:

The Magistrate: Well, what's this woman charged with?

The Overseer: She is a lunatic, Sir, and we want to pass her to –

The Lunatic: It is false, your honour.

The Magistrate: Hold your tongue, woman. You don't understand. They say you are mad. Now you don't look a bit like a mad woman at present; but we shall see. Where is the medical gentleman?

The Surgeon: I have seen her twice, your worship, but she has been calm on those occasions. I understand that she has some very wild notions – and talks of her rank [a laugh] and the property she has been robbed of.

Magistrate: What's the matter with you, woman? What are your notions?

Lunatic: It is false, your honour. They are conspiring against me.

Overseer (nudging the lunatic): Is not Queen Victoria your daughter? [More laughter.]

Lunatic: Lord no, Sir, I should think not. What next!

Overseer: When did you see Prince Albert last? [More laughter]

Lunatic: I never saw Prince Albert.

Overseer [to the bench]: The fact is, your worship, she is putting this all on. They are very often cunning. She knows where she is.

In this case, to the best of my recollection, the patient was eventually proved mad by her running into a strain of abuse of someone who, she declared, had robbed her of several thousand pounds, etc.

On other occasions we have had two or three lunatics, of both sexes, brought into court at the same time by way of expediting business, and they are sometimes pinioned, ... in most cases I have noticed they evince great indignation at being taken before a magistrate in a public police court.

In a few instances I have known the presiding magistrate to refuse his signature to the order, owing to the rational appearance of the patient; and on those occasions have been struck with the air of disappointment and vexation shown by the parish officers, who attribute the 'failure' to the cunning of the person examined, and go out muttering (like policemen who fail to get their prisoners convicted), "Never mind, we shall have 'em up again soon."

But what pains a reflecting man more than all – to say nothing of the feelings of the relatives who may happen to be present – is the degree of levity with which these proceedings are almost unavoidably conducted on the one hand, and regarded by the populace on the other. The overseer once said that a woman was mad because she "talked so much" all day. The magistrate remarked with a smile, which it would have been difficult to suppress, "Dear me, if that is to be the test of a woman's sanity, God bless them." The spectators laughed, of course; but, if any of them thought as well, what must have been their notion of our estimate of humanity? I have seen the Court literally convulsed with mirth at the wild ravings of an idiot, whose appearance should have excited very different feelings in the breast. Is the practice, then, of exposing these unfortunate, afflicted beings a wise, a just, a humane one?

I think I have said enough, perhaps more than enough, to command for this subject some consideration at your hands. Imperfect though this hasty sketch may be, I can assure you that it is not an exaggeration of the

An 1855 broadsheet, as displayed at the Metropolitan Police 150 Exhibition in 1979, referring to the incident which led to the seige of Marlborough Street.

A horse-drawn prison van of 1860.

A horse-drawn prison van picking up prisoners, around the turn of the century.

'The Black Maria', an illustration from *The Graphic*'s three-part series on the three major London police courts in 1887.

'A Detective inspecting new arrivals.' From the Marlborough Street feature in *The Graphic* series 1887.

DISCOVERING THE REMAINS
OF THE MURDERED WOMAN.

MADAME GERARD
THE VICTIM.

M. PAUL GERARD
HUSBAND OF THE MURDERED WOMAN

THE PRISONERS

'Further Incidents in the London
Sack Murder'. Typical grisly
coverage of the Gerard murder in

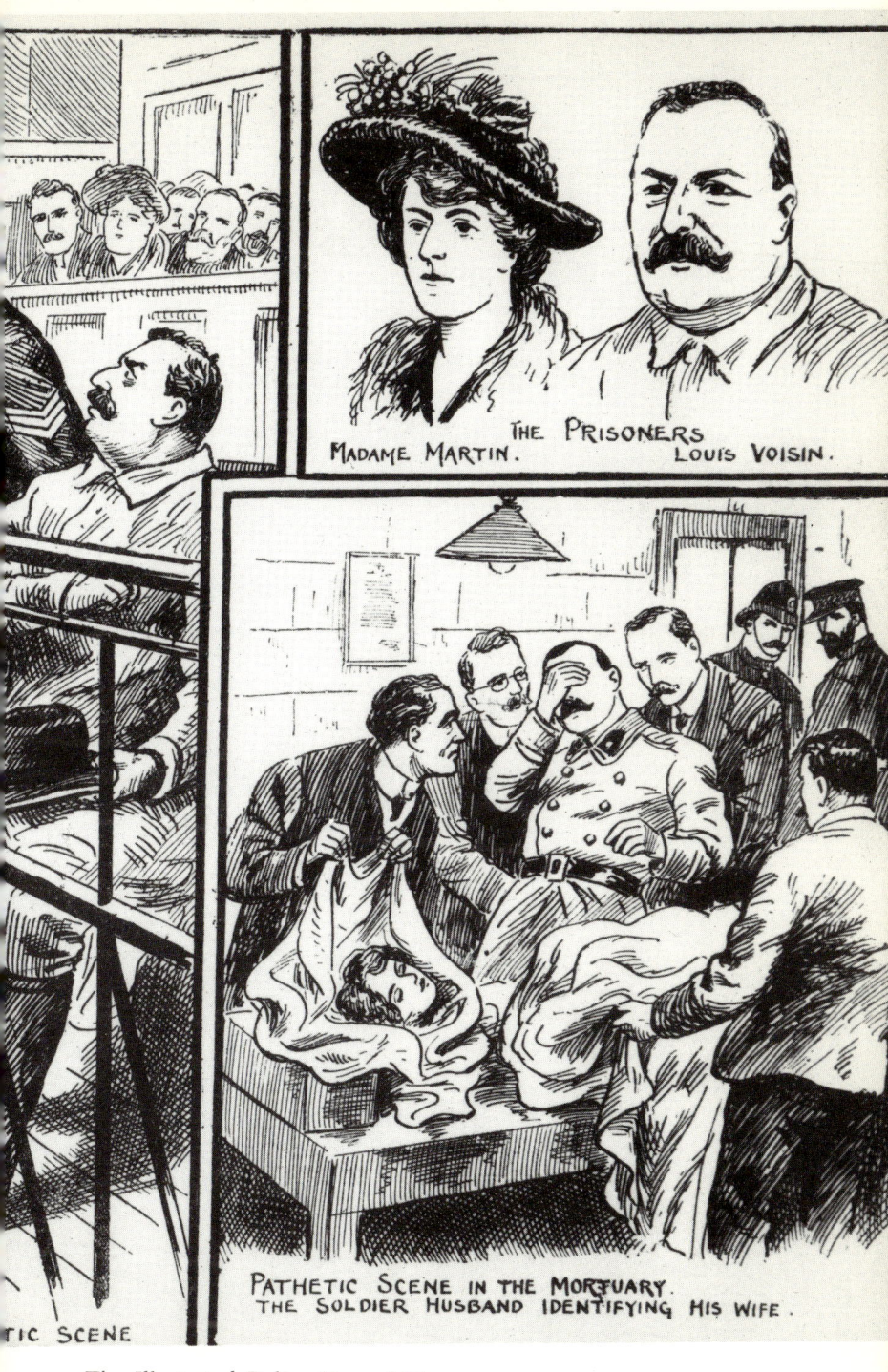

MADAME MARTIN.   THE PRISONERS   LOUIS VOISIN.

PATHETIC SCENE IN THE MORTUARY.
THE SOLDIER HUSBAND IDENTIFYING HIS WIFE.

TIC SCENE

The Illustrated Police News, 15th
November 1917.

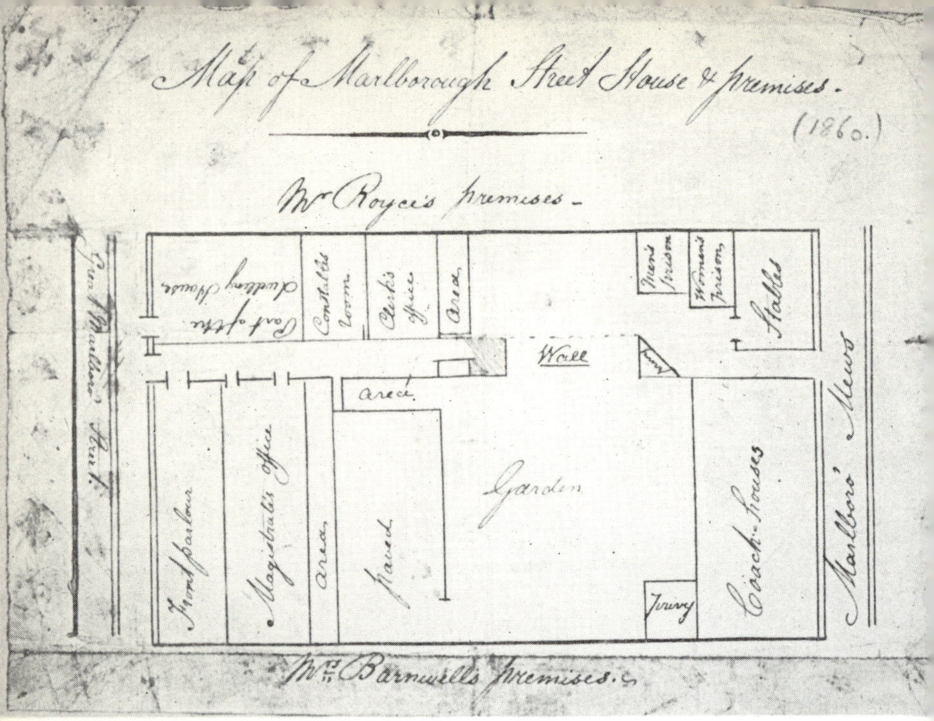

Plan of the interior of the police-station and court in 1860.

More pictures from Marlborough Street feature in *The Graphic* series: 'A consultation with his solicitor' (left) – the solicitor is probably Arthur Newton, and (right) 'Anxiety'.

Also from *The Graphic's* Marlborough Street feature, 1887.

'Night-charges going into the Court.'

Although titled 'Identification' this is also illustrates the line-up of night charges at Marlborough Street. Third from left is a regular, 'Robert the Devil', whilst the men on either side of him are detectives Drew and Elliot, "drawn", the reporter states, "with unerring fidelity".

'The Interpreter'—possibly Augustus de Ballo.

Overleaf: *The Graphic's* series on London's Police-Courts begins, on 16th July 1887, with 'Great' Marlborough Street.

SKETCHES AT THE LONDON POLICE-COURTS.

In Three Parts.—Part I.—Great Marlborough Street

DRAWN BY PAUL RENOUARD.   WRITTEN BY F. W. ROBINSON, AUTHOR OF "GRANDMOTHER'S MONEY," ETC.

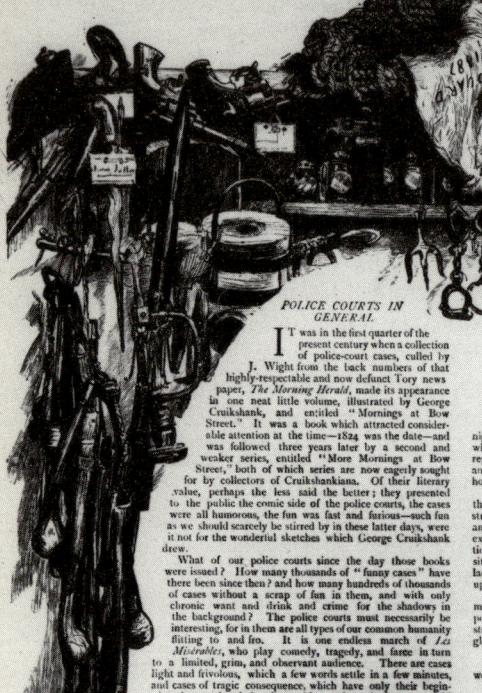

THE CRIMINAL MUSEUM AT SCOTLAND YARD.

POLICE COURTS IN GENERAL

IT was in the first quarter of the present century when a collection of police-court cases, culled by J. Wight from the back numbers of that highly-respectable and now defunct Tory newspaper, *The Morning Herald*, made its appearance in one neat little volume, illustrated by George Cruikshank, and entitled "Mornings at Bow Street." It was a book which attracted considerable attention at the time—1824 was the date—and was followed three years later by a second and weaker series, entitled "More Mornings at Bow Street," both of which series are now eagerly sought for by collectors of Cruikshankiana. Of their literary value, perhaps the less said the better; they presented to the public the comic side of the police courts, the cases were all humorous, the fun was fast and furious—such fun as we should scarcely be stirred by in these latter days, were it not for the wonderful sketches which George Cruikshank drew.

What of our police courts since the day those books were issued? How many thousands of "funny cases" have there been since then? and how many hundreds of thousands of cases without a scrap of fun in them, and with only chronic want and drink and crime for the shadows in the background? The police courts must necessarily be interesting, for in them are all types of our common humanity flitting to and fro. It is one endless march of *Les Misérables*, who play comedy, tragedy, and farce in turn to a limited, grim, and observant audience. There are cases light and frivolous, which a few words settle in a few minutes, and cases of tragic consequence, which have only their beginnings here and end elsewhere with penal servitude, or scaffold and rope.

To magistrates, clerks of the court, gaolers, policemen, and all the numerous subordinates attached to police courts and police-stations, the proceedings, as a rule, must be a trifle tedious; there is a dreadful similarity in crime and its consequences, and a sad lack of anything like originality in the general run of proceedings. This is particularly apparent in the "night-charges," which are heard first at all the courts. The same procession files in, day after day, month after month, year after year. The female "loiterers" in the streets—*toujours les femmes*—with their asseverations of innocence, their protests against their fines, the police favouritism in court, and the levying upon them in the streets of a regular black-mail (a matter that might be inquired into more stringently); the men who have assaulted their wives, and the wives who have assaulted their husbands after a drop too much at the Connubial Arms; the silly swell, who has been noisy at the "Troc," or the "Pav'," or the "Ox," and disputations and pugnacious and very drunk, and the swell's silly friends who have been dragged with him into the conflict and finally into the station-house; the man who has "done nothing, your honour, but call a cab for the genelman," and got "collared" for his officious zeal (there appears to be some misdirected zeal on the other side also in the bagging of this very poor game for the morning's supply); the cabman who has been insolent to his fare, or overcharged him, or been found asleep on his box, sweetly oblivious to all fares; the mother who has been neglectful of her children, the grown-up children who have been cruel to the mother, and torn her hair out, or set her on fire with a paraffin lamp; the pickpocket, the burglar, the area-sneak; the man who has betrayed his employer's trust, and stolen his money or forged his name; the little whimpering, red-nosed boy, who has been letting off fireworks in the street, and "didn't know it was wrong, sir," till an indefatigable member of the force had run him in for endangering the lives and disturbing the peace of Her Majesty's subjects. How tired the presiding magistrate must be of these cases; he knows exactly what is coming, what the policeman will say, what excuse the prisoner will make, and what fine he shall presently impose. It is all so stale, flat, and unprofitable, and yet he feigns an interest marvellously well. He acts, with the rest of them; he cannot help acting in these homely, shabby dramas and trumpery little farces, which "play in" the house, and are called "night-charges." But he will wake wonderfully to interest in a case that involves new business, or introduces new and striking features. When that is the case, the magistrate wakes up in real earnest. Here is something that must be thoroughly threshed out—no sensible magistrate will be caught napping in a case of this kind.

For the proper administration of justice in its early stages—its unfledged condition, before, in the matter of big cases, it has taken to itself wings and flown to the airy regions of the Central Criminal and the Sessions Houses—London has instituted twelve police courts, irrespective of the Mansion House and Guildhall, where the Lord Mayor and Aldermen (by rotation) dispense law on their own account. These courts are Bow Street, Clerkenwell, Lambeth, Great Marlborough Street, Marylebone, Southwark, Thames, Westminster, Worship Street, Hammersmith, Greenwich, and West Ham. The salaries of the magistrates are in all instances the neat little sum, and certainly the well-earned sum, of fifteen hundred per annum, the chief magistrate of Bow Street, Sir J. T. Ingham, being the only exception, and having a salary of eighteen hundred per annum. To most of these courts is attached the chief police-station of the district, so that the official witnesses for the prosecution are handy to be called upon when required. The total number of the London police, it may be remembered, is 13,849, exclusive of some 900 constables, sergeants, and inspectors who owe allegiance to the City of London proper. And London is well served, on the whole, we are disposed to believe, by its police. That there are a few erring mortals in their midst it is in the nature of humanity to expect. They are exposed to many temptations and little bribes, their salaries are not large, and there are some districts where "tips" are plentiful. They are not men of such high orders of intellect, and with such educational advantages to the fore as, say, our army contractors, and the gentlemen who adjudicate on the merits of swords and

bayonets; but, notwithstanding, there are heroes in their ranks, men of pluck and fibre, doing their duty honestly, valiantly, and well. After Police-Constable Barker's big fight for life, we think it will be rather hard work—as we have always considered it exceedingly unfair and in execrable taste—to make capital out of the seeming delinquencies of the "stage policeman," who is no more like life than the poor little mountebank who tries hard to impersonate him, and never gets out of the region of very bad burlesque.

GREAT MARLBOROUGH STREET

WITHIN THE COURT

BUSINESS begins punctually at Great Marlborough Street Police Court. There are many extras to attend to before the important cases come on, and the "night-charges" are always numerous. In the matter of night-charges, Great Marlborough Street probably bears the palm as to number and variety, because the great streets in the most fashionable and wealthy part of London draw to one centre the idle, the vicious, and the intemperate, whereupon the predatory classes in all their infinite variety follow at their heels, and wait their chances of spoil. All sorts of all nations constitute the night-charges here; there is not the one common stamp of poverty impressed upon these which is so apparent at the East End police courts, even the industrious classes are chiefly represented by erring cabmen, newspaper boys, match girls, cab-touts, and bus-conductors and drivers who have been careless with their language, or with their vehicles and horses.

The fair sex is more than well-represented at Great Marlborough Street, and overcrowds the waiting-rooms. Certain portions of the fair sex "loiter" a great deal in the West End streets, will not go away when told to do so, wax abusive and riotous when shoved, and finally get "run in." The fair sex is very penitent next morning, as a rule; is profuse of explanation to the worthy magistrate, prolific of excuses for its last night's unfortunate condition, is very sorry even, at times, for its sad bad life, which makes loitering a stern necessity, according to its own awful reasoning. One or two out of some dozen or twenty offenders lack prudence, and are still defiant, and a few speak indignantly of the black mail levied upon them by members of the force, as a fee for leaving them alone.

The English girls are the most excitable, and the most easily reduced to tears by the mild remonstrance or reproof of the sitting magistrate; the foreign element is more composed, more conservative, more bland and businesslike. When a policeman's evidence is very strong against an offender of this class, the lady will shrug her shoulders, spread her out her gloved hands, and appeal to the magistrate direct.

"Oh! m'sieur, ce n'est pas vrai!" escapes in silvery accent and with "tears in the voice." The interpreter is very busy in the early part of the morning's proceedings—his is a well-known face at Great Marlborough Street, one of the stereotyped institutions here,

"FOR PRISONERS ONLY."

facts; as any one I think who has had the same opportunity of observing them will readily testify. And with this assurance I will conclude.

I am, Sir, your obedient servant,

YOUR BOW STREET REPORTER

August 1846

Fortunately these days such determining of mental instability is left in the hands of the Mental Health authority and done in private, and only offenders against the law appear before the magistrates. Some of the saddest of these are not the insane but the simple-minded who do not know the difference between right and wrong. A neighbour of ours in Bloomsbury had just such a problem with his teenage daughter. "What can I do?" he would ask Bob when she was up at Marlborough Street once again for shoplifting. "I can't keep her locked up all the time." As with many other problems in which police and magistrates become involved, there is really no answer; they must prosecute in the hope of keeping some sort of control of the situation.

Phobias too can cause difficulties at courts. Obviously, claustrophobics are not very keen on cells. Those not too extremely affected can usually cope if they are put in the larger cells meant to accommodate several prisoners, if there is one free, that is. Severe cases, once police are assured they are genuine, may sometimes be allowed to roam the cell corridors, but an extra-special eye must be kept on them since the corridors lead to other places as well – such as the outside world.

A rather more unusual phobia came to light one day when the gaoler received a phone-call from the relative of a (non-custody) shoplifter who was appearing at court that morning. The caller subjected the gaoler to a barrage of questions on the lay-out of the court such as would make any policeman uneasy. Most of the questions seemed to hinge on doors (sorry). Since the only prisoner this gaoler had ever 'lost' was a burglar who had run from him then unerringly negotiated the inner maze of Bow Street's corridors that even he could not remember, he was naturally more than a bit cagey. What was puzzling was that the defendant was 'non-custody' so did not need to escape; maybe the caller was not a relative but the 'friend' of someone in custody. It turned out to be something simpler (but more complicated) than that.

The defendant had a phobia about going through doors. Whenever he went into somewhere, he had to come out again through the same door, or he became very disturbed. Many courts, Marlborough Street included, have doors in all directions, and he would not have come out through the door he had just come in. Although a plan was devised to avoid this eventuality, one unforeseen difficulty was that the hardest part of the whole performance was persuading the phobic that he was indeed coming back through the same doors he had been through earlier. His conviction was naught to him beside the agony this doubt caused.

As with most things, the raving lunatic is not always what he seems to be. People will pretend anything, and that includes being murderers when they have never harmed anyone and being insane when all their mental faculties are perfectly intact, even better than normal. Such as person was 'The King of the Gypsies', alias 'God', of course.

A flashing-eyed little Irish gnome who wore one golden earring and occasionally went shoeless, he explained his problem to the gaoler in one of those cell-side chats. Apparently he had been found 'sane', and it upset him greatly. It had all begun when winter was coming on and he had awoken, feeling very cold after spending the night in one of Her Majesty's Royal Parks, and decided it was time he did something to rectify this state of affairs. Spying a lady park-keeper approaching, he stripped off his clothes and leaped out of the bushes at her.

"Oh, but she did run!" he chortled delightedly at the memory, adding a touch of his wild-rolling eyes act for good measure.

When apprehended, he gave his captors, he told the gaoler, the full 'mad' treatment. Two days of continuous yelling – "*I* am God! I – am God!" – followed, the object of all this exertion being to obtain re-admittance to a certain mental hospital where, he claimed, he would be warm and well fed and get plenty of sex.

However, this time the doctors were unimpressed.

"What would you say if I told you I had lots of people in here claiming to be Jesus Christ?" one asked him.

"I'd say: 'Tell them to behave themselves, their father's here!' " he replied unabashed.

But such repartee did not save him. "You know what they went and did then?" he asked the gaoler in tones of one betrayed and persecuted by society once again. The gaoler said he had no idea. "They found me sane!" he spat out. "Sane!"

Once again the gaoler had to agree that you could not rely on anything these days; the whole fabric was disintegrating etc. The 'King' did not want him to be too depressed about it all, however. He would, he said, get the decision reversed by further exertions and be back home in his mental hospital soon. Sadly, this blithe spirit was found dead, sleeping rough, a few months later.

People can pretend to be mad for other reasons than to get inside, and it is a thing hard for doctors to disprove, so it was not surprising that Mr Hardwick did not find it easy, as a report on one of his cases in *The Illustrated London News* of 1842 shows:

MARLBOROUGH STREET — A singular-looking being was placed at the bar among the night-charges. He was attired in a full suite of canonical sables and wore a long beard and moustaches, to correspond like one of Johanna Southcott's disciples*. At the time he was brought in, the worthy magistrate was consulting an Act of Parliament, but was soon roused by hearing the defendant exclaim, "I am that I am."
Mr Fitzpatrick [probably the clerk]: What name does he give?
Defendant (in most solemn tone): I am Christ Jesus. The acts of my father I show, but ye know not his doings, because you are uninformed. Listen to the words which I speak, and judge me thereby. I am that I am, we and the father are one. I speak to you but ye do not understand me.

Mr W. Bulkely, of College Street, Islington, said that he was on the previous night, while waiting for an omnibus, attracted by the defendant, who was proceeding in a similarly incoherent strain to that which he had uttered before the worthy magistrate. A large crowd was assembled, and the defendant then asked him to give him a shilling. The words he used were, "A shilling will not hurt ye, but much rejoice we".
The defendant (most vehemently): I never begged; we do not ask for anything for hire — all is for the credit of our father.
Mr Hardwick (to Inspector Plume): Is the defendant mad or drunk?
Defendant: I am not mad most noble Festus,** but speak the words of truth and soberness, Christ is on earth again.

In answer to the magistrate's question, Inspector Plume handed him a letter the defendant had sent to a friend, whom he addressed as "Madam the Pastrycook", asking her to bail him from Vine Street Watch-House. The letter was gibberish but looked as though it could be a sort of coded gibberish. The inspector added that he had sent an officer to verify the truth of the defendant's story, and they had found it all to be a tissue of lies. The report does not make clear whether the story was, the one where he claimed to be an agent of Christ or his

* Actually Joanna Southcote, 1750-1814, a religious fanatic who had many followers.
** Porcius Festus, the Roman procurator, before whom the apostle Paul was brought.

'story' of lack of sanity. The magistrate was perplexed and remained so after reading the letter. He did, however, come to a decision. "Mr Hardwick observed that the defendant must either be insane or a gross impostor. He should commit him to prison, with hard labour, for a month, and the authorities at the prison would soon find out whether he was a lunatic or an impostor. This decision did not seem to meet the defendant's views, and he was with difficulty removed, most loudly protesting against it."

The *Graphic* reporter of 16th July 1887 spotted two mentally disturbed persons among one morning's list. One, a "wild, weak-faced ... chaney or wall-eyed prisoner with an open mouth and tongue inclined to stray out of it and rest upon his chin" was up for theft of an overcoat and a clothes-brush from the Army and Navy Club. It was a clumsy theft, merely grabbing and running. There was, however, the reporter decided, a certain method in his madness, since the weather was cold and he "scantily clad". Nonetheless, he was "very balmy" and would probably get off lightly at the next hearing.

The other customer typified the eternal difficulty and perplexity such people cause officers of the law, for he was there because the constable had not known what to do with him and admitted it. At three in the morning he had run up to the policeman and announced that Gladstone was dead and then "refused to quit his society", going on to tell him at length about his just coming out of hospital, then further dashing up to any late passer-by with the important but erroneous news about the demise of the ex-Prime Minister.

"I did not know what to make of him," states the policeman, "so, as he refused to go away, I took him into custody."

And now that he is in custody, it is very plainly apparent that no one at Great Marlborough Street knows exactly what to do with him either. The man listens with great interest to all that the policeman has to say against him, and to all questions which the magistrate puts to the policeman; he is not known to the police; he stands there a striking specimen of complete helplessness, a man friendless and alone.

In a weak moment, perhaps, and before dismissing the case, the magistrate asks the prisoner what he has to say for himself, and why he has gone about in the middle of the night disseminating such false and exciting news. At this invitation the floodgates of the prisoner's eloquence are loosed at last; he leans over the dock and proceeds with amazing volubility, and in a jerky, cracked voice, and with many odd contortions of his body, to explain the matter to the best of his ability. And for a few minutes he is allowed a very fair hearing to a marvellously unintelligible story, until it becomes plain to the meanest capacity that the time of the court is being seriously trifled with, when the prisoner is summarily cut short in his harangue and conducted by a side door into the inner offices, there to await the examination of a medical man as to his mental condition, which evidently is a trifle disturbed.

Though the outward manifestations of mental disturbance seem to change little and are, in a way, curiously and somewhat depressingly constant, the objects that the deranged mind fixes on do change with the times. These days, when politicians have lost much of their power and mystery for us all, it is MI5 and electric currents which seem to hold most sway. Also, large and powerful organizations have developed a remarkable ability to enrage (not just the mentally unstable). When arrested, after chucking a large brick through Broadcasting House windows, a young woman told Paul Bennett that she thought the BBC needed livening up a bit. As she had explained to the policeman; "I thought we had been having some lousy programmes lately." Seems quite sane to me.

18

Up the Sunny Side of Regent Street

In an afternoon's lounge up the sunny side of Regent Street, you turn
aside at Argyle Place* – thread as it were, the narrow isthmus of houses
which it presents, and which opens into the broad, quiet street beyond –
furthermore, if keeping to your left, you encounter a group of policemen,
the invariable signs and symbols of police majesty being at hand – mount
the flight of stone stairs which you will see to your left, and push open the
door at the top of it – you will find yourself in a room about the size of an
ordinary parlour – a lightsome, cheerful apartment – with a long low
writing-desk stretched across it at the upper end, and littered with
newspapers, police-sheets and so forth – light rail compartments mapping
out the centre of the room into pens for witnesses, prosecutors, attorneys
and prisoners. You will probably furthermore remark, easily lounging in
the arm-chair placed behind the aforesaid desk, a pleasant, gentlemanly-
looking elderly man, somewhat bald, and with a strong resemblance to Sir
James Graham.** You are in Marlborough Street Police Court, listening
to the decision of Mr Hardwick.

So wrote *The Illustrated London News* reporter in October 1847.

Though nowadays it appears unremarkable, Great Marlborough
Street, in which the court is situated, was once reckoned to be quite
impressive. The street's first bricks were laid in 1704, and by 1714 it
was included by a contemporary writer in a list of squares because,
"though not a square, it surpasses anything that is called a Street, in
the magnificence of its buildings and gardens, and inhabited all by
prime quality".

Another, slightly later writer was not, however, so taken. Ralph, in
his *Review* of 1734, commented that "Great Marlborough Street is
esteemed one of the finest in Europe; but I think it can have this

---

* Since then Great Marlborough Street has been extended into Regent Street.
** Home Secretary under Peel 1841-6.

character on no other account but its length and breadth, the buildings on each side being trifling and inconsiderable, and the vista ended neither way with any thing great or extraordinary."

Most of the original buildings are now gone, including numbers 19-21, on the site of which the court stands. Number 21 was the first to be acquired, as a public office, in 1793. Then in 1856 the police took out a lease on number 20, largely so they could use the ground at the rear to extend the attached police-station. They did not use the house itself but let it off to various tenants. When *The Graphic*'s reporters attended to collect material for a feature in 1887, they found the future of the court in jeopardy and expressed their concern.

We hope Great Marlborough Street Police Court is not to be swept away, as rumour insists just now upon declaring. It is very central; it is fairly spacious; it is not objected to by the inhabitants who, indeed, are petitioning for its remaining in their midst; it is very handy for the nobility, gentry and public in general who may be run in from Regent Street and Oxford Street, without much fuss over the matter – who, in fact, have a very little way to walk in custody, or to be carried, if disposed to be recalcitrant, and insist upon the liberty of the subject. For literary reasons even, it is a pity that Great Marlborough Street Police Court should be numbered among the bygone landmarks of London ... .

Either the rumour was false or the petitioners won, for not only did the court and station stay, they spread themselves. Two years after the above report, number 19 was acquired, and all three were demolished to make way for the new building which, apart from frontal variations, still stands.

Inside are two handsome old marble fireplaces, relics from the original houses. The police, however, were finally swept away to the spanking new West End Central Police Station which opened at the start of World War Two, in time to be bombed. It survived nonetheless and, being only a short way down Regent Street, probably did not incommode the gentry and nobility too much.

The court alone remained and is now the only one of the first London magistrates' courts to stand on its original site, though every now and then there are rumours that it will have to go. However, a second court was constructed in the basement of the building and opened in the early 1960s. Number Two court is more modern and lighter and has air-conditioning, which makes it very popular on a sweltering summer day, though its 1930s-style woodwork has won it the slightly derisory nickname of 'the cocktail bar'.

Although the street has the prefix 'Great', it was probably originally called just Marlborough Street since a stone tablet on one of the original houses says "Marlborough Street 1704" (the year of the Battle of Blenheim, won by the Duke of Marlborough). The court, however, has always been merely 'Marlborough Street' whether as a public or police office or, latterly, magistrates' court.

There is no doubt about the prime quality of past residents. Five peers lived there in 1716, and even in the nineteenth century, when it had started to go downhill, it still had more than its fair share of titles. Two barons and one earl lived at number 12, a house which is now the least altered of those surviving. However, there had always been a sprinkling of professional and trades people, and these gradually took over and the street became the home of doctors, architects, artists, tailors and, of course, legal men. By the beginning of the twentieth century the architects and music firms had come to the fore. Schott's, the music publishers, and the Royal College of Music are still there, but dominant at present are members of the rag trade who have spilled down from their village just above Oxford Street. Add Carnaby Street, which opens out onto Great Marlborough Street directly opposite the court; the great Liberty's department store also opposite, to the right of Carnaby Street, the stage-door of the London Palladium and a couple of pubs and cafés, and you have a pretty lively daytime area. Incidentally, Ramillies Street (which leads off Great Marlborough Street to Oxford Street, just past the court) was the birthplace of John Fielding. He was born there in the winter of 1741, when it was still called Blenheim Street.

The area is nothing if not fashionable, and this has always been reflected in the court's daily lists, which have illustrated changing modes in crime, many of which are, of course, due to social changes and innovations. During much of the nineteenth century, coining went on at all hours in the stews of Seven Dials (now the area around St Giles' Church, at the junction of New Oxford Street and Shaftesbury Avenue), which was near enough to the West End for thieves and coin-passers to pop in and out again, then quickly lose themselves in the warrens of narrow streets and alleys.

Mayhew gives a blow-by-blow account of how to make a coin-mould from a real coin; how to electroplate the counterfeit article once completed, then how to 'slum' it with lamp-black oil so its brightness would not excite suspicion, all of which must have been a great help to amateur coiners. He even warned that, unless properly dried, the mould would fly apart on the insertion of the hot metal. Maybe he was working on the premise that those who needed to coin were probably not very good at reading. Coiners faced up to thirty years' transportation if caught, but Marlborough Street mainly saw the passers. It is not a common crime these days, though fairly recently the court has seen at least two charges of attempting to pass forged currency (one in Harrods – what a cheek) and one of actual forgery, both concerning US dollars.

Of course at one time children used to stand in the dock and be tried in the same way as adults, and, as we know, many of them were professional criminals. Boy chimney-sweeps were considered very good material for house-breaking since they were good climbers, could enter or exit through a chimney if necessary and knew the inside of many grand houses. There were many child prostitutes too, though some of the better Victorians gradually helped control such abuse by getting the age of consent raised, against strong opposition, from twelve to thirteen in 1875, then to sixteen in 1885. But however awful such an abuse was, it was probably better for a child than being down the mines or in a cotton-mill. The West End of London had no mines or cotton-mills but plenty of rag-trade establishments, sweated labour set-ups which employed whole families.

One Marlborough Street report in the *Hue and Cry and Police Gazette* of 25th July 1818 tells of a Captain Beecham's charging two of his servants, one of whom was fourteen years old, with robbing his dwelling-house after he had left it in their charge while he and his family went away for a few days.

Then there was the apprenticeship system which put many children (often orphans or with parents in prison) into bondage – just how much in bondage is illustrated by this odd extract from *Cobbett's Evening Post* of 22nd February 1820:

MARLBOROUGH STREET – *Curious charge against an Apprentice* – Yesterday, Mr Solomons, a Jew, charged his apprentice (likewise a Jew) with having refused to eat cold roast beef and neglecting his work as a glass-cutter.

Mr Solomons stated that the prisoner was formerly an industrious, well-disposed lad, who was, prior to last West-End Fair, making rapid progress in his trade; but having been taken on a false charge of robbery, and brought to this office, his prosecutors swore positively that he was one of the desperate gang who knocked him down and robbed him at

West-End Fair. He was tried at the Old Bailey but was acquitted. Mr
Solomons solemnly declared on his oath that the same night he was seen
to bed safely by himself. After his committal the boy was sent to prison,
necessitated to associate with characters of the worst description, with
whose habits he became familiar, and to which circumstances Mr S
attributed his anticipated untimely end; although he had made application
to the proper authorities to have him separate from the others. The
prisoner would not now eat cold roast beef, which was laid before him,
nor would he do his work.

The prisoner said he had no appetite, and if he had, the doctor ordered
him not to eat anything cold – he was not well. Mr Solomons – *Vel, put
you coult* eat *rost* beef hot the day before; the *Acth* of Parliament will
make you eat it whether or no, and you shall *eath* it. He was ordered to
come to terms with his master or stand committed.

And *The Graphic* of 16th July 1887 provides a 'graphic' description of
an old lag:

Presently a boy appears whom nobody can do anything with – one of
those dreadful boys! ... a poor, whimpering little waif enough, whose
appearance belies the evidence that he is so very very terrible, In court,
and out in the office afterwards ... and cries intensely all the while, he is
the picture of meekness and uncontrollable grief, but the black list of his
offences is a long and startling one. Appearances are remarkably
deceptive in the case of this youngster – who is eleven years of age and
looks about eight – and the humiliating announcement is made by his
pastors and masters that they can do nothing with him. He is wholly
defiant and incorrigible, they say of this poor little atom, whom a rougher
wind than ordinary seems capable of blowing out of court, and the
incorrigible snivels on and is at all events the picture of contrition. The
particular offence for which this small person is put into dock on this
occasion is that of stealing a letter, and adding to the complication by
disappearing with another boy for a few days' 'life in London' together;
the second offender who has been 'going it' with him being a much smaller
youth, and who, though not as tearful as his friend, is much more scared
and has evidently a rapidly beating heart beneath his plum-coloured
worsted comforter. The smaller youth is sent out of court with a caution;
but retribution, or stern justice, or Nemesis 'makes it hot' for the weeping
lad, and has no mercy upon him – that is, from his point of view.

He is not set free and told to go home and be a good boy for the future;
he is summarily sentenced to durance vile in an industrial school, where
the work will be hard and the discipline extra severe, of all of which he is
probably aware, for he continues to cry hysterically when out of court and

whilst waiting for the policeman who is to take him in the first instance to Marylebone. His forlorn condition even attracts the attention of members of the force as they pass in and out on their various errands. "Cheer up, young 'un; it won't be so bad," says one good-tempered policeman, clapping him on the back; but there's no cheering him up for that day. He is going away from all his pals – from the run of the streets – from all that makes 'life worth living' at present, and that he has escaped the prison on account of his youth does not appear to afford the slightest consolation to him .... .

Evidently someone had been poisoning the boy's mind against industrial schools, the writer concluded.

Many offences, such as duelling, omnibus assault, garotting, dog-, horse- and sheep-stealing (Marlborough Street had a case of sheep-worrying in Kensington Gardens on its lists in 1910!) and smashing phone-boxes, were halted by imposing severe penalties and changes in conditions. And the court no longer sees an offence like one reported in the *Observer* of 8th October 1797; fraud by the selling of "fictitious news-walks". In fact, I have been unable to confirm what this *was*, though I surmise it must have been selling newspaper-pitches one did not own.

Particular fashions in clothes or accessories can sometimes cause the upsurge of certain crimes merely by making them easier. Just as the fashion of carrying beautiful expensive handkerchiefs flopping temptingly out of the tails of men's coats were gifts to boy-pickpockets in the nineteenth century, so bucket-bags were to those of the mid-1950s. "These stupid bucket bags!" exclaimed the normally mild Paul Bennett on one occasion. He proceeded to mount his own little campaign against them with pertinent comments, duly reported, whenever a case involving them came up. For those too young to remember, bucket-bags were, rather naturally, of a rigid bucket-shape and a cross between a shopping-bag and a handbag. To put your purse in one, as many women did, was tantamount to placing it on a presentation platter. Mr Bennet certainly brought this risk to public attention: "Bucket Bags Again" said one headline after his latest attack on "the shopping-bag that invites thieves".

Marlborough Street magistrates are forced to keep in touch with changing fashions whether they like it or not, for no sooner is something 'in' than someone is 'up' at Marlborough Street for having stolen it or is wearing it in dock. Boob-tubes, footless tights and endless other passing fripperies come under legal scrutiny.

"What *is* a gent's handbag?" Neil McElligott asked plaintively one day.

"It's a bag for men to carry things in when they haven't got pockets," the constable explained. "It's a fashionable trend."

Fashions in medicine also enter into things. Recently, when a young man was in the dock for stabbing to death his boyfriend, a photograph of the multi-wounded body also showed a beautiful made-up feminine face, breasts and penis. He was not a hermaphrodite but one of those aided by hormones and surgery.

Currently fashionable killings are 'disco murders', committed by usually quiet young men, with knives, early in the morning, outside discothèques. A young man accused of such a crime recently stood impassively in Marlborough Street dock. And impassive he might well be, since he was allowed bail!

But nothing changes the face of crime and petty offences like war. The West End being an area people drift towards when they are on the loose or the run (partly to enjoy themselves, partly in the mistaken belief that it is anonymous), in wartime its courts are packed with deserters and stragglers from the navy. By 1917-18 Marlborough Street was seeing something like half-a-dozen a day. Many had obviously got fed up and surrendered voluntarily, or at least not argued too much, since "by their own confession" was noted alongside the charge of desertion in many cases. (Conversely, such times throw up a regular sprinkling of charges of wearing uniforms and medals to which one is not entitled.)

One of the court's most unlucky deserters must have been 'Albert', who was caught just before the commencement of the Great War. Albert approached a man in Piccadilly and told him that he was a police-officer and was arresting him. He took hold of his arm in the approved manner and began walking him towards Vine Street police-station. A bystander objected, but Albert, not to be deterred, told him to mind his own business or suffer the same fate. However, before he and his prisoner reached the station, Albert had a change of heart and told the man that, for a sovereign, he would be prepared to waive the charge and let him go. The man showed no gratitude for this chance but turned around and arrested Albert, after introducing himself as Police Sergeant Brodie, plain clothes, and his would-be rescuer as Police Constable Sims.

"My luck is out!" exclaimed Albert, as well he might, and after being told he was to be charged with impersonating a police-officer, he confessed that he was a deserter from the First Battalion of the Grenadier Guards.

The end of World War Two saw a very curious deserter case, as one (unidentified) newspaper reported:

SOLDIERS' TWO-YEAR HOAX AS AN 'ALIEN'

The amazing hoaxes of an English soldier who has hoodwinked the authorities since 1944 came to an end at the Marlborough-street Court yesterday when a twenty-five-year-old man, calling himself André Noullett, who had been suspected by the police to be an Austrian named Karl Stürmer, was revealed as John –, a British subject and a deserter from the British Army.

Asking for the withdrawal of a charge of landing in the United Kingdom without permission, Detective Sergeant Moulder said that, after the man deserted from the Army in 1944, he pretended to be an Austrian and was actually sentenced to twenty-eight days' imprisonment for being an 'alien' landing in this country without permission.

Keeping up his pose, he was eventually interned as an enemy subject, and in 1945 he was 'repatriated' to Germany. After wandering in Germany and Austria, he assumed the guise of an alien soldier suffering from loss of memory but eventually gave himself up to the Americans at Munich, pretending he was a Canadian.

"He has now been quite frank and is very sorry for all the trouble he has given," said the officer.

The magistrate (Mr J.B. Sandbach KC): You don't think he is imposing on you again?

Detective Sergeant Moulder: No, sir! He is John –, and his father, who holds a very responsible position, has identified him.

The magistrate allowed the charge to be withdrawn, and – was handed to the custody of a military escort.

All kinds of refugees and displaced people began making their appearance at the court. A century before, Mr Hardwick had seen distressed Poles, and now Polish ex-airmen, possibly distressed that their fight had not won freedom for their country, came up on various charges. A Dutchman on a weird assortment of charges claimed to have been in Dachau: "Let me have bail," he pleaded, "so I can walk about freely." Even Germans had made their way there, having entered the country illegally. Two young ones approached a West End policeman saying they were hungry and asking for help. They had smuggled themselves in by stowing away on a Polish steamer, having been prisoners of the Russians. They had come to Britain, they claimed, because they could not stand the ill-treatment they were receiving from the Poles and were now looking for work. Deportation was what the police had more in mind, especially since so many Germans were 'smuggling themselves in', but Mr Daniel Hopkin thought they looked "healthy, decent-looking chaps" and that Britain might as well make use of them now that they were here. He gave them the address of a Welsh farm where they could begin work immediately.

19

In the Dock

"I couldn't get away from the Palace, sir. The Queen is coming back tomorrow, and the other storekeeper had to go to Balmoral," said the defendant.

Many and various are the reasons given for non-appearance at court. This man, who had merely been drunk and had appeared a day late, was warned by Paul Bennett, "I think the less you say from now on the better."

"The monkey got away, sir," said another, this time a young lady street photographer up for footway obstruction. "When I was dressing him," she explained to Leo Gradwell, "he ran down the stairs, and I had to chase after him." The monkey was her assistant, who posed with the customers, a common practice – Marlborough Street sees quite a few of our hairy brothers.

One man claimed he had received a coded message from an MI5 agent who had sent it via BBC Radio Three, instructing him not to attend, while yet another claimed that his legs had given out – hardly surprising since he had tried to walk to court, he claimed, from Cleethorpes, where he lived.

Having received a summons instructing him to attend Marlborough Street to answer a summons of leaving a car which he had borrowed, in a restricted street in the West End, when he was down there, he went to the local police and told them he did not have the money for the journey. "You've got a good pair of legs, try walking," he reported them as answering. So he did – try, that is. Thirty-six miles on, he called in to another police-station, in Lincoln, where he was advised to keep walking, and a further 16 miles nearer Marlborough Street he called in at Newark and got the same response, he claimed. That was when he gave up and went home.

"I felt I'd rather go to jail for six years then keep on walking," he told Leo Gradwell when he finally made it by raising 5 shillings here and 5 shillings there, from friends. Later he admitted that he had, in fact, been arrested by the local police for failing to attend in answer to the summons, which, in any case, he could have answered by post. Mr Gradwell, giving due regard to his straitened circumstances and waste of shoe-leather, fined him 10 shillings with plenty of time to pay.

Some defendants never appear at all, having died either through accident or from natural causes or, sadly, being unable to stand the shame of appearing, having committed suicide. Sometimes this occurs as a result of what most people would consider a fairly minor offence, one which many would not bat an eye at, and it is particularly distressing for the police-officer or store detective concerned and is enough to make him contemplate never taking any more action.

Occasionally, a criminal does not make it because he kills himself while actually committing the offence – for example, by falling from a building he is busy burgling. One man, who was found lying injured at the corner of Berners Street and Oxford Street in the 1950s, told a policeman: "I have just done a job. I missed the roof and fell." He had fallen 40 feet and died in hospital a month later. Mayhew relates, with some relish, a similar case:

In the year of 1850 a burglary was attempted to be committed at a furrier's at the corner of Regent Street near Oxford Street by three cracksmen ... They went to a public house between ten and eleven o'clock, when the two former went back into a yard with the pretence of going to the water-closet. The publican did not miss them. The house was closed at twelve o'clock, and they were not discovered. The third party went out to give them their signal, but they, being impatient and accustomed to the work, thought they would try it themselves. They went up by a fire-escape and got on to the parapet of the furrier's house, at the corner of Regent Street. Here they cut two panes of glass in a garret window, with a knife, at the same time removing the division between them. The servant, going to bed in the dark, discovered the two men. Giving no alarm, she went downstairs to her master. The master came up, with two loaded pistols in his hands, presented them at the garret-window, telling them that if they attempted to escape he would shoot them. Edward Edgar Blackwell was so frightened that he lost his presence of mind and fell from the parapet into the yard, a height of three storeys, and was killed on the spot. Henry Edgar, being more courageous, made a desperate leap to the top of a house in Regent Street and got through a trap-door, and made his way into a second-floor front in Argyle Street, where people were sleeping, and alarmed them. To prevent their taking him, he leaped from a second-floor window. Some people, passing by, saw him jump from the window and gave information to the police. He was, thereupon, arrested and conveyed in a cab, with the dead body of his 'pal', to Vine Street police-station.

At the police-station he was found to have a dislocated ankle and taken to the Middlesex Hospital, from where one of his friends helped him escape. However, another 'friend' ratted on him, and he was re-arrested and sentenced to penal servitude.

A more gruesome non-appearance, or reason for non-appearance, was put in a letter the court received explaining why the defendant, an Iraqi doctor working in Britain, who had been accused of stealing three cassettes, would not be coming. Apparently he was no longer in existence. A near relative had cut off his hands, stabbed him to death then cut his body to pieces which had been taken back to his relatives in Iraq — or so the letter claimed. This charming explanation concluded: "We are all very sorry and are sure that he didn't do anything wrong but it was just bad luck," which seems to be a massive understatement. A warrant for non-appearance was issued, and the magistrate directed that police make further enquiries. They did, but the warrant was never executed, so perhaps the good doctor was dead, though I think it more likely that he had skipped from his place of employment and sent the letter himself.

Those on bail who do appear await their turn in the front hall. Those in custody, having no choice, wait separately in a room at the rear.

At one time the 'overnights' were lined up in the yard at the rear of the court and station so that they could be inspected by the divisions' detectives, the best of whom were the "watchful and alert Messrs Drew, M'Dow and Elliott", who, according to *The Graphic* of 20th August 1887, were three "very shrewd thief-catchers". "The night-charge who has been at Marlborough Street before, or who is wanted for another case, must shiver in his shoes when he is out on parade in the court-yard, if either of these gentlemen should chance to drop in 'just to have a look round' before the prisoners go into court."

And a motley crew they would see there:

The same procession files in, day after day, month after month, year after year. The female loiterers in the streets — *toujours les femmes* — with their assertations of innocence, their protests against their fines, the police favouritism in court and the levying upon them in the streets of a regular blackmail (a matter that might be inquired into more stringently); the men

who have assaulted their wives, and the wives who have assaulted their
husbands after a drop too much at the 'Connubial Arms'; the silly swell,
who has been noisy at the 'Troc', or the 'Pavy', or the 'Ox', and
disputatious and pugnacious and very drunk, and the swell's silly friends
who have been dragged with him into conflict and finally into the station-
house; the man who has "done nothing, your honour, but call a cab for
the genelman" and got 'collared' for his officious zeal (there appears to be
some misdirected zeal on the other side also in the bagging of this very
poor game for the morning's supply); the cabman who has been insolent
to his fare, or overcharged him, or been found asleep on his box, sweetly
oblivious to all fares; the mother who has been neglectful of her children,
the grown-up children who have been cruel to the mother and torn her
hair out, or set her on fire with a paraffin-lamp; the pickpocket, the
burglar, the area-sneak; the man who has betrayed his employer's trust
and stolen his money or forged his name; the whimpering, red-nosed boy,
who has been letting off fireworks in the street and "didn't know it was
wrong, sir," till an indefatigable member of the law had him run in for
endangering the lives and disturbing the peace of Her Majesty's subjects
... there are larger and finer batches of them [night-charges] to be
disposed of here when Mr Newton and Mr Mansfield comes, than at the
other London courts, an infinite variety of men, women and children.

As now, some were defiant, some anxious ("witness 'Anxiety', as
depicted on page 66," the paper suggested – it is here among the
illustrations between pages 144 and 145), some jaunty, some stolid and
some fuddled.

The prisoners were not the only ones to suffer the indignity of
inspection out in the yard; unmuzzled dogs waited there to be
inspected and claimed. The law on muzzling dogs had not yet been
rescinded, and those seized for offending against it were placed in "a
colossal many-sided kennel constructed to hold a quantity of animals
on the solitary confinement principle" – so that they would not infect
each other. The poor animals were in greater trouble than "their
superiors" (the humans in the nearby cells) for they did not know how
they had offended, *The Graphic* felt.

Policemen too were given the once-over out there – by their
superior officers, before going on duty, this being the yard for the
adjacent station as well. They in turn critically examined the new
supply of clothing there on 'uniform day', "for a policeman loves not
to look baggy, any more than we do, and is very particular about his
cut".

Having eventually been called into court and into the dock, most offenders behave quite reasonably, but there is no knowing what even a most normal-looking person might suddenly do when confronted with this spotlight – start shouting or throwing things, refuse to leave, faint or even try to kill himself.

The gaoler is in the front line there. When one of them, the long-serving and well-known Alf Chaney, saw a sudden flash of a knife as a prisoner repeatedly plunged it towards his stomach, he leaped forward and wrested it from him, sustaining a cut hand in the process. The man, who had a respectable job and could not stand the shame of being accused of procuring his girl-friend to be a common prostitute (which he denied), was later treated for slight cuts to the stomach.

The standard of appearance expected from the defendants has changed a good deal with the years. Immediately post-war, a young actress who wore slacks when in dock got a special mention in the Press. (Green slacks they were, which somehow seemed to make it worse.) It was not the only way in which she was slack, however, for when asked if she was any trouble when arrested for being drunk, the policeman replied, "No – she was unconscious."

Since then, Marlborough Street docks have probably seen more *outré* clothing than a Chelsea Arts Ball used to produce. Some, such as the Santas, do it to make a point and/or get publicity. When the editors and directors of OZ Publications Ink Ltd were accused under the Obscene Publications Act for the material in their Schoolkids Issue, they all turned up in full schoolboy gear of short trousers, long socks, caps and blazers, and swinging school satchels.

Exchanges between the accused and the magistrate or clerk are often the source of the much-vaunted humour in court, but much of it depends for its impact on the normal solemnity of the proceedings' (though they are much more relaxed nowadays) being interrupted by something incongruous, less solemn, the unexpected.

"I do not understand this testeekals," complained a young foreigner accused of assault who had been thought not to need an interpreter and had pleaded guilty anyway.

"It means," answered Mr David Hopkin matter-of-factly, before the clerk of court could summon up a delicate euphemism or the gaoler an earthy one, "that you kicked him in the balls."

Another man, a street trader, complained to Mr Hopkin that he had lately been fined £50 here and £50 there and consequently felt like a man on the edge of a precipice. The magistrate, knowing how much he was raking in, murmured, "£50 today, Mr –. You've just fallen off."

Of course policemen have lewd minds and never let an accidental *double entendre* or a funny pass unacknowledged. As Mr Sandbach noticed, they never miss a chance of livening up the proceedings. Thus a homosexual, excusing his charge of gross indecency by saying, "I'm sorry sir, I haven't been feeling myself lately," had no hope of avoiding the signs of barely controlled mirth any more than did a probation-officer who, speaking for a working girl who had gone out soliciting, said her work had been getting on top of her lately; or Mr St John Harmsworth, giving fatherly advice to another on the downward path: "Young women who stop men in cars in Hyde Park often come to a sticky end."

When one is familiar with court procedure, it is difficult to visualize how it must seem to an offender who is not. It certainly must be disconcerting to be whipped out of a quiet waiting-room or corridor and suddenly find oneself centre-stage and the focus of the attention of a roomful of people whose appointed tasks are mostly halted while your name and reputed misdeeds are read out. It is small wonder that confusion sometimes sets in and they begin to tell their side of the story straight away, despite being told to wait. In some ways, foreigners and deaf-and-dumb people with interpreters are at something of an advantage: not only is there someone standing beside them, but that someone knows the procedure and can not only translate into their language but possibly put it in simpler terms.

Some defendants, however, are not only used to being centre-stage, they are used to courts. Such a man, charged with causing footway-obstruction with his snake-charming act, was most put out when the court inspector, in the brief facts given, suggested that the snake was probably artificial. It was no such thing, the defendant said indignantly and offered to prove it to the magistrate. It was not strictly germane to the charge, but magistrates can be curious too and appreciate a little light relief. Very well, Mr St John Harmsworth agreed, prove it. From the inside of his underpants the busker hauled a four-foot long, writhing bundle of North American King Snake, causing the lady court usher to flee from the room in a panic.

It was a constrictor, the defendant agreed, but was not poisonous and was quite a nice pet really – economical too, requiring only one mouse a week. Duly impressed at this addition to his knowledge, and joining in the court laughter, the magistrate gave him and his snake an absolute discharge (a conviction without a penalty).

Due to the court's central position in the capital, Marlborough

Street Court dock has seen more than its fair share of the famous: actors, writers, academics turned television pundits, singers and musicians, and MPs of all parties. It has seen them more for possession of drugs or drunkenness (especially drunken driving) than for anything else, and this includes people on the way to killing themselves by either means – for example the Rolling Stone Brian Jones with drugs, and actor Robert Newton with drink.

Driving with excess alcohol in the bloodstream has always turned up a motley selection of people, but two of the most ironic were 'Maigret' and the MP who nurtured the legislation under which he was arrested. 'Maigret', of course, attended as the actor who played him in the television series, Rupert Davies, a charming man whose adopted son was a policeman neighbour of ours at the time. As for the MP, he was Ernest Marples, who had not long before, as Minister of Transport, seen the new and more stringent legislation with regard to excess alcohol put into action. (Previously it had been a disgraceful shambles.) Both took their medicine like men.

Although drug cases only started to make news when pop-stars began to appear in court during the 1960s, these offences have fluctuated there for many years. During the First World War cocaine was hawked around the West End, and one of the first policewomen was employed undercover to help catch the traffickers. From time to time the London Chinese would be hauled up after a raid on what was always referred to as 'a Chinese Opium Den'.

"POLICE USE CHINESE PASSWORD," said the headline to a report of such a raid in 1940. The password was not quoted, but we did learn that Low Yow, who stood in dock accused of smoking opium, claimed that the drug relieved his asthma.

Marijuana was always used on a small scale by those dreaded foreigners or members of the Commonwealth. Paul Bennett told a couple of West Africans, accused of possessing Indian hemp, that he wished he could send them back from whence they came, which was their right place in his view.

Drugs and popular music have always had an affinity. "DRUG AIDED HIM TO SWING MUSIC", said a headline in the late 1940s, while by the fifties it was "DRUG-FIND IN BEBOP RAID". The latter told of cocaine, opium and hemp being used at a private party in Carnaby Street, just opposite the court. The street was a Soho backwater then, dim and murky. That time not only foreigners had been using the stuff; apparently some natives had too.

However, the real thin end of the wedge came in the early 1950s when a Serpentine angler was accused of baiting his hook with hemp-seed. Was nothing sacred? Paul Bennett was puzzled by the charge. "What's the point of all this?" he asked the police sergeant in the case. Hemp-seed, as bait, was banned, explained the sergeant.

"If he uses hemp-seed, the fish will not be attracted by any other bait," he told the magistrate. And, if everyone else began using it, all the fish would soon be caught – hooked in more ways than one, you might say.

Paul Bennett found all this "most interesting" and fined the man 5 shillings.

20

Women in Court: *The Precocious Piglet*

Women do not commit crime nearly so often as men, and their crime-rate has even decreased since Marlborough Street's earlier days, though it is currently rising a little. In the middle of the nineteenth century the ratio of indictable offences in certain areas was roughly three committed by men.to one committed by women. Nowadays it is more like seven to one. Women are also much less violent than they used to be. Those employed on heavy work such as loading coal at pit-heads were often quite as tough and aggressive as their male colleagues, and even in the West End they were no shrinking violets. Many took part in the garotting epidemic of the early 1860s, usually as prostitute decoys but sometimes doing the job themselves. One "respectable-looking woman" garotted a distinguished old man who had been walking between Bond Street and St James's Street, with such ferocity that she crushed his throat and he died a few days later.

An earlier case showing the violence of some of the ladies of the town was reported in the *Observer* of 13th May 1798:

Saturday night, about eleven o'clock, as Mr Barry of Great Queen Ann Street, barrister, was passing through Wardour Street, he was suddenly attacked by two prostitutes, one of whom struck him a violent blow on the groin, which instantly deprived him of the power of breathing and caused him to stagger against the wall, the other wretch, meanwhile, robbed him of his pocket book containing £70 in notes. On his recovery he followed the women into the house, the door of which was shut upon him, and two ruffians rushed from the back parlour, who, after knocking him down, beat him most barbarously with a quart pot and a bludgeon. His cries alarmed the neighbours, who, on forcing open the door, found Mr Barry weltering in his blood on the parlour floor. The ruffians had locked themselves in the parlour, from whence they made their escape through the window; the two women were taken into custody on the spot.

Later the two women were 'examined' at Marlborough Street and sent for trial. But it is pertinent that the women were the ones who were caught.

What makes women less crime-prone than men has never been properly investigated, though there are, of course, plenty of theories: that men are under more pressure to provide money and food; that they have more opportunity due to the relative freedom to commit crime and are physically stronger so more able to do physical damage to another. And, while women do fewer naughty deeds than men, there have always been plenty of them willing to live off the proceeds – though when they are financially dependent, there is often no choice.

The reason for the higher female crime-rate during the last century is probably that women who were unprovided for and had families to support were in a more desperate situation. Work open to them was extremely limited and pitifully paid, thus there was often little choice except crime or prostitution or an amalgam of both. This pressure did not, of course, prevent the dear old Victorian moralists from regarding female crime as more depraved than male.

Marlborough Street has always seen an exceptional number of female offenders due to the high preponderance of shoplifting and vice in the area. Shoplifting is, of course, the female crime, but prostitutes are often brought in for stealing from clients, which gives some weight to the opportunity theory.

No female offender (until the First World War) ever saw one of her sisters standing in judgement or taking any part in judicial proceedings. The whole system was run by, and for, men – and it showed. There were no women magistrates, police, clerks of court or ushers, so, not surprisingly, the male view tended to prevail, especially as far as the poorer women were concerned. In cases involving indecency, even when a woman was a victim, women were also cleared from the public gallery, and the victim would often then metamorphose into the accused trying to defend herself among a sea of hostile men. Even child victims suffered this way, accused of being sexually experienced and of having lured the poor unsuspecting male.

Men and women fighting against the white-slave traffic began to notice this bias, as did the suffragettes brought before courts – but they were tougher and fought back. A ban on women's suffrage meetings in Hyde Park brought two of the movement's more colourful characters into Marlborough Street dock: Nina Boyle and Mrs

Drummond. Both were women of wit, humour and intelligence and
noted for their beguiling public speeches, though the court did not see
them at their best in this respect.

Mrs 'The General' Drummond (also known at different times as
'Bluebell' and 'The Precocious Piglet'), was a fiery little thirty-five-
year-old Scotswoman, who, by the time she stood before Mr Denman
in April 1914, was an old campaigner. Since meeting Christabel
Pankhurst as she left prison for the first time in 1905, she had helped
in a campaign against Winston Churchill which had substantially
reduced his votes in a by-election; she had seen the inside of 10
Downing Street and the House of Commons before being ejected,
graced the cells of Holloway when well-pregnant, led an Edinburgh
suffrage procession on horseback shortly after the birth of her child,
and danced a Highland fling outside the gate of Holloway to greet a
lone Scots girl being released a day later than her group. Now, while
Mrs Pankhurst was being cat-and-moused* out of prison in the
process of serving three years' penal servitude, they had the nerve to
tell her she could not even speak in Hyde Park in a counter-
demonstration to that of the Ulster Unionists. What particularly irked
was that the Unionists were advocating violence to people, not just
property as did the suffragettes, yet were allowed to say their piece.

However, a procession was allowed in the park, and Mrs
Drummond brought up its rear in a dog-cart. Being already
acquainted with the lady, the police stopped her and diverted the cart
towards the Serpentine, away from the crowds. They must have been
somewhat surprised when she mildly acquiesced. But, when nearly
there, she jumped out, climbed the railings and made back across the
park towards the throng. She had no platform, of course, but she did
have two male supporters who obligingly held her aloft while she let
rip, to much cheering and jeering. Inevitably, she and her companion,
Miss Margaret Rogers, were arrested, and consequently on the
following day Marlborough Street was in for one of its more difficult
mornings.

Miss Rogers went on first and, according to *The Times*, "took no
interest in the proceedings but sat in dock reading a newspaper". She

---

* 'The Cat and Mouse Act' enabled the authorities to release suffragettes whose
condition became critical due to hunger-striking, then re-arrest them when they had
recovered, and to do this continuously.

was given a fine of 20 shillings or fourteen days in prison for obstructing the police, then invited to leave but declined and was forcibly removed.

'The General's' technique of illustrating her contempt for the proceedings was different. She had to be forcibly put into the dock, which she entered shouting: "Where is Carson and all those Unionists? The militants of Ulster who are prepared to take life, why are they not arrested and we are! – Simply and solely because you want to do the Government's dirty work and hound us down." She was not going to be tried here, she went on, and, for a while, she was not. The magistrate, Mr Denman, unable to make any headway against her shouting and refusal to co-operate, had her 'put back'. Four policemen removed her, to shouts of "You devils!" from her supporters in the public gallery, who were soon subjected to similar treatment. After the second abortive attempt to hear the case, only two constables did the job, and after the third attempt the case went on without her. However, it was by then getting rather late, so after hearing police evidence the case was adjourned until Wednesday.

When she came up again, she began by shouting while the clerk was speaking to her, then dashed out of the dock, careering into the counsels' box. "Do sit down," pleaded prosecuting counsel. "You sit down, you Jack-in-the-box!" she retorted before being overpowered. After "vigorous resistance" she was dragged back to the dock, where her remarks about the Ulster movement were encouraged by "Hear, hear!", "Well done!" and "Bravo!" from the public gallery.

Suddenly she seized a policeman's whistle and hurled it towards Mr Denman, yelling, "I suppose you have been to see Bluebeard at the Home Office* – the man who tortures women!"

"Forty shillings or one month," said Mr Denman.

Then The General was removed, shouting, "You have not seen the last of me!" – which cannot have been a cheering thought.

Marlborough Street had been the particular target of another group of suffragists, the Women's Freedom League, for quite a while. The League's magazine, *The Vote*, had been keeping a watching brief on courts since early in 1912, noting the unfair sentences given to women offenders as compared with male and publishing the details in a column cynically titled "The Protected Sex". In October 1913 they had devoted a great deal of editorial space to an attack on Frederick

---

* Harold McKenna, the Home Secretary, who brought in 'The Cat and Mouse Act'.

Mead's severe handling of some suffragettes (not belonging to the WFL) arrested outside the London Pavilion for selling suffragist literature and had compared it with his behaviour during the 'Queenie Gerald Case', during which, they alleged, he had been party to the cover-up.

Mr Mead was also, they claimed, one of the more determined ejectors of women from courts, and Nina Boyle, their political and militant organizer, wrote him a long letter about this, to which he replied that he would at all times give facilities for the presence of ladies having "a *bona fide* interest in such cases". In fact, he still cleared the court when he felt like it and was to continue doing so for many, many years to come.

Nina Boyle, later described as "one of the finest and friendliest figures of the women's movement" and a "delightful racy talker", did attack men in her speeches but also reasoned with them and made them laugh as well. A one-time actress, writer and journalist and, while living in South Africa, a "fighter for freedom of Women of Native Races", Nina Boyle had a style rather more sophisticated than that of Mrs Drummond. Pricking pompous male dignity was her speciality, and the establishment and police never forgave her for that. The police particularly disliked her, as, during her campaigns (always against the government, never private concerns), she had made them look foolish on more than one occasion.

Like Mrs Drummond, she had been at Marlborough Street for making banned speeches in Hyde Park and had subsequently led a campaign against conditions of police prison-vans, which she claimed to have won.

Finally, in July 1914, she commenced her Police Court Protest Campaign. Possibly it was the presence of Frederick Mead at Marlborough Street which made it the lucky first venue selected. On the appointed day Miss Boyle and five other ladies fired their opening salvo. One of the five was Edith Watson, who had collected most of the data for "The Protected Sex" column over the years and who had even bravely sat tight when the call "All women out of court!" went up.

Since the court was temporarily removed (due to rebuilding) to other premises in Francis Street off Tottenham Court Road, it was thence the ladies repaired. They chained themselves to the court door and each other, successfully bringing the proceedings to a standstill until the police managed to wrench the handle from the door and threw them out into the street, where, eventually, they were arrested for refusing to go away.

Their names, they informed the arresting officers, were Ann Smith, Louisa Smith, Lillian Smith, Annunziata Smith and Edythe Smythe. They were in the cells, half disrobed inspecting their bruises, when, Nina Boyle later complained, five detectives burst in and "gazed insolently" at them. "That's Nina Boyle!" one exclaimed. Subsequently troops of police came to gawp at them. Despite the fact that women were expected to be demure and pure in those days, they were looked after largely by men when in police cells, which not only gave them a distinct lack of privacy but put them at the mercy of predatory male policemen. They even had to wash in the cell corridors within view of policemen and male prisoners in other cells. Miss Boyle lost no time in mounting an attack on this situation after her release.

When they finally came up before Mr Graham Campbell, they held up proceedings as long as possible by cross-examining witnesses at great length until pulled up. Then they would admonish magistrates, prosecuting counsel and police ("I know it is not fashionable in this court to tell the truth, but do try") as though they were small boys, which cannot have pleased them. Finally, the women obtained an adjournment by asking for a witness, the Marlborough Street janitor, who was not available.

Meanwhile they went to Holloway Prison, where they made contact with their WSPU* sisters in long-term solitary confinement. As Nina later reported in *The Vote*: "There are a number of them in prison, several being in hospital in a very wretched condition; but their spirits and courage are wonderful, and it was a heartbreaking thing to hear them shouting encouragement to each other, often in cracked and strained voices, two or three times a day."

After their next appearance at Marlborough Street, the six women received a short sentence in Holloway. The opening incident in their Police Court Protests had succeeded beyond their wildest dreams, said Nina, whose Irish ancestry tended sometimes to show. In fact, it turned out to be their closing shot as well, since within two weeks the Great War had begun and they suspended hostilities for the duration. The Women's Freedom League, however, unlike the Pankhursts' WSPU, never stopped fighting for women's rights during that time,

---

*WSPU – Women's Social and Political Union – led by Mrs Pankhurst. The WFL was a breakaway group.

nor did they let patriotic fervour lead them to do anything silly. Indeed, their attitude was that these silly men have got us into this mess, but we will have to make the best of it.

Nowadays there is a matron permanently on duty at Marlborough Street Court, and the women's cells and transport are kept separate. When the matron is off duty, a policewoman may take her place – a duty I have done on several occasions.

21

The Siege of Marlborough Street

The mob which had begun to gather around Marlborough Street at such an early hour was not friendly, nor was it there merely out of curiosity: it was feeling aggrieved and aggressive – very aggressive. When the magistrate, Mr Hardwick, appeared in the street, reactions were various. Some cheered, some hooted, some shouted: "Act with Justice!", and one person threw a stone which missed Mr Hardwick and hit another member of the crowd.

Once inside, the magistrate was still in some danger, for a stone shattered a pane of glass as he was passing a window, but he remained unruffled. He must have known this was not going to be an easy day. However, he did "intimate to an inspector", as *The Times*, in one of its more understated moods, put it, "that if the persons outside persisted in their disorderly conduct, he would procure the assistance of sufficient civil force and cause the streets and avenues of the court to be cleared".

Despite the magistrate's attendance, the sitting was to be much delayed "in consequence of a doubt as to the Home Office allowing the charges to be heard at that court". They *could* have them removed to Bow Street. This had been done on more than one occasion and was a move strongly deprecated by *The Times*, as it always caused great inconvenience to all parties and even, in one instance, nearly led to the defeat of justice, "as important evidence was furnished to this court which only by something like an accident reached Bow Street in sufficient time to ensure the conviction of the murderer of Lord William Russell".

After a three-hour wait, a defence counsel, Mr Ballantine, entered court in a fighting mood. When were they going to have the accused brought in? he wanted to know, or did the police inspector not wish for them to be brought before an impartial tribunal? Inspector Lester retorted that he had no wish in the matter at all; he was merely waiting for orders.

Another hour passed, during which time the number of prisoners was considerably augmented, "in consequence of the mob outside and the necessity for police interference". But soon Mr Hardwick announced that the cases would be heard at Marlborough Street, for now they were merely waiting for Crown counsel to appear.

At 3 p.m. another defence counsel, Mr Herring, spoke out. His client, an apprentice, with his character at stake as well as future prospects, had been in custody since 3 p.m. the day before and was now in a crowded room below, almost suffocating from the heat (it was mid-July).

Mr Ballantine weighed in again:

I must say that I never in the whole course of my life witnessed anything so scandalous as the conduct of Government from the beginning to the end of this business. The disturbance that occurred yesterday, it is well known, was occasioned by the bad management of those in authority, and after the persons who were apprehended have been in custody so many hours, I really think they have a right to know why they are there detained. You hear, Sir, that a respectable lad is in custody, and yet there is not a soul present to tell you on what ground or to explain any charges against him.

The two lawyers continued to attack in concert, Mr Herring on behalf of his client and one or two others, Mr Ballantine on behalf of the proper proceedings and most of the other ninety defendants. Mr Hardwick was sympathetic but unmoved. He was awaiting police action. This stalemate was momentarily interrupted while two stone-throwers, culled from outside the court that very day, were brought in. Both had thrown stones at the police; an officer duly exhibited his cut face to prove it, and they were fined 40 shillings, despite a plea for leniency from the father of one, who claimed that his boy was "marked out by police because he was known to be the son of a publican".

The 'pause' continued. The counsel also. What insolence from the police to himself! they goaded Mr Hardwick. There were ninety prisoners in the cells; it was 3.30 p.m., and still no charges had been placed before him. The magistrate announced that the court would close at 5 p.m. and that if anyone had any complaint about the police, he should make it to the proper authorities.

Another pause. The crowd, who had been noisy and riotous in fits and starts, were now getting tired, and a "smart shower" soon dispersed them. At 4.45 p.m. several police superintendents suddenly entered the court, and the day's list began, but only after Superintendent Hughes had given a *résumé* of the affair. He and Superintendent O'Brien, also present, had played leading roles in the previous day's happenings in Hyde Park.

The cause of the happenings had been a highly unpopular Bill, introduced into Parliament by Lord Robert Grosvenor, against Sunday Trading. The intention was to prevent all markets and even the opening of pubs on Sundays, mainly with the object of forcing people into church. (It was not deemed necessary to close gentlemen's clubs.) What was particularly monstrous about the whole idea was that those this ban would affect the most were the working classes who laboured fifteen to sixteen hours a day, from Monday to Saturday, leaving them only Sunday to shop and relax.

At first no one took the proposal too seriously, though it attracted much caustic comment and meetings were held in Hyde Park to voice objections to it. Then the last, and biggest, meeting was banned, an action which brought out the largest crowd seen in London up to that time, about fifty thousand; 450 policemen were deployed to prevent the meeting's taking place. Lord Grosvenor had left for the country.

London had enjoyed a long respite from mob violence since 'the New Police' had at last gained control. The first pitched battle had been at Hyde Park Corner in 1830, a year after their birth. There had been several skirmishes before and after, the worst being in 1833 at Coldbath Fields, where a constable was stabbed to death and such was the anti-police feeling that the inquest jury brought in a verdict of justifiable homicide (later quashed). Since then there had been comparative peace in London. However, the police still were, as David Ascoli points out in *The Queen's Peace*, walking "a precarious tightrope of public opinion", hampered by an ageing and by then out of touch Commissioner, Richard Mayne.

Superintendent Hughes now told the court that on the previous day, Sunday 1st July 1855, at 2 p.m., he had been on the south side of the Serpentine in command of 250 men. By 3 p.m. a large crowd of about forty to fifty thousand had assembled, and, whenever a carriage or person on horseback passed by, there was "a great tumult, shouting, hooting and cries of 'Go to church!' 'Who bought you that horse?' " and so on. His orders were to disperse the crowd when any disturbance arose and to keep the mob back from the rails. Some stones were thrown at the constables, and one or two struck him though did not hurt him.

Shortly after 4 p.m. several persons were taken into custody and conveyed to the station-house in cabs. On several occasions he had spoken to the assembled persons to induce them to go away quietly. No one had paid any attention, "neither the well-dressed nor the evil-disposed" (nice distinction that). The latter class of person impeded the police as much as possible.

Mr Clarkson, on behalf of the Crown, asked the superintendent whether the assembly was such that would "prove a terror to those not taking part".

"I'd say it was," he replied. "The mob were swaying about and making much disturbance. Later in the day an application was made for a body of constables, as the mob were throwing stones at the soldiers in the barracks. When it was getting dark, I consulted with my brother officers as to the best means of getting the people quietly out of the park, and formed a hundred constables in a line and paraded them towards the throng, and by that means the park was tolerably well cleared."

Mr Ballantine's examination revealed a slightly different picture:
"Were many people injured?" – "Yes."
"How many?" – "I did not see how many."
"Was there a child half-crushed?" – "I heard so."
"Did not several people sustain serious wounds from the police?" – "I heard some persons were injured."
"Don't you know that several were wounded?" – "Yes."
"Did you see the police use their truncheons?" – "I gave orders to the constables to use their truncheons."
"They obeyed and struck right and left at the people, did they not?" – "Not right and left."
"Violently?" – "Not violently, in my opinion."

And so it went on. The crowd's only offence, Mr Ballantine claimed, was their being there and their hooting and shouting.

Mr Clarkson came back and re-examined the superintendent, to put it all in a more favourable light, and elicited the information that the mob had been obstinate and riotous and that the superintendent had had orders from Sir Richard Mayne himself that they must be dispersed. He had asked them to do so, five or six times, before weighing in, and he had ridden around on horseback among the people, "making observations on the state of things".

It seemed obvious that the police had lost their heads a little, but, given the odds, this was scarcely surprising. And there was a precedent for the superintendent's action: in 1830, when a vast mob (equally opposed to the lack of mention of reform in the recent opening-of-Parliament speech and to the New Police) decided to invade the West End, an unexpected baton-charge had caused them to turn and run without any battle's being joined.

The police constable who had actually arrested the first accused person on Marlborough Street's list gave evidence next. He had seen "bushels of stones" being thrown, he declared, including, of course, one by the prisoner. Mr Ballantine then cross-examined him, and, despite his alleged concern for the prisoners still incarcerated, he launched into a long speech as to why *he* was there acting as general defence counsel. He had been retained, he informed Mr Hardwick, not by the defendants but by "Messrs Travers and Smith – most respectable persons", who had, though not acquainted with the accused, arrived at the opinion that the present charges should be watched and that persons of the condition of the defendants should not be left unprotected.

He continued into a harangue against the proposed legislation and government action against the meeting, which was responsible, he claimed, for driving people to excess, and it was this, his retainers felt, that should be brought to the attention of the magistrate. To add insult, they had been kept waiting all day while all sorts of "tricks and traps" had been resorted to in order to get the charges heard at Bow Street, "as if an independent magistrate was not to be trusted, or as if the magistrates at this court were not as competent to deal with the charges as any magistrates in the metropolis". In fact, he went on, no magistrate was ever placed in a more important position than the magistrate he was addressing at the moment. A great national calamity had occurred, owing to the improper use of authority, and so on. He hoped therefore that the defendants would be leniently dealt with and this particular one sent home without a fine or disgrace to his character. There was scarcely a person in Hyde Park who had not a friend or relative shedding his blood for his country elsewhere (the Crimea), and this was no time to stir up class-hatred. He concluded, *The Times* reported:

Let the people feel that the poor man's errors were dealt with leniently and kindly, and he therefore addressed the magistrate on the bench – one of the oldest magistrates – a magistrate he had known for years and respected – he might even use a warmer term – and whose opinions on these matters he believed he knew – with a view of calling his attention to the importance of administering the law that it should have a good effect not only on defendants but on the country.

Mr Hardwick responded to all this rhetoric by saying that he would adjourn his decision until he had heard more evidence. If it was an isolated case of stone-throwing, he would not be disposed to deal with it other than leniently, but if it turned out to be a case of riotous character, it would require severe treatment.

It was past 6 p.m. when the court adjourned, the prosecution solicitor having passed on the message that the Government would allow all those *not engaged in violence* to be set at liberty. Mr Ballantine did not see why this could not apply to all the prisoners, who could be bailed in their own recognizance, but Mr Hardwick would not accept that.

The day was not yet over for Marlborough Street police, however. The mob not only reassembled, it grew larger and more hostile, and battles ensued during which, *The Times* reported, "severe injuries were inflicted on both sides. One police constable was stated to have had his jaw broken, and more than one was cut about the head with stones, a large quantity of which were at hand in consequence of the macadamized road having just been repaired."

Smaller mobs roamed around pouncing on lone police-officers. One group, headed by several foreigners – including two Frenchmen, yelling, it was claimed, "Bravo Englishmen! A republic, a republic!", caught up with Police Sergeant Laws, who was coming down a street near the court. One of the Frenchmen promptly struck him on the face, while the other hit him as he fell, resulting in serious wounding.

In nearby Regent Street a Mr Medcalfe observed a mob attacking a policeman with stones and brickbats and ran to his aid, telling them not to be so cowardly, whereupon they turned on him, causing him to flee. He took shelter in the house of a furrier named Barclay. The mob demanded Mr Medcalfe be handed over and, when he was not, proceeded to break the windows. Eventually he was able to get home under an escort of "respectable persons".

On Tuesday morning the mob gathered outside the court and station once again and exhibited "indications of renewing attacks on the police court and police".

Mr Hardwick instructed that a body of constables be "in attendance" in the garden at the rear of the premises, "a precaution which, in all probability," said *The Times*, "saved the neighbourhood from premeditated outrage". It did not save the gaoler, Welch, however, or his assistants, when they were placing the first batch of prisoners, who could not pay their fines, in the van. They were pelted with large stones "and would have been roughly handled but for the precautions which had been taken".

Halfway through the afternoon some of the police guard had to leave and add their weight to the guard on the residence of Lord Grosvenor, which was also being besieged.

Inside the courtroom, when the first batch of prisoners was brought forward, the prosecuting counsel made an announcement as to the course the Government intended to pursue. In cases where no violence had been done, such as with the first ten prisoners in dock, who had merely been part of the unlawful assembly, no proceedings would be taken. He hoped they would consider they had been dealt with leniently, for, despite the cause so well put by the learned counsel on the previous day, they had been part of an *unlawful* assembly. However, in consequence of what had passed in the House of Commons the previous evening, the Bill had been withdrawn. As for the charges involving assault, they would be proceeded with as normal assault-charges.

Mr Ballantine thought this a wise course and a pity it had not been adopted earlier, since the prisoners had not committed any offence.

It was Mr Hardwick's turn to have his say now, and he made a long speech which amounted to the fact that he could not agree that no offence had been committed: the law was quite clear on the subject of unlawful assemblies, no matter how just the cause. Huge angry crowds tended to get out of control and often ultimately did things they would never do individually.

Mr Ballantine, though pleased that the Bill had been withdrawn, added (pushing his luck), that if it had not been for the meeting and subsequent activity, it would by now be law. Could not the Government go all the way and let everyone off? The prosecuting counsel declined to oblige, and the remaining nineteen cases went on, most resulting in convictions and fines (with alternative prison sentences) amounting to 10 shillings or seven days, or 20 shillings or fourteen days.

A couple of people counter-charged assault by the police, and during the day several other people came in to complain about the violence of police the preceding evening. They had attacked men, women and children indiscriminately, it was alleged.

Police Inspector Mahoney, who had obviously had enough by then, retorted that this was a strange assertion when three police-officers were seriously injured, one so badly as to make it doubtful he would recover.

Several noblemen and gentlemen were in court, during the hearings, reported *The Times*, one of whom, the Marquis of Stafford, was much cheered as he left. The police were not much cheered as they did. Once the mob had realized that the prison-van was being taken round the back and not, as usually happened, loading at the front, they dashed around there. Eventually they were kept out of the back mews altogether. They wanted to attempt a rescue and, when this likelihood was frustrated, so were they. They rushed round to the front and began to smash the court and station windows. *The Times* continues the story:

> The police, who had not up to this time made their presence apparent, were formed into two bodies in the court and suddenly let out into the street by the two doors, but with strict injunctions not to use their truncheons. The rioters at once dispersed in all directions. As soon as the police had retired to their old post, the mob returned and committed various acts of mischief, breaking more windows at the police-court, twenty-eight squares of glass in all, and breaking the windows of some of the inhabitants, the principal sufferers being Mr Garratt, No 5 Great Marlborough Street, Mr Rutherford, of No 7, and Mr Clipperton, of No 3. The strength of the police being considerably augmented, the mob, about twelve o'clock at night, gave up their attempts and dispersed.

Two of Marlborough Street's longest days were at an end. The incident was not closed, however. A Royal Commission of Enquiry was appointed to look into police behaviour, and it decided that the majority of officers had shown moderation and forbearance but that Superintendent Hughes had lost his head. He and Superintendent O'Brien were reprimanded and six constables dismissed.

A week after the siege of Marlborough Street, Mr Medcalfe begged permission of Mr Hardwick to make a statement of some public importance. Mr Hardwick agreed and was given information as to how Mr Medcalfe had attempted to rescue a beleaguered policeman but had been forced to take refuge in the furrier's in consequence. The furrier, Mr Medcalfe went on, had promptly sent him a bill for the damage to his windows. He had paid it, but what he wanted to know was, was he liable?

The magistrate thought him neither legally nor morally liable. Had he a right to seek shelter? Mr Medcalfe persisted. The furrier had since told him, politely, that, had he been at home when Mr Medcalfe ran in, he would have kicked him out of the house. Mr Hardwick assured him he had a right; he would have done the same under the circumstances.

Public Order was to continue to be a Marlborough Street speciality, Hyde Park Corner being the chief venue of demonstrators (Trafalgar Square was served by Bow Street). The next big riot occurred at the 1866 Reform Meeting in Hyde Park (once again banned, but this time the park was closed as well). It was much more serious, resulting in the Commissioner's being mildly injured (though his reputation took another battering since he had been in personal command) and twenty-eight of his men being disabled for life. Marlborough Street was once again inundated with 'bodies' (police parlance for arrested persons) but this time was not put under siege.

Since then, every cause known to man has been aired in the court's catchment-area. People for or against the bomb, sex-shops, Queen Frederika of Greece, Belgians in Biafra, Americans in Vietnam, British/Greeks/Turks in Cyprus, Black Power, Gay Lib, the Welsh Language, the Shah of Iran and so on, have marched, sat down, fought hand to hand or with staves and banners and even hurled jam at the BBC. All had understandable aims, with perhaps the exception of the counter-anti-apartheid movement, which title tends to stop the brain a little until you have repeated it slowly and out loud.

The causes have brought to the court, either as offenders or as involved onlookers, a motley mix of people, including Robert Bolt (ban the bomb), Tariq Ali, Colin Jordan, Michael X, Pat Arrowsmith and Oswald Mosley's son, but no more Frenchmen shouting '*Vive La Republique!*' (they did catch them, by the way). I think they got tired and went home. It is a good job that someone does now and again.

22

Business of Living – "The warm precincts of a cheerful day"

Paddy was a road-sweeper – a job, one imagines, which gives ample time for rumination, and Paddy had been ruminating, soul-searching even. There he was, happily doing this job for all these years, but what had he done for mankind? Nothing. It was his attempt to right this imbalance which brought him into the dock at Marlborough Street.

It transpired that, after receiving a visit from Paddy, his doctor noticed that he had lost some of his prescription-forms. When Paddy was approached on the subject by the CID, he was sweeping a road some miles away from the surgery. On him were a wad of the missing forms. At first he insisted that he had just swept them up from the gutter and was keeping them in safe custody about his person in case they got into the wrong hands. How did they get to be in a road so far away from the doctor's? those unreasonably suspicious detectives wanted to know. Obviously they were not schooled in the wayward ways of litter, so Paddy enlightened them: "I expect they blowed about a bit."

Eventually Paddy confessed that he had taken them. He was soon to retire, you see, and had an unfulfilled desire to help his fellow men and had decided that the best way to do this was to become a doctor – not straight away, you understand, he was going to practise a bit first. That was where the prescription-forms came in. He had been practising on them and had not yet, he assured the detectives, issued any of them to his patients.

A likely story, I can hear you say. He intended to use them to get into drugs-traffic or induce bored ladies on housing-estates to remove their clothes for a quick and furtive 'medical check-up'. All I can say is that the world-weary cynical detectives believed every word of it, for Paddy was a sincere, if rather simple soul, and he was sent on his way with a warning that he must curtail his generous impulses.

Paddy was an exception. The impersonators usually have more mercenary motives or are hooked on the feeling of power and authority. True, Paddy may have acquired this craving once his career had got underway – we shall never know. Another 'doctor' (who was actually a real medical student), who did a bit of private practice on the side, usually treating leg-ulcers or giving the odd injection, eventually went as far as performing a circumcision on a seven-month-old baby and was charged at Marlborough Street with obtaining money by false pretences.

Charges of impersonating a police-officer are more frequent, possibly because the skills required are less obvious and the aura of power greater. Money and sexual favours are the two other motives for the pretence. Heaven knows which of these motivated one man who grabbed a woman in Hyde Park and told her he was arresting her. Unfortunately for him, he grabbed the wrong kind of woman, for she was a cool customer. "All right," she said, "I'll come along" – at which he turned pale. "If you run, I shall scream," she told him firmly. And, as he walked her towards Hyde Park Police Station she called out to a number of people they passed, some of whom fell in behind them.

"So he had to go to the police station. He had no option," she later told Paul Bennett. Indeed, when they arrived, she pushed the now terrified man through the station door. He was fined £5 for his odd little escapade but was more concerned about what his wife was going to say.

There is no doubt about the motives of another impersonator, who posed as an equerry to the Queen. Her Majesty wanted, he told a jeweller, a gold and diamond brooch in the shape of a trotting horse. It was to be a present for a foreign visitor. He even met the jeweller in the royal mews to discuss the matter, but when he took away the finished glittering object, he did not set it before the Queen. The jeweller heard no more, and there was no money forthcoming. Although he was 'of no fixed abode', he did have a long record of fraud and was eventually run to ground and appeared at Marlborough Street.

Another type of offence concerning identity turns up now and then, though in these cases while the offender removes one identity with his/her clothes, he/she does not replace it with another. He runs about 'starkers', in fact. During my years both as a nurse and as a policewoman, I could not help but notice that the habit of stripping to the buff is much indulged in by the deranged, and, while I never figured out the reason, I made a few informed guesses.

Sometimes, the sane have a go either for obvious sexual reasons or as a bid-for-freedom, cock-a-snook gesture, which could be a reason that the unstable do it.

Of course, for a period, it was the fashionable thing to do. "I have nothing to hide," claimed one Hyde Park streaker, while his brother told Mr McElligott that they merely wished to brighten up everyone's afternoon – a laudable desire but surely over-estimating their charms. Mr McElligott thought so and fined them £20. Mr Bennett was more lenient with a twenty-two-year-old naked swimmer in the Round Pond, who claimed his intentions were absolutely honourable. "In the Round Pond though?" enquired Mr Bennett. "Where children sail their boats and the expert old men their models! Fined 40 shillings."

"I always do it," claimed a young man in a Camden Town launderette at midnight wearing only his underwear. He was merely washing his jacket, trousers and socks, anyone could see that. When told that a woman had complained, he commented that he did not expect to find women in a washeteria at midnight – now what kind of strange behaviour is that, going to a washeteria at midnight; what will women do next? "Wear an overcoat next time," said Mr Gradwell and fined him a pound. Equality has not yet come to public stripping. A woman who behaved in a similar fashion was conditionally discharged.

Rather in the same vein of what-the-hell offences, which usually result is now-what-do-we-charge-them-with reactions, came the incident where two young men jumped on the track in the underground and ran along it – for a dare. They were charged with trespass, though attempted suicide might have been more appropriate.

"The work of magistrates' courts is too bloody multifarious," one of the magistrates used to say to Stanley French, the clerk. What he meant was that too much business-of-living legislation had been heaped on their shoulders, social problems rather than crime, such as the charge of attempted suicide, non-payments of all kinds of licences, gas and electricity bills, hygiene and dangerous structure legislation for premises, landlord and tenant disputes etc. At one time magistrates even had to decide whether minors should have permission to marry!

The 'suicide law' was one of the most misunderstood we have had. It was abolished due to an understandable feeling that people should not be punished for wanting to take their own life, which they had a perfect right to do. The legislation was probably clumsily used in earlier days, but certainly during my service it was used largely as a means for assisting attempters.

"If you are determined to commit suicide, no earthly court can prevent your doing it," Clyde Wilson once told a woman brought before him, and he was right. "But it is a very serious step to take," he went on, "because once you have 'left the warm precincts of the cheerful day' [Gray's Elegy ...], it would be useless to 'cast one longing, lingering look behind'." Making sure they were looked after until they could again appreciate the cheerful day was what those of us who operated the law felt was its purpose.

I dealt with many attempters, both as a nurse and as a police-officer operating in lonely, high-risk, bed-sitter land. We used our power over these people, the threat of prosecution, merely to see that they would consent to be looked after by someone for a while. Warm human contact was what most of them needed, till they got back their sense of perspective. Once over the hump, most were very grateful and happy to have been helped. We took statements from them, saying why they did it and hopefully promising not to do it again. This too had a therapeutic effect, giving them someone to spill their troubles to – a principle, I believe, on which the Samaritans work. Making a promise, albeit under certain duress, can sometimes hold a person back, at least for a while – hopefully for long enough.

Only one of those I dealt with ended up in court – at Marlborough Street. This was done as much for our sanity as hers. We felt that, should we have to rescue her once more from one of her 'attempts', we would be ready to take the death-leap ourselves. Final cries for help from a phone-box, mouth full of half-chewed aspirins or wrists slightly scratched, were her favoured mode. The ambulance-service were pretty sick of her too, not to mention the public who wanted to use the phone, so we charged her, and she was put on probation, which did not exactly please the probation-service either.

A genuine double attempt landed one elderly couple in front of Rowland Thomas. The woman, in an attempt to regain some of the money she had lent a friend who had since died intestate, had obtained £18 via the late friend's savings-book. Consequently she had been accused of fraud. The couple decided that the shame of this was more than they could bear, so they took a hundred aspirins each and turned on the gas-tap. Fortunately they were stopped in time and sat, holding hands in dock, while the police inspector told the story of their previously blameless lives.

"A very sad case," said Mr Thomas. He gave them a conditional discharge, urged them to forget all about it and, a little later, was able to tell them that someone had written to the court and offered to pay back the money for them – £18 was then about three weeks' wages for most people. They were to take heart from all this kindness that had been shown them by many people, he said. And they did.

Mr Robey did not marry until very late. This and his rather privileged circumstances would hardly, one imagines, give him the right experience to be able to judge whether one should marry early or get started in a career first. However, these were just the kind of judgements he was called upon to make. He granted permission to one nineteen-year-old lad who wanted to wed his seventeen-year-old girl-friend, despite the fact that the father, a major from Chelsea, preferred that they should wait until the boy was launched in a career, "such as the law or police". 'Careerism' was a dirty word among the young at the time, and when the youth declared himself more than happy to remain an ice-cream salesman, Mr Robey saw no harm in that. "Merely because somebody is not ambitious does not mean he cannot be happily married," he said.

He did not prove so sympathetic to the cause of the eighteen-year-old kennel-maid who wanted to marry a young man who actually had 'a career in the police'. They had met when she started work at Hyde Park Police-Station and the twenty-three-year-old policeman had been assigned to show her the ropes – or the leads. She (the daughter of an Indian princess) was too young to marry, Mr Robey decided, and he adjourned the case indefinitely.

The age of freedom to marry without parental consent is now down to eighteen, so this task rarely arises these days, and in any case the permissive society has rather reduced the likelihood. Similarly, it has reduced the incidence of bigamy, though the court has seen at least one this decade (a night porter) and plenty in the past. The *Hue and Cry and Police Gazette* of April 1818 gives a graphic description of one such:

John Caulion, a young man, an artist, was committed for trial from the Marlborough Street Police Office, on a charge of bigamy, in intermarrying with Miss Margaret Evans, his former wife, Mary Bigland, being alive. Miss Evans, who is about twenty years of age and was dressed very elegantly, with a gold watch and appendages suspended from her bosom, proved that the prisoner represented himself to be a widower and married her on 3rd February last at St Pancras Church but soon after left her in distress, taking away her watch and other property.

However, Marlborough Street has never had so much business-of-living work as some courts, in the East End for example, where they tend to have to sort out more personal squabbles. Those it does have often tend to have a certain flourish and imagination about them. It was imagination gone nasty in 'The Case of The Voodoo Woman and the Major'.

A major's wife, living in Chelsea, had been receiving one or two choice items through the post: a model dagger wrapped in bloodstained paper; a miniature coffin with a doll's head inside, to which was stuck a picture of the recipient; and much abusive correspondence and telephone-calls. Her cook was sent a brown cockerel's head with a message to say that, when a white one arrived, plus blood, she would know that 'the rites' had been performed. All this was wearing the woman down, and the final straw came when some undertakers' men arrived to measure her up and arrange for her funeral — they, of course, thinking she was dead. The woman collapsed, and it was decided that something must be done.

The culprit was soon found, and she claimed to have had a 'romantic relationship' with the major, until he had thrown her over. The major denied all knowledge of this, and the woman was brought before the court for 'conduct likely to cause a breach of the peace' (such a useful power, that). When she appeared, she was bound over in the sum of £100 not to bother the major or his wife, or communicate with them again; and to my knowledge she never did.

War always brings a great deal of extra legislation, to do with rationing, official secrets, aliens etc. Quite apart from the forged clothing-coupons and personal-points cases which most courts handled, the West End Courts saw fraud cases connected with "that magic word, nylon" (when street traders tried to sell nylons which were full of holes to the unsuspecting public) and many restaurant prosecutions. The latter concerned the serving of too many courses. One restaurant was even found not only to have served three courses but to have accompanied them with *bread*, while a Mayfair hairdresser had illegally served tea, coffee and sandwiches to clients who were being shampooed.

The defence pleaded that it was difficult to tell a marchioness that she could not have a cup of tea but added that they were relieved that they could refuse "now that the authorities had shown they thoroughly disapproved", and the rest of the country would doubtless follow suit. This was after, not during, the last war.

One business-of-living act which could do with some implementation nowadays is the Litter Act. It does not get it, as it was given no teeth. If a litter-lout refuses to give his name and address to a constable, the latter must summon him on description! Most will not bother to try to put into force such a derisory procedure, so London disappears under a sea of rubbish.

Contrast a prosecution in 1820, as reported in usual style by *Cobbett's Evening Post*:

CONVICTIONS UNDER THE NEW STREET ACT

MARLBOROUGH STREET
Yesterday the Marquis of Waterford, Thomas Madden, Esq, of Portland Place, James Parker, Esq, John Daniels, a poor tradesman, together with several others, were summoned to this office under the New Street Act, for neglecting to sweep their doors or cause them to be swept, in frosty weather, on or prior to the hour of ten o'clock in the morning, which subjects them to a penalty of 10 shillings, and not less than five.

The Marquis of Waterford and others were severally convicted in the mitigated penalty. Mr Daniels, one of the party, asked for what he was to pay the penalty. For the offence, was the answer.

"Good God!" said he. "You are not going to *rob* a poor man like me! If you were to *shake* me for a day, you could not shake 5 shillings out of me.
Magistrate: You ought to have swept your door.
Defendant (who is a tailor): My God! I did, until I had not a dry *thread* in my shirt.
Magistrate: But that was after ten o'clock.
Defendant: This was on a Sunday, Your Worship; is there any human law that binds man to break the sabbath?
Magistrate: The act of Parliament binds you to sweep your door every day.
Defendant: Then, in that case, we are bound to serve man more than GOD; now that's very pretty isn't it?
Magistrate: Well, you must pay the penalty, or a distress warrant will be issued against you.
Defendant: No! I can't pay it; come and rob me; I had rather you would meet me on the highway and take it from me in an honest way; it's hard

that there should be such laws; I want no law to teach me my duty.

Officer: The magistrate don't care whether you pay it or no; you must go out, Sir.

Defendant: Well, if *he* don't, I am sure I don't; so good day; thank you your Worship.

When about to leave, he was told that a distress warrant would be issued against him, he said, "That would be *distressing*." The above answers were given with such an air of *sangfroid* that they caused much laughter. He at length very reluctantly paid the fine.

23

Wanted on Warrant

"I was gently awakened by an officer who politely gave me the summons in bed and actually wished me a Happy New Year," a student told the Marlborough Street bench of JPs. "It was rather nice because it was also my twenty-first birthday." The officer who did the waking was a member of the court's warrant-office staff.

Police staff at the court are divided into two working groups, those who run the daily court lists and look after the prisoners and those who execute the warrants for non-payment of fines and deliver summonses which for some reason have not been served by post. The man in charge of this department is the warrant-officer, and those under him are assistant warrant-officers; each has his own batch of warrants and summonses to expedite. Usually this is merely a matter of catching the offender at home, perhaps early in the morning or after work, but sometimes it can mean tracking them down elsewhere.

'Elsewhere' could be somewhere such as Aberdeen, which is where one of the warrant-officers ended up recently after a 'we've got your man' phone-call. The man was wanted on a committal warrant (he was to be deposited in a prison since he had failed to respond to gentler tactics and now had to serve the alternative sentence), but it had to be an English prison, since he had committed the offence in England. So the Marlborough Street officer made the long journey north, picked up the man, took him back over the border and dumped him in the nearest English 'stir', which happened to be Durham Prison. The whole exercise cost more than the fine he had failed to pay.

Since warrant-office staff get out and about more in plain clothes, they tend to run into 'incidents'. In 1951 PC Fred Stone walked into a jeweller's shop smash-and-grab raid and tackled the three thieves who resisted him with bricks and iron bars. The assistant warrant-officer was seriously injured and forced into an early retirement, which was hard since he loved the job. PC Stone BEM QPM had demonstrated his bravery on other occasions, once, in 1927, by jumping into the Thames to save a drowning man (he took the man, a suicide-attempter, home, where he and Mrs Stone nursed him back to equanimity and got him a job), and another time, during the war, by entering a dangerous building which had just received a direct hit to rescue people trapped there. Some time after, his story was told on *This is Your Life*, on television.

Indeed, two things strike anyone who does research of this nature. The first is that a good many more police-officers than one realized or is happy about are arrested for petty dishonesty, and the second is how many more police-officers, more than we have a right to expect, show great physical courage when up against it and even risk their lives on our behalf. Marlborough Street records are full of commendations and words of praise from magistrates about such acts.

Warrants for non-appearance of offenders, or apprehension of them on information supplied, are not usually dealt with by the warrant-office but by the individual officer involved in the case. The far reaches of Scotland are not, of course, the limit of their effectiveness. One of Marlborough Street's warrants which proved most difficult to enforce involved a US citizen.

The story began on the morning of 19th September 1967, when an eighteen-year-old French model, Claudie Delbarre, was found dead in her Chelsea flat. Her body, clothed only in a bra and pyjama-jacket, lay face downwards on her bed and was surrounded by half-sucked oranges. She had extensive bruising to her scalp and about 8 inches of sheeting stuck down her throat. Death was from suffocation. Near the body stood a large, heavy-based tumbler which had been broken.

Claudie had been last seen alive by friends with whom she had dined three nights before. In the party had been her companion, Robert Lipman, a thirty-six-year-old American real-estate agent who, like her, took drugs. The friends had deposited them both near her flat at 3.30 a.m., and on the following morning a dishevelled Lipman had rushed into his Knightsbridge Hotel, dashed up to his room and was soon down again with his bag, agitatedly demanding his bill. Then he was off to a travel-agent's, where he requested an immediate flight to Lisbon. There was not one until 2.30 p.m. that afternoon, so he took the twelve-forty plane to Copenhagen, which is scarcely *en route*, then an onward connection to Lisbon.

Next day police discovered the body and picked up Lipman's trail. They also found his tie in Claudie's flat, his fingerprints on the tumbler and a witness who had seen him hurrying away down the street that morning. They began to suspect that he could help them with their enquiries. The USA, where he soon turned up, did not quite see it that way.

"The battle for extradition began," says ex-Commander Bob Huntley in his book on his police career, *Bomb Squad*. "It was to be a difficult one, because no American citizen had ever been extradited before."

The battle ended the following March when a district judge in Hartford, Connecticut, eventually decided that Scotland Yard had shown "probable cause for a murder charge", despite the defence claim of insufficient evidence. A month later the American Secretary of State, Dean Rusk, endorsed the extradition, and Bob Huntley travelled over and escorted Lipman back.

En route, the wealthy American said he was glad he was returning to clear it all up and described what had happened on the night of Claudie's death. "They had gone to her flat for an LSD orgy," writes Huntley, "and on his trip he met a monster he had to kill. That 'monster' was Claudie. And when Lipman came round, he found she was dead, with a sheet down her throat." He also told Huntley that he hoped he had now 'kicked' drugs and that he planned to write a book about their ill-effects.

On his second appearance at Marlborough Street, his defence solicitor, David Napley, protested his client's innocence and elected to have reporting restrictions lifted in the hope that witnesses might come forward. There had been a certain amount of acrimonious comment about the fact that this wealthy man had been granted legal aid on his first appearance, but Mr Napley now assured the court that this had occurred through a misunderstanding and that Mr Lipman was quite able to provide the means for his own defence.

At Crown Court Lipman pleaded 'not guilty' and claimed that he was an alcoholic as well as a drug-addict and that on the night of Claudie's death he had been, via LSD, on a trip to the centre of the earth. Coming back, he found Claudie with a sheet stuffed down her throat and her face all puffed up and realized that there was something amiss. When she did not respond to his shaking, he panicked and did not remember anything after that.

He was acquitted of murder but found guilty of manslaughter, and the judge had one or two pungent things to say to the effect that one is still responsible for one's actions while on drugs when those drugs have been taken voluntarily. He also commented on the fact that the accused had done nothing to assist the girl when he had come around. (When prosecuting counsel had asked him why he neglected to inform anyone, he had replied, "I was afraid of police brutality.") Lipman received a six-year prison-sentence, and the police learned something new – that the latest trendy way to take LSD was to suck it up from an orange.

I am coming to the end of my Marlborough Street saga, having, of course, only touched on the variety of cases and events which have taken place there since 1795. There have, for instance, been a lot more minor trends other than LSD orgies. Many have been to do with sex. The 1950s and early 1960s saw a great deal of to-do about Soho strippers, and the public were regularly regaled with tales of "WHAT THE POLICE SERGEANT SAW", "MY STRIPTEASE DANCE, BY THE PLATINUM BLONDE" and "THE ADVERTISEMENT IN GREEN INK IN A SOHO SHOP". Bouts of prudery with regard to the scanty attire of Serpentine sunbathers were usually followed by pictures of same offenders (if they were ladies), and the Press were also much preoccupied with the activities of 'the Hyde Park ladies'. Not surprising. Even the stolid Paul Bennett expressed some wonderment at the goings-on in "those shrubberies" about which he kept hearing so much.

It is scarcely surprising either that some of the first shots in the battle for the permissive society were fired in that court. John Aubrey Fletcher was saddled with the task of deciding whether pictures of male and female genitalia displayed in a Mayfair Art Gallery were obscene (they were, he thought); Leo Gradwell had to contemplate the book *Last Exit to Brooklyn* to see whether it was likely to deprave or corrupt (it was, he thought) and St John Harmsworth had to make decisions on some explicit John Lennon prints which had much shocked some art-lovers: he decided that they had not, as had been alleged, been exhibited to 'passengers' and dismissed the case.

"Oh yes, it was Friday," said Clyde Wilson when told of a daylight wages-snatch. "Friday is cosh day, and Saturday is gelignite day, isn't it?" – which tells you all you need to know about that trend. Unfortunately the cosh was soon to be replaced more and more by the firearm, though, strangely enough, despite the use of firearms still being on the increase, the number of firearm raids fell quite dramatically in 1978. As far as Marlborough Street is concerned, firearms victims tend to be either policemen or ladies who have rejected a man's advances (both Shirley Bassey and Christine Keeler have been targets in such cases, and it was the attempt on Christine Keeler coming up at Marlborough Street which, as one newspaper put it, "caused the Profumo/Ward case to burst into the news").

Currently fashionable crime centres round disco-murders, terrorists and bomb-threats, all of which Marlborough Street has seen. It has even had a 'threat to depose the Queen', attempted by three Irishmen. Who knows what the next fashion will be? Whatever it is, you can be sure Marlborough Street will be one of the first to know.

Selected Bibliography

Ascoli, David, *The Queen's Peace: The Origins and Development of the Metropolitan Police, 1829-1979* (Hamish Hamilton, 1979)

Babington, Anthony, *A House in Bow Street: Crime and the Magistracy, 1740-1860* (Macdonald, 1969)

Brome, Vincent, *Reverse Your Verdict: A Collection of Private Prosecutions* (Hamish Hamilton, 1971)

Browne, Douglas G. and E.V. Tullet, *Bernard Spilsbury, his life and cases* (Harrap, 1976)

Chesney, Kellow, *The Victorian Underworld* (Temple Smith, 1970)

Chester, Lewis, David Leitch and Colin Simpson, *The Cleveland Street Affair* (Weidenfeld & Nicolson, 1976)

Collins, Philip, *Dickens and Crime* (Macmillan, 1965)

Day, John R., *The Story of the London Bus* (A London Transport Publication, 1973)

French, Stanley, *Crime Every Day* (Barry Rose, 1976)

Goodman, Jonathan, *Bloody Versicles: The Rhymes of Crime* (David & Charles, 1971)

Huntley, ex-Commander Bob, BEM, QPM, *Bomb Squad* (W.H. Allen, 1977)

Jones, Marjorie, JP MA PhD, *Justice and Journalism* (Barry Rose, 1974)

Jullian, Philippe, *Oscar Wilde* (Constable, 1969)

Mayhew, Henry, *London's Underworld, Selections from 'Those that will not work', the fourth volume of London Labour and the London Poor, 1862*, ed. Peter Quennell (Spring Books, 1950)

Monsarrat, Nicholas, *Life is a Four-Letter Word: Breaking Out* (volume two) (Cassell, 1970)

Montgomery Hyde, H., *The Cleveland Street Scandal* (W.H. Allen, 1976); *Crime has its Heroes* (Constable, 1976); (ed.), *The Trials of Oscar Wilde* (Hodge, 1948)

Robey, Edward, *The Jester and the Court* (William Kimber, 1976)

Sandbach, J.B., KC, *This Old Wig: Recollections of a London Magistrate* (Hutchinson, undated)

Sheppard, F.H.W. (ed.), *Survey of London*, Vol XXXI and XXXII (Athlone Press for LCC, 1963)

Simpson, Professor Keith, *Forty Years of Murder* (Harrap, 1978)

Wiggin, *My Court Case-Book* (Sylvan Press, 1948)

Williams, Guy R., *The Hidden World of Scotland Yard* (Hutchinson, 1972)

Index

Index